SLEEP **IN ART.**

S L E E P **IN ART.**

Edited by Regine Pötzsch

with contributions by

Hartmut Schulz

Irene Tobler

Piero Salzarulo and Lorenza Melli

Pier Luigi Parmeggiani

Silvia Evangelisti

David Parkes

Katharina Eder Matt

Annemarie Seiler-Baldinger

Robert Th. Stoll

Editiones Roche, Basel, Switzerland

Caption to the painting reproduced
on the dust jacket and opposite the title
page:

Auguste Renoir (1841–1919)
Young Girl Lying in the Grass, ca. 1915
Oil on canvas, 20.5 × 31.5 cm
Kunstmuseum, Basel

In 1907 Renoir bought 'Les Colettes', Cagnes, west of Nice. Although he moved into his newly-built house a year later, he never painted it. The old farmhouse, however, was kept in repair and appears in several paintings. We know from the painter's son Claude that Renoir was very attentive to detail and intent on preserving the rustic character of his surroundings. He even instructed the gardener to leave the grass growing in the pathways. Renoir wanted to enjoy his property not as a 'Villa' or 'Garden', but as untouched nature. What the pond of water-lilies in Giverny was to the elderly Monet, the Mediterranean world alive with young women, brightly-dressed washer-women and glistening bathers was to the sage Renoir. From it he continued to draw inspiration for his poetic paintings, whose colour caught and reflected the light of the southern sun. In this paradise on earth the young girl reclines dreamily on the ground, in all the fresh round firmness so beloved of Renoir.

The captions to the plates in this book were written by Robert Th. Stoll.

⟨Roche⟩

© 1993, Editiones Roche
F. Hoffmann-La Roche Ltd, Basel, Switzerland

71 353

Layout: Markus Hodel
English translation by BMP Translation Services
Lecturer: Paul Zimmermann
Photolithographers: Photolitho Sturm AG, Muttenz
Typesetting and printing: Kreis Druck AG, Basel
Binding: Grollimund AG, Reinach

ISBN 3-907946-95-2

Foreword

In *The Tempest,* Shakespeare's Prospero says: 'We are such stuff as dreams are made on, and our little life is rounded with a sleep.' The physiological fact that we spend two-thirds of our lives awake and the other third asleep did not interest him in the least. Neither would he have been impressed by a concise definition such as the one coined by the well-known Freiburg neurologist Richard Jung, who has described sleep as an 'active, biological, regulatory process controlled by the brain'. He was even less aware that there are different stages and gradations of sleep and that it is mainly during periods of paradoxical, or REM sleep that we dream.

Like Shakespeare, and Goethe, many poets and dramatists over the years have been fascinated by sleep, 'god of the night', 'brother of death', and have dealt with the phenomena of sleep and dreams in a wide variety of ways. Small wonder, then, that countless famous artists, representing almost every epoch and style, have also explored what is still, despite modern experimental sleep research, the mysterious 'dark third' of our lives. Using pen, colour and brush, chisel and hammer, their aim has been to capture the many and varied faces of sleep.

Why this fascination with sleep? Perhaps because the tranquil security of healthy, undisturbed slumber discloses our true selves to us and, like death, palliatively erases every trace of pain, exertion and passion from the human face.

Regine Pötzsch

Contents

Pablo Picasso (1881–1973)
Siesta, 1919
Tempera on paper, 31 × 49 cm
The Museum of Modern Art, New York

A survey of the genius Picasso's life work that takes note of his manifold evolution of form will bear out the view that his drawings and paintings are by way of being a visualized diary. It is hardly surprising that, after the revolution in visual philosophy which, before and during the First World War, influenced the analysis and synthesis of the facetted forms of Cubism in Braque and Picasso, the Spaniard should have followed up with a collection in the style of the new Classicism. In this post-war period of the much-longed-for return to a lush and lusty world, Picasso drew and painted lush and lusty people. Such pictures of the human form prompted the remark that a new race of titans and giants had been born. It is against this background that the tempera work *Siesta* with its precise draughtsmanship and strong colours must be seen. The composition is vigorously bold. The couple have bedded down against a stook of corn sheaves. The bronzed man is sitting, inclined to one side, his face shaded by his straw hat. The fair-skinned woman has placed her head in the man's lap, her right arm thrust under her head. The white chemise reveals her snowy bosom. In such physical propinquity, they are blissfully asleep.

I woke when it was almost tolling the hour for the evening meal. I felt dull and somnolent, for daytime sleep is like the sin of the flesh: the more you have the more you want, and yet you feel unhappy, sated and unsated at the same time.

Umberto Eco (The Name of the Rose)

Daytime Sleep
by Hartmut Schulz

At night no one can evade the dominion of the gentle tyrant we call sleep. And if, during the hours of darkness, sleep proves elusive, one feels miserable and out of sorts. Daytime, by contrast, is the time set aside for active life. That is why daytime sleep has a rather dubious reputation. It is not death's younger brother but rather the accomplice of the sin of accidie and therefore one of the more reprehensible vices. For Bruegel yawning is the ugly symbol of sloth.

Sleep during the day is also the result of gluttony indulged in but also of sheer boredom. However, it is not always this culpable side we see in pictures. Daytime sleep, in the form of rest or respite, can also be refreshing and replenish energies for the rest of the day.

Siesta

Midday rest, when half the day's work is accomplished, has figured in pictures since the Middle Ages. The sleeping reaper from the *Brevarium Grimani* has left off his laborious task and lies asleep near his implements. His arm serves him as a pillow and his broad straw hat shades him from the meridional heat. There is little time for rest before work begins again.

A short break during work in the open air, the noontide rest, is depicted in a number of paintings. The toilers use the time to snatch a short respite. Always fully clad, they plump themselves down, just as they are, without fuss or ado. They rest in the hay, or against a bale of straw, with rake and sickle by their side, ready to hand.

Perhaps the finest expression of this state of respite and relief from exhaustion is to be seen in Picasso's *Siesta*.

Midday sleep needs little protection, the air is warm, and even the body reaches its maximum daytime temperature at this time[4]. What appears to be the careless posture of the midday sleeper, with clothes awry and limbs outstretched, serves as a safeguard against overheating. It is hardly surprising, then, that the body adopts a greater variety of positions during diurnal compared with nocturnal sleep, when heat retention is the first priority. Human midday sleep is closely akin to the torpor of animals living in an arid climate[7].

9

Giovanni Segantini (1858–1899)
Resting in the Shade, 1892
Oil on canvas, 44 × 68 cm
Private collection, Zurich

This picture occupies a special position in Segantini's development as a painter, since it marks the last of his attempts (which commenced with *Ritorno all'ovile*) to structure his pictures by the use of horizontal planes. As in *Sul balcone,* the village of Savognin is painted against the light, at midday. The picture is composed of contrasts: a shady foreground with a high fence through which the light-drenched backyards and houses can be seen; a second plane of masonry up to the upper edge of the canvas, instead of a horizon. Of all of Segantini's works *Riposo all'ombra* displays the greatest fidelity to humanity's everyday existence. In the confined space above the fence where light and shadow meet, life is proceeding on a farm: two cows are about to feed, a peasant woman, seen in semi-profile, is going about her work. Her form, diminutive in the distance, contrasts sharply with the fine figure of the country lass in the foreground, who has lain down on the ground out of sheer exhaustion. The face turned to the grass and the hoe lying parallel to her body emphasize how completely relaxed she is. Her depleted energies will be replenished by vitalizing Nature.

Camille Pissarro (1830–1903)
Country Lass Lying in the Grass, 1882
Oil on canvas
Kunsthalle, Bremen

Over a meadow that fills most of the picture the eye roves towards a path in the background and the wall of a house that is only just visible. All the more striking, then, against this horizontal pattern is the diagonally disposed figure of a girl lying on the ground with a simple wooden rake by her side. She is wearing a striped blouse and a brown skirt; round her waist is a blue pinafore. Restrained though the cool colours of her clothing are, they strike a formal note amidst the green of the summer meadow, but it is to the warmth of the face and the soft pink of the bonnet that the beholder's eye is drawn. The girl's body is relaxed. Her right leg is extended slightly in front of her left; her right arm is bent a little and her hand lies in the grass. She has placed her left arm under her cheek. The girl is lying in the sun, which, to judge by the shade of the tree in the foreground and the shadow cast by her bonnet, dispenses a gentle warmth. Weary with the toil of raking the grass, she has probably lain down in the shade of the tree to snatch a short nap. Meanwhile the sun has moved in the sky but the sleeping girl has not noticed.

Such an inclination to midday napping is not confined to the bucolic scene and is not – like the siesta – cultivated in southern countries only. We all tend to feel the need for sleep peaking a second time midway between two nights. The noontide saddleback with its increased drowsiness and lowered capacity has been demonstrated in the laboratory under a variety of test conditions[9]. It is even detectable when the test subjects are observed during 24-hour bed rest[5]. The increase in the number of naps in the early afternoon, combined with a marked drop in functional capacity, prompted the conclusion that sleeping and waking display not only a circadian rhythm but also a circasemidian rhythm of the tendency to fall asleep[3]. In this case the midday rest would not be simply an individual or socially cultivated habit but rather the expression of a biologically based tendency to fall asleep for a second spell in the 24-hour day. The risks inherent in the increased drowsiness of early afternoon are reflected not only in diminished functional capacity[6] but also and in particular in a marked rise in traffic accidents due to the driver 'dozing off' at this time of day[13].

Sleep in the open air

Sleeping out of doors is not confined to a particular time of day, for the tendency to fall asleep during the day depends on a number of very different factors, such as, say, the lack of any work to be done. Open-air sleep is often felt to be a pleasant and beneficial doze or snooze. The sleeping boys are good examples.

Albert Anker (1831–1910)
Boy Asleep in the Hay
Oil on canvas, 55×71 cm
Kunstmuseum, Basel

His feet bare and dirty; his pale shins protruding from the well-worn blue dungarees; the straw hat cast away carelessly; the brown waistcoat unbuttoned, revealing the light-coloured shirt over his chest: thus the rapscallion lies spread-eagled in the hay. He has slipped away into the shed, stretched out on his back and fallen asleep. Anker had a masterly gift for portraying the world he lived in and his contemporaries. The composition of the picture with its variable diagonals is done with skill; the lighting and the colouration are subdued. There is a particular charm about the way in which the young lad's complete relaxation in sleep is portrayed: in the position of the body, the slight turning of the head, the slackness of the hands.

Jan Steen (1626–1679)
The World Awry, 1663
Oil on canvas, 105 × 145 cm
Kunsthistorisches Museum, Vienna

In the Golden Age of Dutch painting, distinguished by such luminaries as Rembrandt and Vermeer, there were also a number of lesser masters at work who prospered because the well-to-do middle class was anxious to have a pictorial record of its milieu, life and customs. Jan Steen was a brewer and tavern-keeper but also and more particularly a sardonic painter who openly depicted in his works what he was continually witnessing anew. Under the perhaps not entirely apt title *The World Awry,* he portrays a slovenly household. Someone has left the bung out of the barrel. The child is playing with a pearl necklace. The dog on the table is relishing the leftovers of the meal. A girl is rifling the cupboard and a monkey is playing with the chains of the clock weights. The world is out of joint. The fiddler and the elderly man reading prefer to ignore what is going on. But the old woman is addressing urgent appeals to the young man, who, of course, just laughs as he makes up to a tipsy young woman who is smirking at him. The greatest contrast is provided by the well-dressed woman who is sleeping, oblivious of the fiddling, jabbering, giggling and champing. She notices nothing, so deeply is she sunk in sleep in the broad light of day that streams in through the window. On the blackboard at the bottom right are written words of warning: 'In weelde siet toe' – Lay by for a rainy day. One never knows what the morrow may bring. Sword and crutch are hanging in the basket over the centre.

Sleep during travel

Caspar David Friedrich (1774–1840)
Boy Resting by the Tree Stump, 1802
Pencil and sepia wash, 18.1 × 11.6 cm
Kunsthalle, Bremen
(Lost during the war)

Friedrich was born in Greifswald in the north of Germany and moved to Dresden, where he taught at the academy from 1816 onwards. His work is the epitome of German Romanticism. This pencil and sepia wash, which was unfortunately lost during wartime evacuation, is a detailed study for a painting. The preliminary sketch was done in pencil and then executed in pen and given a sepia wash. With its angular bough and writhen branches, the bare tree stump forms a framework for a youth who is lying sleeping, it may be surmised, on a rock. The high-necked clothing, shoes, tight trousers, jerkin with large buttons, lavaliere and epaulettes suggest a man in uniform who is taking a rest. The forester, the count's huntsman and the castle servant are familiar figures in German Romanticism, or is it rather the image of Eichendorff's *Good for Nothing* that is being evoked? His right hand is stuck in the side pocket of his trousers and the left arm is raised to support his head. His finely lined features with the hair sweeping softly over his brow appeal to the beholder. At the same time they excite the curiosity of the large bird that has perched fearlessly on the branch to look down on the sleeper.

If a number of people are asked in turn what situations have caused them to feel sleepy, 'long journeys and rail travel' will be the commonest reply. Monotony, heat and cramped conditions, which are inseparable from most travel, are typical sleep-inducers. Unfortunately this is true not only of rail travel but also of car-driving with its attendant risk of dozing off at the wheel, particularly at critical times of the day[12].

Evidence that loud noises and music do not disturb our sleep but may even encourage us to drop off, provided they are rhythmical, was adduced by Oswald[11] in a series of experiments. The test subjects received mild electric shocks at regular intervals coupled with flashes of light and loud jazz. Although they could not close their eyes because their lids were lightly fixed with plasters, the test subjects' degree of vigilance fluctuated according to electroencephalogram (EEG) criteria and finally most of them fell asleep. In addition to quiet and inactive waiting, obviously an excess of stimuli can also induce sleep.

Electrophysiologically, a distinction can be made between different grades of waking and levels of vigilance by measuring the EEG and the electrooculogram (EOG). In the EEG fatigue is reflected primarily by an increase in the low-frequency components of the spectrum of EEG activity, and in the EOG by slow deviations of the eyeball[14].

In a study in which 274 persons of various age groups were interviewed, a statistical analysis of their replies showed that there are four sleep-inducing conditions which can be described as satiety, relaxation, reduced stimulation and physical exhaustion. It comes as no surprise, therefore, that, in addition to travel, sleeping in church also became a subject for painters and authors[15].

Adolph von Menzel (1815–1905)
*Man Yawning in a Railway
Compartment,* 1859
Oil on canvas
Staatliche Museen, Berlin

A well-dressed gentleman is sitting in a first-class compartment of a railway carriage and, it may be imagined, is on a protracted journey from one city to another. The man has ensconced himself in the corner, near the window with its blue curtain. His head is powerfully shaped; his hair is smoothed back; his eyebrows beetle over large eyes; under his prominent nose flourishes a brown moustache. His dark brown suit has been rumpled by long hours of travel and is gaping at the front, revealing his white shirt front; his wing collar sports a bow tie. A heavy gold watch chain is hanging from the row of buttons on his waistcoat. He is wearing light-coloured leather gloves. This traveller appears to be well-bred and might hold an important position in the business world. But he is alone in the compartment, with no one to talk to and no reading matter with which to wile away the time. And so he indulges in a hearty and uninhibited yawn with his mouth wide open. It is popularly said there are three types of yawn: the yawn of fatigue, the yawn of boredom, and the yawn due to oxygen deficiency during mental exertion. Menzel the painter was an outstanding psychologist and observer of humanity. In this work he has portrayed the yawn that comes with the weariness of boredom.

This subject was perfectly expressed in the depiction of the little girl who fell quietly asleep during the sermon. The child in her Sunday best, her hands tucked into the warming muff, has nodded off. Unlike the siesta scenes in which the farmers shaded themselves from the midday sun with broad hats, there is something nonchalant about this form of napping: she has laid aside her hat; clearly, it is difficult to reconcile sleep and perfect social decorum. This may be another reason why daytime sleep is held in such poor repute. The sleeper pays no heed to his surroundings, he is deaf to what others say and is clearly not interested in the social context.

Daytime sleep can be both an expression of pleasant relaxation or the result of severe exhaustion. This double nature of daytime sleep is also reflected in the great variety of places the sleeper chooses for his slumbers.

Sleeping in church

Sir John Everett Millais (1829–1896)
My Second Sermon
Oil on canvas
Guildhall Art Gallery, London

Encouraged as a child prodigy, of independent means, and congenial to contemporary taste, Millais was a successful painter; he became President of the Royal Academy. This picture, which attests to his skill, is redolent of Victorian sentimentality and a typical example of his late work. A little girl with chubby cheeks is seated on a wooden bench covered with moss-green cushions. Behind the high back, also moss green in colour, a strip of window glazing can be seen. We are in a church. The little girl has blissfully fallen asleep during the sermon. She has laid her feathered hat by her side. The bench on which she is sitting is too high for her, so that her feet, clad in stockings and shoes, dangle down and, caught in the stream of daylight, cast shadows on the boards of the church floor. The little girl has tucked her hands in a fur muff lying on her lap. Her blue frock with its black borders and her red cape contrast with her pale face under the curly golden-brown hair held with a black hair-band. Her tiny red mouth over her little chin is closed; her eyes on either side of her snub nose are lowered. The little girl remains blissfully asleep throughout the long sermon; one can almost hear her regular breathing.

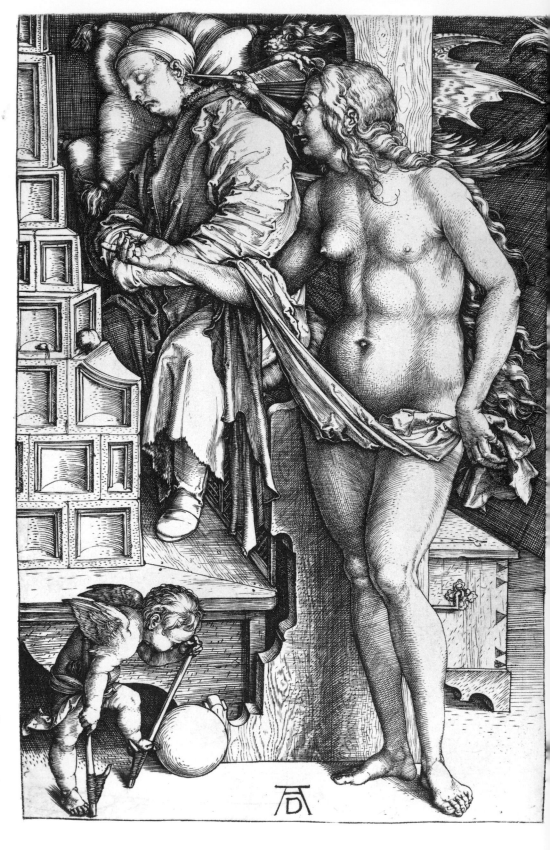

Albrecht Dürer (1471–1528)
The Doctor's Dream, ca. 1497/98
Copperplate engraving, 18.8 × 11.9 cm
Print Room, Basel

Albrecht Dürer was familiar with the goldsmith's burin by virtue of both his upbringing and his training. The son of a goldsmith, he was also a trained practitioner of this craft. At least secondarily, prints like the above were intended as a record of his insights into the human form, and, since reproducible, they were also available to other studios for use as models. During his stay in Venice in 1494/95, the German master had his first encounter with antiquity, as reflected in Italian art, and he made a close study of the technique of drawing from the nude. He liked to work his depictions of the nude body into scenic tableaux, a predilection illustrated here. The sturdily built woman in this engraving is a symbol of temptation, which has visited the sleeping man in a dream. He is resting, fully clothed and almost upright, on a bench near the warm tiled stove, his covered head laid sideways on the pillows. With a bellows a winged demon is blowing an erotic dream into his ear. Fortuna's ball, lying on the floor, and the small cupid attempting to mount his stilts intimate how unlikely this dream is to be fulfilled. Self-assured and supremely aware of his skilful handling of theme and form, the artist has engraved his initials at the bottom centre.

Whereas for night sleep, the places chosen must be safe and afford protection — be they trees, nests or dens for natural creatures or bedrooms and beds for human beings —, the brief daytime sleep or nap can be enjoyed almost anywhere. The sleeper may be seated or relaxed in a recumbent posture. The body is held loosely, the lower part often slips forward. The head seeks a support, whether it is the back of the chair or the sleeper's own arm. The nap is usually short and easily broken: it often appears to be unplanned, a fact suggested by the places and positions chosen. Daytime sleep is most commonly the result of overtiredness or monotonous activity.

Sleeping places

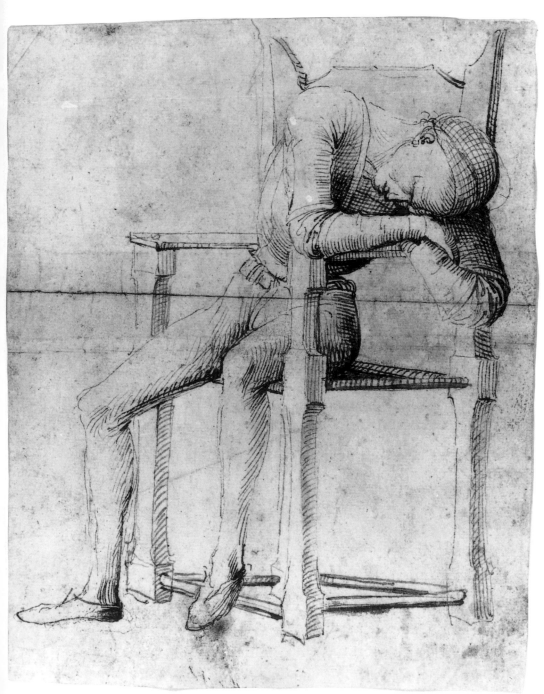

Anonymous German master
Second half of 15th century
Man Asleep in a Chair
Pen drawing
Universitätsbibliothek, Erlangen

This tall wooden chair, it may be well imagined, is not the most comfortable place to sleep. But the man is very tired. With narrow trousers, jerkin, tight-fitting cap and slip-on shoes, he is dressed like a journeyman. Or is he a colleague in the studio of the anonymous draughtsman? To judge by the pen drawing, the artist was a minor German master of the type frequently commissioned at the height of the Gothic period to produce designs for altars, goldsmith's work and decorations. This drawing was composed with great care; the structuring intent is evident in the verticals of the chair leg. The contrast between the flowing organic lines of the body and the picture's geometric elements serves to heighten the artistic effect. The man's weariness is acutely observed. We find here in a work of late Gothic art an intimation of that conception of the body which was later to attain its apogee in Albrecht Dürer's depictions of the human figure.

Sleep and work

Jan Vermeer van Delft (1632–1675)
Girl Asleep, ca. 1656
Oil on canvas, 86.5 × 76 cm
The Metropolitan Museum of Art,
New York

Vermeer, who was Rembrandt's most prominent contemporary and his antithesis in terms of formal composition, was an enigmatic personality. There are only a few of his works extant. We know virtually nothing about his life: apart from being a painter he was also an art dealer and was elected chairman of the Guild of St Luke. No autographic documents have come down to us; when he died, he left behind debts and eight children who were minors; no purchaser could be found for any of the pictures left in his studio. Yet today his works compel our admiration. They are infused by a vibrant tranquillity, and this painting is no exception. The eye goes questing from the parlour via a half-open door through a corridor into a second, almost empty room. Hanging from the light-coloured walls there are a few pictures, mirrors and maps. The immediate foreground is barred by a diagonally placed chair and a table upon which are textiles, a jug and bottle and a bowl of fruit. The sleeping girl is seated at the table. Her left hand is resting lightly on the table's edge while her head is supported by her closed right hand, the elbow propped on the table. She is wearing a close-fitting black cap; round her neck is draped a scarf; a bodice of copper-coloured damast reveals her opulent white bosom. The woman seems to have nodded off while waiting by the open door for a visitor to arrive.

Monotonous activities and jobs readily induce woolgathering and dreaming, as shown in the pictures by Vermeer or Nicolaes Maes. Women doze and dream rather than sleep properly. The head propped on the arm was familiar as the attribute of the dreamer, even back in medieval iconography[2].

Sleep at work can also be a sign of exhaustion, as in Dega's ironing woman or Courbet's spinning woman, who have dropped off to sleep over their work.

Another common motif is the sleeping shepherd boy or the journeyman who has taken a rest on the way. And, of course, sleeping by day and in the open air may also be an expression of sheer destitution.

Adolph von Menzel (1815–1905)
The Artist's Sister Asleep, ca. 1848
Oil on canvas
Kunsthalle, Hamburg

Menzel loved his sister, and he painted her more than once. Her black hair is pinned up like a crown over her youthful face. In keeping with her temperament, she displays a very quiet taste in clothes. Her woollen dress, olive in colour, is widely spread and is heavily wadded at the shoulders over narrow sleeves. Fine white linen shows at the collar. The woman is lying asleep on a chaise longue in the living room. There is a flat cushion on the scroll-shape end, all in a warm reddish ochre, which, nuanced a shade, is also the colour of the back. Contrasting with this is the cool sand colour of the walls and, again, the dark blue of the damask cushion, decorated with an embroidered border in silver. The woman has nuzzled her face into the cool cushion; incident light falls over her brow, cheek, collar and left hand, which she has laid in her lap. The liquid folds of the skirt, cast into a triangle by the concealed posture of the legs, contrast with the rounded forms of the shoulders and head. Yet it is the restful diagonal disposition of the whole that lends the composition its beauty and makes the unruffled slumbers of the young woman almost palpable.

Gustave Courbet (1819–1877)
Woman Sleeping at the Spinning Wheel, 1853
Oil on canvas, 91 × 115 cm
Musée Favre, Montpellier

This painting conveys an impression of the country life dear to the heart of Courbet, who hailed from the farming village of Ornans in the French Jura. *'Le réalisme'* was his watchword; he rejected all grandiose subjects; he wanted to depict unvarnished reality in all its gripping truth. There is something homely about this woman who has nodded off while spinning. She is seated in the parlour in a thickly upholstered chair by the window.

A shaft of light falls directly on her brown hair done up in a knot, her strong, pale throat and her white-and-blue striped shawl. There are reminiscences of Rembrandt's *chiaroscuro* but here there is nothing mysterious as in the Dutchman's pictures. The woman has simply been lulled by the whirr of the spinning weel and has dropped off to sleep. Now the wheel and bobbin are still and the distaff has dropped onto her lap; but the thread still passes loosely through the lightly sleeping woman's right hand. For all her rotundity, this woman has shapely hands; her left one is lying loosely on her flowered garment as if it, too, were asleep.

Romanesque ceiling painting
from Zillis
Joseph's Sleep, ca. 1160
Tempera on wood
Single panel, ca. 92×92 cm
Zillis, Grisons, Switzerland

The Church of St Martin's in Zillis, which stands on the Via Mala, a pass route in the Swiss Canton of Graubünden, houses one of the most beautiful wooden ceilings in the Romanesque style. It comprises 153 square wooden panels painted in tempera. They extend the full length of the nave and, framed by fabulous monsters, depict the life and miracles of Jesus and the first incidents of His Passion. This splendid work was executed sometime after the mid-12th century, probably by a studio in Rhaetia to judge from its character and style. No one knows who the artist and his journeymen were, who commissioned the work, or why it should have been painted in this unpretentious village church. It bears witness to a profound faith and expresses an insight into the human heart that still touches us today. This panel shows the sleep of Joseph, a Joseph still burdened with doubts and apprehensions at the sheer incomprehensibility of the nativity. He is sitting at a slant on a bench, his head resting on his left hand. The outline and interior lines are boldly drawn; the colours are austere. For the faithful the ceiling of St Martin's was a kind of picture book, each panel telling a story. Joseph appears to be listening with an inner ear to the angel that hovers nearby, urging him to flee to Egypt with mother and child.

Auguste Renoir (1841–1919)
Sleeping Girl, 1897
Oil on canvas, 81×65.5 cm
Reinhart Collection, Winterthur

Degas said of the amiable Renoir's painting with its pearly lustre that it was like butterfly's wings. Renoir came from a poor tailor's family in Limoges and, at the age of thirteen, was apprenticed to a porcelain manufacturer to paint flowers and amatory scenes on china. Eager to learn, he found his models in the Rococo painters Boucher and Fragonard in the Louvre. Renoir became a past master in the observation of light and the modulation of colour, and in the impressionistic reproduction of whatever delighted his eye. His later work shows great sensitivity in its handling of a discreet eroticism. This painting of a beautiful young woman asleep is a masterpiece. It attests to his mature genius in the management of colour and form. The colours of the garment laid over her lap are concentrated in the embroideries as if in a palette where colour is conceived in utter freedom out of sheer joy in the play of light. The outlines of the body are mellifluous but tutored by observation and reproduced with sensitivity and precision. Its beautiful contours are modelled through grey and violet nuancing of the flesh tints by glazing in translucent films in the style of the old masters. The beholder dare barely breathe, so golden are these slumbers.

Nicolaes Maes (1634–1693)
The Dreamer
Oil on canvas
Musées Royaux des Beaux-Arts, Brussels

This minor master of the great Flemish tradition worked in Dordrecht, Antwerp and later Amsterdam; otherwise we know little about him. Maes was one of hundreds of painters who turned out well-composed, technically superb genre studies to satisfy the desire of prosperous burghers to decorate the walls of their homes. He was also a recognized portrait painter. Maes recorded the details of any situation with great thoroughness. The play and effects of lighting were a very popular subject of painting in that age. In our picture, the shafts of sunlight fall through the window. In the shadow we can distinguish on the cupboard against the rear wall one candlestick, one lidded tankard and some books. The table is covered with a red tablecloth. On it a large book lies open, and next to it a lace cushion with bobbins and unfinished lace trimming. The old woman is wearing a headscarf and jacket, and has a fur cover over her knees for warmth. She was too tired to carry on with what she was doing, i.e. reading something in the illustrated book in her lap. She has removed her pince-nez and fallen asleep, with her chin resting on her left fist. Might she be dreaming? Maes excels at details such as the play of shadows on her haggard face as well as on the heavily veined hand which still clasps her spectacles and the ring of shadow they cast on the book.

Daumier, the social critic, painted the squalid conditions in the night shelter, where the sleepers, with no bed of their own, can rest their weary bodies only by slumping over a rope. There is not even anywhere to put down their hats; they keep them on while asleep. And in conclusion Scharl has sketched the sleeping clochards in Paris — wretches who must sleep at times and places undreamt of in the bourgeois philosophy.

The sleep of the poor

Honoré Daumier (1808–1879)
The Dosshouse
Lithograph

Impossible to provide enough beds in the dosshouse for so many beggars. What can one do? A bench is placed along the wall and a strong rope stretched in front of it. The poor unfortunates take their places in a row on the bench, hang their arms over the rope and try to forget their misery for a while. Some sleep with their hats on, which affords them some sense of protection, and safeguards this one belonging against theft. But even this brief rest is continually disturbed by the movements of the others. This scene of destitution is not a product of Daumier's imagination. The tremor in the artist's hand betrays his compassion: Daumier has seen this scene for himself.

Diurnal sleepiness

Even with the healthy subject there are many reasons for daytime sleep and it may take many forms, all of which have been reflected in works of art. At the same time, however, daytime sleep may be the expression of a profound disturbance of the sleeping-waking rhythm and the regulation of levels of vigilance. Hypersomnias with their increased daytime somnolence represent a form of disease which is greatly underrated in regard to frequency and importance.

There is a very impressive description of a case of daytime somnolence in Charles Dickens's *Pickwick Papers*. The obese boy Joe, known as Fat Joe, is in the habit of falling asleep at any moment, appropriate or otherwise:

'Mr. Lowton hurried to the door. The object that presented itself to the eyes of the astonished clerk was a boy — a wonderful fat boy — standing upright on the mat with his eyes closed as if in sleep. He had never seen such a fat boy, in or out of a travelling caravan; and this, coupled with the utter calmness of his appearance, so very different from what was reasonably to have been expected of the inflictor of such knocks, smote him with wonder.

Jean François Millet (1814–1875)
Midday Break
Oil on canvas
The John G. Johnson Collection,
Philadelphia Museum of Art

Pictures like this one of carefree peasant life won Millet the acclaim of Parisians. Like his fellow-members of the plein-air school, he painted outdoors in the countryside. His pictures capture the light of the fields, and the essence of the peasants' simple life reflects his careful observation. At the same time, his pictures are very carefully composed. His division of the surface into two halves is very effective: he achieves variety through lighter and darker tones of the same natural colours. The contrast between sunlight in the distance and the shade of the trees in the foreground, whose foliage lets through just the odd circle of light, gives the picture great strength. It is midday; after hours of labouring in the fields the peasants are enjoying their break. But they are not asleep; one feels that one can almost follow their simple exchange.

"What's the matter?" inquired the clerk. The extraordinary boy replied not a word; but he nodded once, and seemed, to the clerk's imagination, to snore feebly.

"Where do you come from?" inquired the clerk.

The boy made no sign. He breathed heavily, but in all other respects was motionless.

The clerk repeated the question twice, and receiving no answer, prepared to shut the door, when the boy suddenly opened his eyes, winked several times, sneezed once, and raised his hands as if to repeat the knocking. Finding the door open, he stared about him with astonishment and at length fixed his eyes on Mr. Lowton's face.

"What the devil do you knock in that way for?" inquired the clerk, angrily.

"Which way?" said the boy in a slow sleepy voice.

"Why, like forty hackney-coachmen", replied the clerk.

"Because master said I wasn't to leave off knocking till they opened the door, for fear I should go to sleep", said the boy.' (Dickens, C.: *The Posthumous Papers of the Pickwick Club*. London: Chapman.)

The syndrome underlying this excessive daytime somnolence comprises obesity, alveolar hypoventilation with an elevated carbon dioxide tension in the blood, and also cor pulmonale. The mystery remained unsolved until it was found that these patients were suffering from sleep apnea caused by obstructive changes in the respiratory tract due to narrowing of the oropharynx by depositions of fat. Today we know that overweight is a risk factor in sleep apnea but that sleep apnea is not necessarily connected with obesity.

Sleep apnea that lowers the oxygen concentration in the blood to pathological levels and causes frequent arousals is probably the most common cause of daytime somnolence[8].

Another disease which is characterized by a serious disturbance of the sleeping and waking rhythm and increased daily somnolence is narcolepsy[10]. Narcoleptic patients are unable to remain continually awake during the day. They complain of pronounced daytime somnolence and are continually nodding off, even in situations which may be dangerous or socially inacceptable. A second component of the syndrome is cataplexy, i.e. attacks of momentary paralysis. At such moments the patients are incapable of speaking comprehensibly, they cannot move, or may even slump to the ground. Cataplectic attacks are very often triggered by emotions such as joy, anger or surprise. There is much evidence to suggest that neurophysiological mechanisms that are normally activated in sleep and precede REM sleep (REM = rapid eye movements) may also operate in these patients in the waking state and are responsible for the cataplexy and also for the sudden sleep attacks.

Daytime sleep thus embraces a wide spectrum of phenomena, ranging from wholesome napping for relaxation to narcoleptic attacks that are a symptom of a pathological change in the sleep-regulating system.

Night sleep is undoubtedly the most important restorative for our bodies, but there is in addition a tendency to rest for short periods during the day which is biologically based and then shaped by cultural factors. Finding the right measure and the right time is part of our 'sleep culture'.

References

1. Aldrich, M.S.: Automobile accidents in patients with sleep disorders. *Sleep 12,* 487–494 (1989).
2. Bagliani, A.P., Stabile, G. (Ed.): *Träume im Mittelalter. Ikonologische Studien.* Stuttgart, Zurich: Belser, 1989.
3. Broughton, R.J.: Three central issues concerning ultradian rhythms; in: *Ultradian rhythms in physiology and behavior,* pp. 217–233. Ed. H. Schulz, P. Lavie. Berlin, Heidelberg: Springer, 1985.
4. Campbell, S.: Duration and placement of sleep in a 'disentrained' environment. *Psychophysiology 21,* 106–113 (1984).
5. Campbell, S., Zulley, J.: Napping as a biological rhythm: disentrainment of the human sleep/wake system; in: *Sleep '86,* pp. 3–10. Ed. W.P. Koella, F. Obal, H. Schulz, P. Kisser. Stuttgart, New York: Fischer, 1988.
6. Colquhoun, W.P.: Circadian variations in mental efficiency; in: *Biological rhythms and human performance,* pp. 39–107. Ed. W.P. Colquhoun. London: Academic Press, 1971.
7. Glotzbach, S.F., Heller, H.C.: Thermoregulation; in: *Principles and practice of sleep medicine,* pp. 300–309. Ed. M.H. Kryger, T. Roth, W.C. Dement. Philadelphia, London: Saunders, 1989.
8. Guilleminault, C., Dement, W.C. (Ed.): *Sleep apnea syndromes.* New York: Liss, 1978.
9. Lavie, P.: Ultradian rhythms: gates of sleep and wakefulness; in: *Ultradian rhythms in physiology and behavior,* pp. 148–164. Ed. H. Schulz, P. Lavie. Berlin, Heidelberg: Springer, 1985.
10. Meier-Ewert, K.: *Tagesschläfrigkeit. Ursachen, Differentialdiagnose, Therapie.* Weinheim: Edition Medicin, VCH, 1989.
11. Oswald, J.: Falling asleep open-eyed during intense rhythmic stimulation. *Br Med J 1960/1,* 1450–1455.
12. Pratt, P.: When did you last drive asleep? *Drive 39,* 17–23 (1976).
13. Prokop, O., Prokop, L.: Ermüdung und Einschlafen am Steuer. *Dtsch Z Ger Med 44,* 343 (1955).
14. Santamaria, J., Chiappa, K.H.: *The EEG of drowsiness.* New York: Demos, 1987.
15. Sterne, L.: *The life and opinions of Tristram Shandy Gentleman.* London, 1759.

Karel Čapek (1890–1938)
Dashenka, 1932

'Dashenka could sleep and eat right from birth, without having to learn. That's why she did it eagerly, every hour of the day, and I think she also slept just as conscientiously at night when no one was looking – she was such a diligent dog.' The book written by the Czech author, Karel Čapek, to record how his dog Dashenka grew up is illustrated with charming sketches and photographs. Using Dashenka, Čapek closely observed and depicted the ritual many animals perform before sleeping. Like wolves and foxes, dogs look for a quiet, comfortable spot, pawing the ground to create a hollow if they are in the open. They may then be observed briefly attending to 'personal hygiene' before turning on their own axis several times and finally rolling into the prepared resting place. Sleep will then come rapidly to an undisturbed animal. In our pet dogs, only vestiges of this behaviour can be observed. The lower half of the work shows little Dashenka's behaviour on waking and 'getting up'.

Sleep in Animals

by Irene Tobler

Sleep behaviour

In many animals a large diversity of preparatory behaviour can be observed before the onset of sleep. Most people have had the opportunity to watch a cat or a dog (Čapek, a Czech writer, was inspired to write a book filled with many sketches and photographs of his dog, Dashenka, going to sleep and waking up) suddenly performing digging movements, circling around the body axis, and finally curling up and lying down in a typical position. Such behaviour has also been seen in the fox and wolf. As long ago as 1867, K. Möbius, a German biologist, published his observations of the resting behaviour of fish in the aquarium. In fact, aquarium owners can easily observe that many species of fish have a very different appearance during the day and the night: marked changes in the daily activity pattern can be observed in, e.g., wrasses: reduced overall activity, fidelity of place in the evening hours, investigation of 'sleeping places' and building of nests. Some wrasses normally just rest on the sand while others bury themselves into the sandy bottoms. Parrot fish and the cleaner wrasse secrete a mucous envelope in which they remain motionless all night. Many reptiles, lizards and non-tree-dwelling snakes search in the evening hours for an appropriate dwelling in which to spend the night. The chameleon, for instance, climbs a tree, changes its colour and spends the night in a typical position on a branch.

The choice of a sleeping site is an element of species-specific sleep behaviour and varies with the mode of life and social organization of the species in question. Burrows, caves and trees are common sites because of the safety they afford, but some species (e.g. zebras) rely on the presence of vigilant conspecifics for protection. The seal and hippopotamus sleep under the water some of the time.

Nests and pillows

Unknown artist
Husky Sleeping

Of the more than 400 breeds of dog, the husky is very special. Even today, huskies are working animals essential for drawing sledges and as companions for Arctic and Antarctic travellers. Huskies are related to wolves, which they resemble in many respects. With its black-and-white mask of a face and steel-blue eyes, this particular husky is beautifully depicted. Konrad Lorenz, founder of ethology and winner of the 1973 Nobel Prize for Medicine – along with Karl von Frisch and Nikolaas Tinbergen – described the remarkable qualities of this breed and the closely related chow-chow in his book entitled *So kam der Mensch auf den Hund* (How humankind discovered dogs). Most dog-related species – including foxes and wolves – lie on their sides and tuck in their heads when sleeping, like the husky in the picture. The head is supported on the paw, the tail wrapped around the body. This protects sensitive parts such as the belly and the soft paws from hypothermia while the animal is asleep. Sleeping dogs (and cats) can frequently be observed making sounds and abrupt movements of various parts of the body. The ears, hairs of the muzzle and tail are the most prone to this twitching. The animal will then be in the REM stage of sleep: the muscles, especially in the neck, are highly relaxed, but repeated muscle twitchings occur in phases.

Construction of a nest in the branches of a new tree each evening is typical of chimpanzees, whereas an improvised nest on the ground is more typical of mountain gorillas. Not all apes have developed the habit of constructing nests, e.g. the gibbon sleeps sitting on a branch. Many species prefer more hidden sleeping sites. Thus, most rodents disappear into burrows to sleep and are more difficult to observe. Fruit bats return every evening to their 'sleeping-tree' around which they circle until it becomes dark and where they spend the night in large groups. Other bats can be found sleeping in 'sleeping-colonies' by the hundreds, hanging from the ceiling of caves. Some such caves have been used by bats for generations. Peacocks, which spend most of the day on the ground, are found perched on tree branches after the onset of darkness. Herons can fly for many miles to their preferred 'sleeping-tree', where many spend the night together. Starlings sleep by the hundreds in small patches of reeds. Although many birds are known to construct nests, they are mainly used for breeding. Most birds prefer to sleep on a tree branch and do not spend the night in the nest.

Elephants have been observed to collect some hay with their tusks and form it into a 'pillow' before lying down. The function of this behaviour is unknown, although the interpretation that it serves to rest their heads on a soft surface is tempting.

These ritualistic pre-sleep activities are a characteristic of each species and they have led to the consummatory act 'sleep', which is recognized by ethologists as an appetitive, instinctive behaviour.

François Boucher (1703–1770)
Pastoral Idyll
Oil on canvas, 243 × 254 cm
Alte Pinakothek, Munich

The paintings of François Boucher convey something of the frivolity that pervaded the epoch of Louis XV of France. Whether he was painting ladies of the Court in their boudoirs or the pastoral idylls that were so popular at the time, plain and simple enjoyment is everywhere in evidence. Boucher's technique is precise but his images are dreamlike and often imbued with echoes of playful mythological themes. Boucher was more susceptible to the *rococo* of the Venetian Tiepolo than to the classical sobriety of the Renaissance masters whose work he had seen in Rome. He was extremely successful, becoming a favourite of high society. He illustrated the works of Molière, decorated palace rooms for the king's mistress, and was much in demand as a portrait painter. His renderings of pastoral idylls were also intended for this luxury-loving society. The sky's gentle light suffuses the scene, which appears to unfold before the viewer like a stage set for amateur performers. The human and animal worlds are one in their paradisiac harmony. Flirting, playing, sleeping: this is not the world as it is, but as it should be – gay and unproblematic.

Sleep postures Apart from the well known 'curled up' sleeping posture of cats, dogs and many small rodents such as squirrels, mice and hamsters, a very common sleeping posture is lying on the side with legs outstretched (dog, cat, rabbit, elephant)[3]. The preference for one or the other position is often determined by the structure of the ground (hard, straw, etc., and ground and environmental temperature). For example, many species such as bears, mice and some hamsters sleep tightly curled and entwined, thereby keeping one another warm. Such a situation was captured as early as 2000 BC in the bowl representing two hippopotami tightly entwined during sleep. In contrast, lying on the back with the abdomen exposed and limbs stretched away from the body is a position that can be observed in lions in the middle of the day, in the house cat, and sometimes in bears. It is a posture that is favoured when the ambient temperature is high.

Lateral or sternoabdominal recumbency, with eyes closed, is the posture most commonly associated with sleep in larger mammals (horse, sheep). But there are some striking variations: the horse and the elephant, for example, are able to sleep while standing. Sleep in a standing posture has been described by Julius Caesar, who reported that elks cannot lie down, and that they sleep standing on stiff, stretched legs while resting their bodies against a tree! The recording of brain waves has shown that herbivores can sleep while they are ruminating, either lying or even standing. Thus, cattle and deer sleep for several hours with their eyes open, ruminating. When they enter paradoxical sleep, rumination stops and the animals rest their head on the flank of a hind leg or on the ground. This has led to the opinion published by several behaviourists in the sixties that this stage represents 'deep sleep'. It also contributed to the notion that ruminants can get by with very little sleep. It was assumed that in the sitting, ruminating position sleep could not take place. For example, only 36 minutes of sleep per day had been reported for cows! Similarly, giraffes rest their head on the flank of the hind leg, thereby twisting their long neck backwards and downwards when they enter paradoxical sleep; otherwise they sleep either in a sitting or standing position. Dolphins sleep while floating in the water in a position that allows the breathing hole, which is located on the back of the head, to remain above the surface. Seals often sleep in the water while floating in circles close to the surface, performing small movements of the flippers to keep the nose above the surface to allow breathing.

The lateral, recumbent sleeping position seems to be typical of mammals. Birds never lie on their sides to sleep: the flamingo and stork stand on one leg, whereas others, e.g. the pigeon, duck, swan and penguin, sit resting on the abdomen. Often the entire head, including the beak, is tucked under a wing, a position which can be easily observed in swans and geese. Some exceptionally conspicuous sleeping positions are known for the ostrich and some parrots. In completely undisturbed animals in the zoo, one may come upon an African ostrich or a South American nandu lying with its long neck completely stretched out on the ground. Some parrots hang like bats upside down in trees with their heads pointing downwards. Zoological gardens provide unique opportunities to observe the sleeping habits of many semi-wild animals. Thus several directors of zoos, such as Hediger, Meyer-Holzapfel and Immelmann, have described their observations.

Ancient Egyptian bowl with hippopotami
Gabbro stone
Height: 7 cm; diameter: 24 cm
Middle Kingdom, around 2000 BC
Archeological Institute of the University of Zurich

After the traditional dignity of the Old Kingdom, the Middle Kingdom was ushered in by deep-seated political and philosophical changes. These are etched into the faces of the Pharaohs of the XIth and XIIth Dynasties. The private art also reveals a surprising realism. This round bowl is made of bedrock, difficult to work because of its hardness. In the smooth curve of its interior, the bowl reveals two sculpted, raised hippos arranged ovally. The animals are lying on their sides, and we look down on their heads. It is not clear whether they are sleeping or only resting. Hippopotamus representations were popular in the Middle Kingdom. The goddess Toeris, in the guise of a pregnant hippo, was generally believed to be the patron of maternity. The inhabitants of Egypt experienced their country as a gift of the Nile since at the time – although unfortunately no longer – its annual floods brought the fertile black sludge that meant new life. This is the deeper reason for the status of hippopotami, dwellers in the waters of the Nile, as guarantors of a divinely sanctioned regeneration. This masterly ritual bowl richly illustrates the numinous dimension.

Fritz Hug (1921–1989)
Ox Dozing

A large ruminant – such as the ox in Fritz Hug's painting – will spend a great deal of time asleep on the ground in the midday heat and at night. It will rest half on its belly and half on its side, but with the head and neck raised and the eyes half closed. Apart from occasional flicks of the tail and ears to ward off flies, these animals hardly stir. The transition from the waking state to sleep is fluid. Only during REM sleep – often referred to as 'deep sleep' – is the side of the head supported by the flank. Even though it is dozing, the ox in the painting makes an extremely lively impression. Fritz Hug – born in Dornach near Basel in 1921 – succeeds in capturing the essence of the ox in an almost sketch-like way, a quality he achieved with most of his animal representations. It was Hug's joy in nature and his talent for meticulous observation that led him to painting. Zoo animals, game and pets, crocodiles and roosters, predatory cats and domestic dogs, all served as his models.

Many insects, e.g. the honeybee, sit still in a particular region of the bee-hive for hours during the night. There are many indications that this 'resting' behaviour could be related to sleep in mammals. It is obvious that sleep needs to be strictly defined: it is noteworthy that many authors have reported that species such as the horse, cow, elephant or guinea pig never sleep because they rarely assume a recumbent position with their eyes closed. It had been overlooked that many species are very susceptible to noise in the environment and can therefore rarely be 'surprised' by an observer while sleeping. Modern technology has provided the means to observe animals and reveal some of their 'secrets'[1]. Thus time-lapse video recordings with sensitive infrared light cameras allow the continuous observation of animals in their undisturbed night-time environment. I have recorded many nights of Asian elephants in the zoo and in the circus, and have described the amount of time the adults sleep per night (4–6.5 hours). An infant slept eight hours per night! Sleep onset started after 21.00 hours, increased progressively and reached a maximum between 1.00 and 4.00 hours. Sleeping bouts in the recumbent position had an average duration of 72 minutes.

Franz Marc (1880–1916)
Horses Resting
Coloured woodcut
Städelsches Kunstinstitut,
Frankfurt am Main

For a long time, it was thought that horses do not lie down to sleep. The reason for this assumption was that adult horses lie down to sleep mainly late at night, when people are also asleep. However, it is a fact that horses can also sleep when standing up. A stable will often be too confined for a horse comfortably to lie down and attain its usual sleeping position. Instead, the animal will then doze for several hours a night, with its head supported. Horses can sometimes be seen sleeping in a meadow, undisturbed and frequently in groups – as in this picture. They will be lying down, with the head tucked in. The young generally lie on their sides; they sleep more frequently during the day and for longer periods than adult horses.

Many years ago, in 1913, Henri Piéron, a French physiologist, introduced a set of behavioural criteria which defined sleep as a state that is periodically necessary, with an inherent rhythmicity relatively independent of the external conditions, and characterized by complete interruption of the brain's sensory and motor functions which link it to its environment. Although this last aspect is not quite correct, his definition of sleep, based on behaviour alone, has been adopted over the years and consists of several criteria:

1. Specific sleeping site.
2. Typical body posture.
3. Physical quiescence.
4. Elevated arousal threshold.
5. Rapid state reversibility.

The example of the crocodile, which can sit immobile with eyes closed for prolonged periods, but immediately reacts to a stimulus, illustrates the importance of including the criterion of an elevated arousal threshold to distinguish a sleeping animal from a resting animal.

Flanigan applied these criteria to define sleep in several reptiles: the caiman, iguana and turtle. Later the presence of sleep in these species was also corroborated by measuring the brain waves.

I have suggested the inclusion of a sixth criterion to define sleep: 'sleep regulation', i.e., compensation after sleep loss (see page 53).

(see page 53)

Criteria for defining sleep

Paul Gauguin (1848–1903)
Fleurs et chats, 1899
Oil on canvas, 92 × 71 cm
Ny Carlsberg Glyptotek, Copenhagen

While recovering from an arsenic intoxication in hospital in Papeete in October 1898, Gauguin wrote to his friend Daniel de Monfreid in Paris: 'I should like to ask a favour of you: I should like you to send some flower bulbs and seeds. Simple dahlias, nasturtiums, different sunflowers, flowers that will stand up to a hot climate. As you know, I love flowers more than anything else.' In February 1899 Gauguin was convinced that he had been cured. He built himself a hut, which was surrounded by tropical trees, and moved into it with his Vahine. De Monfreid had sent sixteen different kinds of seeds. Gauguin wrote to thank him: 'Most of them have come up. Will they ever reach their full size? When I am able to paint again, I shall do some studies of flowers. My life is so sad because of this illness, which is sapping all my strength.' The composition of this lovely flower study is marked by clear lines and harmonious proportions. Gauguin, who was struggling with serious financial problems, hoped that de Monfreid and Vollard could sell such paintings for him in Paris. The cool background to this particular example – echoing in some ways the style of Cézanne – accentuates the warm colours of the blossoms and leaves. Gauguin did not simply paint a bouquet of flowers that was placed in front of him. He wrote that he was 'not a painter of nature – even less so today than in the past. Everything takes place in my uncontrollable imagination.' His imagination fed on what he observed. In this example, the bunch of flowers becomes a dream of beauty, of nature's bounty and the music of colour and form. A contrast is formed by the two cats, the one on the right alert while that on the left is curled up and sunk unto itself.

Sleep polygraphy

Franz Marc (1880–1916)
Weisser Hund, 1910/1911
Oil on canvas, 62.5 × 105 cm
Städelsches Kunstinstitut,
Frankfurt am Main

For Franz Marc, animals were a rich source of metaphor for every kind of human behaviour. He painted many species of animal, but favoured horses and cats. Form in his paintings is simple to the point of abstraction, but he used it to enhance the symbolic dimension of his colours. In this example, the dog, wearing a collar to indicate ownership by somebody, is sleeping peacefully in the open air, perhaps in a woody glade. The colours are tranquil. Varying shades of white surround the animal. A touch of violet close to the body communicates the dog's vibrant warmth. Lost in sleep in the middle of the day, the animal is painted in a bright yellow that is enhanced by its proximity to the cool blue and related green. This rendering of an animal is a vision of peace. Together with Kandinsky and Gabrielle Münter, Franz Marc was a founder of the revolutionary group of Munich artists known as *Der Blaue Reiter.* He was a religious man, inspired by the spirit of St Francis, and he sensed and feared the danger inherent in the upheavals of his times. In 1913, he painted *Tierschicksale* (Animal destinies), which has come to be regarded as his masterpiece. It shows nature being submerged by storms and fire. Animals – as exemplified by the pig, horse and deer – respond. Marc intended this vision as an apocalyptic warning. On the back he wrote: *Und alles Sein ist flammend Leid* (And all being is scorching pain). The painting has come to be seen as a vision of the approaching First World War. The painter himself was to be consumed by this war – Verdun, on 4 March 1916.

Although the origin of the polygraphic history of sleep research is attributed to Berger (1930), who, in the 1920's, discovered the human electroencephalogram, which led to the first detailed investigations of sleep in man, as early as 1875 Caton had discovered changes in the EEG elicited by sensory stimulation in the rabbit and monkey. The first polygraphic record of an EEG was obtained in a dog by Pradvich-Neminsky in 1913. Although there were many early experiments in animals, sleep research, and therefore the definition of sleep stages, was largely based on the findings in humans. Over the years analogous sleep stages were described for mammals and even later for some of the non-mammalian vertebrates, i.e. birds, reptiles and even fish.

Even so, humans, cats and rats have been the most frequently employed subjects for sleep research. With the help of EEG recordings it has been possible to define sleep in the guinea pig, which does indeed sleep relatively little (seven hours per day) and only for short episodes (five to six minutes), and thus can no longer be considered 'not to sleep at all'. Similarly, Lev Mukhametov, a Russian biologist, has shown by means of electroencephalography that deer can sleep while they are ruminating.

In those animals in which the EEG can be measured the changes in brain waves have been taken as the clearest markers for defining sleep. This leaves us with the problem of whether species whose rest-activity behaviour cannot be correlated with changes in the brain waves can also be considered to sleep. The question is whether the prolonged periods of behavioural quiescence, e.g. in snakes, toads or invertebrates such as snails, octopus and insects, resemble sleep as it is defined for mammals. Application of the behavioural criteria for sleep have shown that for some species this may be the case. Furthermore, there is general consensus that most vertebrates sleep, behaviourally and electrographically. Amphibians, however, have rarely been investigated, and it is not clear whether they sleep at all. For fish there are many behavioural observations and very few EEG recordings to indicate that there may be EEG correlates of sleep in fish. In all snakes and in several lizards the eyelids are lacking, and so they cannot close their eyes in sleep. Nevertheless, reptiles have been shown to sleep both by behavioural and EEG criteria. In most reptiles the EEG changes differ from those found in mammals and birds at the onset of sleep: during sleep the EEG exhibits large spikes, and slow waves are absent. Michel Jouvet postulated that the neocortex is necessary for slow waves. Because the neocortex of reptiles is very thin, it may not be capable of generating slow waves.

Most studies of invertebrates have focused on their active behaviour or on the rest-activity rhythm, while rest has been dismissed as an uninteresting 'non-behaviour'. In arthropods, the honeybee, scorpion, flower moth and cockroach, arousal by a stimulus was systematically measured. It was possible to demonstrate that certain body and/or antennae positions correlated with decreased responsiveness to stimulation. These experiments led to the notion that arthropods, by behavioural criteria, may also exhibit 'sleep-like' states.

Reports of sleep-like behaviour in invertebrates other than arthropods (e.g. bees or scorpions) are anecdotal. However, observations of the sea-hare, *Aplysia,* a marine snail which returns to a particular location in the aquarium every night to 'sleep', suggest that sleep-like behaviour may also be found in non-arthropod invertebrates.

Rest-activity: circadian rhythmicity

Most animals exhibit a daily rest-activity rhythm, which is considered a basic biological rhythm. It can be assumed that sleep, as we know it for mammalian species, evolved from rest. It is important to note that a rhythmic, diurnal change from rest to activity *per se* is not a criterion for sleep. Many species (including the human species) can spend several hours per day in rest, and not sleep at all. In addition, experiments in which the internal clock (the nucleus suprachiasmaticus of the hypothalamus) was lesioned and all behaviour became arrhythmical have clearly shown that these animals still exhibit sleep: it is regularly dispersed within a 24-hour period and is no longer organized as a daily rhythm.

Because the sleep-wake rhythm most often coincides with the rest-activity rhythm, the measure of the latter can provide information on the 24-hour sleep-wake pattern in animals in which recording of the EEG is difficult or impossible. From telemetric studies or behavioural observations in the wild, particularly on full-moon nights, the natural rest-activity pattern of many species has become known. Thus the wolf exhibits a bimodal, crepuscular rest-activity pattern, with a marked episode of prolonged rest during the noon hours. In contrast, the domestic dog has adapted its rest-activity cycle to the human species. Activity monitors worn by dogs on the collar and simultaneously by the owner on the wrist have shown that the dog is active when his master is active and rests when his owner does not move around. In isolation, dogs are diurnal and exhibit a regular rest-activity pattern. However, if there is noise from the environment, the rest-activity pattern resembles the activity of the environment: for example, the activity patterns on week-ends differ markedly from those of the week-days.

The polygraphic sleep patterns of most mammals are very similar and closely resemble sleep in humans. In contrast to humans, where non-REM sleep is subdivided into stages 1–4, in most animals a distinction only between non-REM (non rapid eye movement) sleep and REM sleep is made. However, in apes, e.g. the chimpanzee, four sleep stages can be defined. But in monkeys, it is difficult to distinguish more than one NREM sleep stage. Several authors have subdivided NREM sleep into 'light' and 'deep' NREM sleep in cats, according to the number and amplitude of slow waves in the electroencephalogram. However, more sensitive methods for the analysis of the EEG, such as spectral analysis, have shown that NREM sleep represents a continuous process, and its subdivision is based on arbitrary criteria.

REM sleep, which was first described by Aserinsky and Kleitman (1953) in humans, was named 'paradoxical sleep' by Jouvet (1959). This designation was based on his studies in the cat in which he discovered the paradox-

Francisco Goya (1746–1828)
Charles III, King of Spain, around 1788
Oil on canvas, 210×127 cm
Prado, Madrid

This is a curious and certainly a memorable painting. There are several versions – identical apart from minor details – housed, for instance, at the Banco Externo de España in Madrid and the Madrid city hall (the latter version having earlier been in the royal palace). These large paintings are official royal portraits in multiple variations and executed in the tradition of Velázquez. They were painted by Goya in his capacity as court painter, head of the royal carpet manufactory and Member of the Royal academy of the fine arts. The academy was founded by Charles III, who looked towards Versailles. He also summoned Tiepolo to Madrid.

The style of the painting is thoroughly Rococo – as evidenced by the colours of the King's damask waistcoat and his medal ribbon, as well as a landscape resembling a set with the actor on the forestage. Wearing the costume of a hunter, he holds a flintlock in his gloved left hand and the other white glove casually in his right. On his head is a dark three-cornered hat. A white dog – symbol of loyalty to the master – sleeps at his feet. The animal's collar displays a royal inscription. All this is very much to be expected for an official court portrait – and yet a closer look at the face shows that this is not one of the usual court paintings aimed primarily at pleasing.

This is the unvarnished, unadorned truth: the large nose, the reddened eyes, the furrowed cheeks – it must have been Charles's own wish for his image to be reproduced with such honesty. The fact that this is a royal portrait that reveals the man is what makes it so memorable. Charles III was an enlightened, absolute ruler who limited the power of the Church, expelled the Jesuits (in 1767), organized the administration of his kingdom, liberalized trade – including with the colonies – and promoted the arts. His successor, Charles IV, under whom Goya was to become chief court painter, unfortunately lacked his stature.

Giovanni Segantini (1858–1899)
Knitting Girl in Savognin, 1888
Oil on canvas, 54 × 88 cm
Kunsthaus, Zurich. On loan from the
Gottfried-Keller-Stiftung

When the motherless Giovanni Segantini, whose father was from South Tyrol, left the orphanage in Milan in 1873, he began an apprenticeship as a house-painter. He later attended evening classes at the Brera, but he was too revolutionary-minded to stay there. His encounter with the art of Jean-François Millet was to be his epiphany, discovering on the one hand, Millet's use of light, and on the other his spiritual dedication to the harmony of man and animal in nature. Segantini decided that this was how he, too, was going to live and paint. In 1886, he found his ideal home in Savognin, a village in the Grisons region of Oberhalbstein, where he settled with his family and, painting in the open air, produced his mature work. He composed his pictures with delicately contrasting brushwork, applying complementary colours in the narrow spaces between the strokes and thereby creating the impression of luminosity. This example epitomizes his *Weltanschauung* and his art. The girl is seated on the meadow, watching over her sheep and knitting. The sun is shining down on the village, the fence, the girl and the sheep – the light-coloured ones standing and the brown ones asleep. Peace reigns supreme.

ical occurrence of muscle atonia concomitant with an EEG resembling waking. Although most animals exhibit rapid eye movements during episodes of REM sleep, many authors still prefer to use the term 'paradoxical sleep'.

Sleep has been studied in at least one species of each of the mammalian orders. With the exception of the dolphin and porpoise, all placentals so far studied have exhibited both NREM sleep and REM sleep. Marsupials (e.g. kangaroos) also sleep in a way that is similar to sleep in the placentals. There is a notable exception: REM sleep was absent in the spiny ant-eater, the only species of monotreme (the other living species belonging to the monotremes is the platypus) that has been recorded polygraphically. Because they are the most ancient group of mammals, the presence or absence of REM sleep in these animals is of interest in tracing the origin and evolution of this vigilance state. In the two species lacking REM sleep, the dolphin and ant-eater, only adult animals have been recorded. It is still possible that REM sleep may be present in the young or that REM sleep is absent in these animals because they are particularly sensitive to the recording procedures.

While a night's sleep in human subjects can be subdivided into four or five NREM sleep-REM sleep cycles of approximately 100 minutes, sleep in most animals consists of relatively short cycles: 10–12 minutes in the mouse and the rat and 28 minutes in the cat. The sleep cycle length in the elephant has not been determined by polygraphic recordings, but, assuming the cycle cannot be longer than an episode in a recumbent position, the duration of a cycle is approximately 72 minutes, and not the 124 minutes that have been reported in textbooks. The length of the NREM sleep-REM sleep cycle has been found to correlate negatively with an intense metabolism and long sleep duration[6]. Snyder in 1966 proposed that a short cycle could be advantageous because it allows animals to scan the environment during the brief awakenings which are typical of many animals at the end of each cycle.

Sleep cycle

Napping, monophasic and polyphasic sleep

While in the human subject as well as in several primates, sleep usually occurs in a consolidated (monophasic) phase (except for children, elderly people and habitual nappers) in most animals sleep is polyphasic, i.e. the sleep period is often interrupted by long activity bouts and the active phase of the 24-hour day is interrupted by sleep episodes[4]. This is particularly evident in cats and lions, which can be seen sleeping at any time of the day or night. A daily 'siesta' is by no means a privilege of humans alone. Many animals rest or sleep in a recumbent position during the noon hours: elephants, giraffes and zebras in the wild, or sometimes in the zoo, and cows, sheep and horses on pastureland. Nocturnality is particularly obvious in pets such as the golden hamster, which prefers to sleep when there is light, and which is active during a large portion of the night when the human species would prefer to sleep. Similarly, the crepuscular activity pattern of the domestic cat results in the disturbance of many a night's sleep for the owners, when the cat wakes up in the late hours of the night and manifests its wish to leave the house. Thus, the timing of daily sleep varies according to the species: some are diurnal, others nocturnal, and many more are crepuscular, whereas only few are almost arrhythmical.

Sleep in aquatic animals

Interestingly, there is a close relationship between EEG and behaviour in virtually all mammals studied thus far. However, in 1969 the studies of Shurley and Serafeditines in dolphins and later of Ridgway in seals revealed a peculiar phenomenon: these animals are capable of sleeping with only one brain half for several minutes or hours, while the other half of the brain shows a distinct waking EEG pattern, i.e. unihemispheric sleep. Observations of the animal's behaviour, which included swimming activity and eye closure, did not allow any classification into sleeping or waking. Lev Mukhametov and his co-workers from Moscow have been investigating this phenomenon in many aquatic mammalian species for several years. Their studies include recordings in an Amazonian manatee (sea cow), which relevaled the presence of unilateral sleep episodes in this species as well.

There are indications that some bird species may have very short episodes (lasting a few seconds) of unihemispheric sleep, besides the normal bihemispheric sleep pattern. However, in contrast to the dolphin, these unihemispheric sleep episodes are accompanied by closure of one eye. Many bird species can be observed closing one or the other eye for a few seconds.

There are also experimental situations in which a discrepancy between the EEG and behaviour can be elicited. For example, during a period of sleep deprivation in the rat, after a few hours the animal engages in waking behaviour and the EEG is of low voltage and high amplitude, resembling the EEG in sleep.

Effet de lunes

Voilà le moment (passe minuit) ou le calme et la paix regnent veritablement dans les heures
...nages. Vaut mieux tard que jamais.

Honoré Daumier (1808–1879)
Effet de lunes
Lithograph

Daumier was a penetrating observer of life among the petty bourgeoisie. This was, after all, his own class. The former Marseilles man earned his living by producing caricatures for newspapers in Paris. Many of his lithograph series are about the little pleasures, hopes, disappointments and tribulations of these people. He knew them all, and depicted them masterfully with free chalk strokes on Solnhofer stones. In his caption to this litho reproduction, he revealed the full truth: the entire family is asleep, the child in its cot, the cat on the blanket, husband and wife in the marital bed – draped with curtains because they want a bit of refinement, just like richer people. The scene is lit up by a full moon, which we perceive as a malicious voyeur, shining directly into the room and throwing into relief dark, shadowy areas. Daumier uses his caption to poke fun: these are the after-midnight hours, when peace and tranquillity reign even in married life – after all, late is always better than never.

Sleep duration

There is an enormous difference in sleep duration among mammalian orders[2]. Moreover, the proportion of sleep spent in REM sleep and NREM sleep is very different. Many correlations have been computed to make use of these differences in order to understand the significance of sleep and its substates[5]. Thus, Allison and Cicchetti have shown that mammals that are relatively secure during their sleep (e.g. small rodents and large carnivores) have longer periods of REM sleep than more endangered species which are exposed to predators. Large herbivores have only short periods of REM sleep.

Sleep duration varies between 2.9 hours in the horse and 19.9 hours in the little brown bat. It is the large herbivores which exhibit only a few hours of sleep compared with species such as the opossum and hedgehog, which sleep for 17–19 hours. Based on the assumption that sleep duration reflects the 'need' for sleep in each species, two main theories concerning the function of sleep have been proposed. Sleep has been viewed either as behaviourally adaptive immobility and non-responsiveness at a time of day when activity is disadvantageous, or as a process with a primarily restorative function. Obviously, the two theories do not conflict and can be combined. Zepelin and Rechtschaffen[6] examined, in 53 mammalian species, the possible relationship between sleep duration and lifespan, as well as between the duration of NREM sleep and REM sleep on the one hand and variables such as metabolic rate, brain-weight and body size on the other. Since sleep duration correlated positively with metabolic rate, the hypothesis was proposed that one function of sleep is to enforce rest and to limit metabolic requirements.

The amount of NREM sleep and REM sleep was generally found to be positively correlated. Allison and Cicchetti included ecological variables (severity of predation, security of the sleep site and a general estimate of predatory danger) in the correlation of the amount of NREM sleep and REM sleep with constitutional variables (brain-weight, body-weight, lifespan and gestation time) of 39 mammalian species. NREM sleep was mainly related to the animal's size and the weight of its brain (i.e. large animals have less NREM sleep), while REM sleep was associated with overall predation danger during waking or sleeping (i.e. animals who are in great danger have less REM sleep). Recently, Zepelin[5] further analysed the relationship between duration of REM sleep on the one hand and such factors as gestation time, precociousness, encephalization (i.e. size of the neocortex), litter size, metabolic rate, body size, predation and others on the other hand. He found, for example, a negative correlation between the amount of REM sleep in the adult, and brain size and degree of development at birth.

As in the human infant, many mammalian species have more sleep, and particularly more REM sleep, in the early development stage. In the course of maturation the amount of sleep decreases. For example, the kitten, young rat, piglet, lamb, seal and elephant all exhibit larger amounts of sleep during their maturation than as adults. In animals that are born more mature, e.g. the guinea pig, the total amount of sleep is only slightly above that of adults. Sheep have even been recorded as fetuses, in which an 'active sleep' stage in many ways resembling the REM sleep of mammals occurred most of the time.

Ontogeny of sleep in animals

Many species of birds have been electroencephalographically recorded. It can be concluded that the sleep EEG of birds and mammals is similar. They exhibit both NREM sleep and REM sleep. However, the REM sleep episodes are relatively short. It has been speculated that the REM sleep episodes must be short to ensure that birds do not fall off the branches during this sleep stage. This interpretation is improbable because many birds which sleep floating in the water or resting on the abdomen also exhibit only short REM sleep episodes. A study in the pigeon showed REM sleep rebound and a prolongation of REM sleep episodes after sleep deprivation, indicating that birds may also compensate for loss of sleep.

One challenge for modern technology and ethology is the question whether birds can sleep during the long periods of migration when they cross the ocean and cannot land. Can they sleep in flight? Do they sleep with one hemisphere? Or are they sleep-deprived? If the latter is true, then a marked rebound would be expected when they end their flight. Any capacity of birds to sleep in flight can be determined only by measuring the EEG. It would be very interesting to record birds during their long flights, and it would be particularly revealing to record them when they arrive at their destination. Many anecdotes report that swifts have never been seen to sleep. On the contrary, they seem to gather in the evening hours and have been observed gliding at very high altitudes throughout night.

Sleep in birds

Pieter Jacob Horemans
After the Hunt, 1729
Oil on canvas, 90.5 × 111.5 cm
Deutsches Historisches Museum, Berlin

The painter of this picture is the younger brother of Jan Joseph Horemans I (1682–1759), who was the most prominent of the Horemans family of painters and minor master in the production of Flemish society paintings, similar to the one we see here. A fine day is drawing to its close; the light is already cast at a very low angle. The hunt has been successfully concluded and the party has returned to a slightly dilapidated castle. The bag has been displayed, the guns have been put away, and the dogs have settled down. The castle fountain is spurting; it has already slaked the first thirst. A light meal of bread, fruit and wine has been prepared for the hungry hunters by the stylishly attired ladies. The company is engaged in conversation, picturesquely grouped round the broken columns. In the centre a man clad in blue is making overtures to a woman dressed in golden finery. A huntsman in courtly green garb is lying propped against a fluted column, overcome by fatigue, while his hunting dog lies sleeping at his feet. Another dog has placed its forepaws on the sleeper and is sniffing at him. But there is no response.

Sleep regulation

From our own experience we know that the need to sleep becomes stronger the longer we stay awake. Indeed, a very interesting finding in sleep research is the compensation that takes place when sleep is allowed after an unnaturally long waking period. Although this phenomenon has been investigated in great detail in humans and rats, the method of sleep deprivation as a tool to discover the function of sleep has a long tradition in sleep research. Thus, in 1921, Piéron walked throught the streets of Paris with several dogs to prevent them from sleeping; similar experiments were performed almost at the same time by Ishimori in Japan. Crile (1921) and Nicholls (1922) performed sleep deprivation in the rabbit and the guinea pig by placing the animals in a slowly rotating drum.

All animals that have been sleep-deprived have exhibited compensatory sleep during recovery. Thus, when sleep is recorded after, for instance, 24–36 hours of waking, recovery sleep is somewhat prolonged, with an increase in NREM sleep and paradoxical sleep. But the most striking feature is a marked increase in slow waves in NREM sleep. They are considered to indicate an 'intensification' of sleep. Such compensation for loss of sleep has been found in many mammals: humans, rats, hamsters, chipmunks, rabbits, cats, guinea pigs and dolphins. In the latter species, investigations which disturbed the animals only when one brain hemisphere showed signs of going to sleep, as ascertained by the slow waves in the EEG of that hemisphere, showed that the animals slept more in that hemisphere during recovery. These results indicate that sleep is needed by each hemisphere *per se*.

It is interesting that sleep deprivation in two bird species, the pigeon and barbary dove, several reptiles (e.g. caiman, iguana, tortoise), and even fish (perch, carp and gudgeon) revealed that these vertebrates also compensate for the loss of sleep. Because sleep deprivation in mammals is followed by compensatory mechanisms during recovery, the question whether disturbances of rest are similarly compensated in insects has been investigated. Cockroaches and scorpions that were disturbed during their resting period showed a decrease in active behaviour in the subsequent recovery period. These results could be interpreted as compensatory responses to the preceding deprivation of rest that are similar to those observed in vertebrates.

In a natural environment, there are many disturbances that prevent animals from achieving their normal daily quota of sleep. Although the function of sleep has still not been clarified, the development of the mechanisms which have been found in many animal species to compensate for the loss of sleep is a strong indication that sleep is a form of behaviour that is needed for survival.

References

1. Borbély, A.A: *Secrets of sleep.* New York: Basic Books, 1986 (Original in German: *Das Geheimnis des Schlafs.* Stuttgart: Deutsche Verlags-Anstalt, 1984) (out of print). New edition: Ullstein Sachbuch, 1991.
2. Campbell, S., Tobler, I.: Animal sleep: a review of sleep duration across phylogeny. *Neurosci Biobehav Rev 8,* 269–300 (1984).
3. Hassenberg, L.: *Ruhe und Schlaf bei Säugetieren.* Wittenberg Lutherstadt: Ziemsen, 1965.
4. Tobler, I.: Napping and polyphasic sleep in mammals; in: *Sleep and alertness: chronobiological, behavioural, and medical aspects of napping.* Ed. D.F. Dinges, R.J. Broughton. New York: Raven Press, 1989.
5. Zepelin, H.: Mammalian sleep; in: *Principles and practice of sleep medicine,* pp. 30–49. Philadelphia: Saunders, 1989.
6. Zepelin, H., Rechtschaffen, A.: Mammalian sleep, longevity, and energy metabolism. *Brain Behav Evol 10,* 425–470 (1976).

Asmus Jacob Carstens (1754–1798)
*Night with Her Children
Sleep and Death,* 1794
Black chalk, 74.5 × 98.5 cm
Schlossmuseum, Weimar

Carstens is the perfect representative of German classicism. Born in Silesia, his path was strewn with obstacles. Only after he had completed his apprenticeship as a cooper could the young man take his first steps towards realizing his goal – an art imbued with the purity and clarity of antiquity. From Copenhagen he moved to Lübeck and then Berlin, where he became a professor at the *Akademie.* However, he soon left Berlin for Rome, where he was to spend the rest of his life. Landscape painting had never appealed to him, and portraits were but his daily bread and butter. His interest was scenes from classical mythology in which he strove to render the human form in the spirit of classical beauty. This large and ambitious drawing, in the Weimar state art collections, is one of the finest examples of his work in this field. Goethe called Carstens a genius and the founder of a new age in German art. As he recorded in his notes on the year 1806, he had purchased some drawings from the late artist's estate on

behalf of the Grand Duchy's *Schlossmuseum* – and we can well understand why. According to Greek legend, Sleep and Death were twin brothers born of Nyx, the Goddess of Night. In the centre of the picture, the powerfully built nude Goddess sits on a cushion and is in the act of spreading out her veil. Between her knees is the boy Death, with the lowered torch in his hands. Sleep is leaning on her left thigh, holding poppy seed capsules. Behind this well-balanced group stands a row of figures with a whip, knife and stone. Carstens portrays Death and Sleep as helpers of mankind – an unavoidable but necessary part of life.

Infant Sleep: The Focus of Many Eyes

by Piero Salzarulo and Lorenza Melli

Various approaches have been used to investigate sleep in childhood. The oldest, used mainly in clinical and population studies, is observation of the child. The eyes of the observer note particular features believed to correspond to sleep: closed eyes, absence of body movements, regular respiration. The observer may be the researcher himself or, quite often, the mother, as in the Kleitman studies[7]. The observer may also be the eye of the painter.

More recently (from 1950 on), other techniques have been used for objective evaluation of infants' sleep. The most widely used, i.e., electrophysiological techniques, have provided descriptions of the biological components, in particular the EEG, the electrooculogram, the electromyogram, respiratory rhythm, the electrocardiogram and a distinction between two main types of sleep (see below for terminologies), as well as the time course of each variable within each sleep state (see, for instance, Salzarulo et al.[17], for the EEG). In other words, we can monitor the biological variables for periods ranging from a few hours to 24 hours, including waking[5]. Other 'objective' recording systems have been used: video tape with time-lapse camera, motility recordings, etc. Though these systems are less 'precise' in the evaluation of sleep parameters, they have the advantage of being less 'invasive'.

The use of a technique depends, of course, on the technological developments and research goals. In fact, the source of information may be experiments done in a laboratory setting (as in the majority of electrophysiological studies) or field studies. Until recent years, the latter, which are very informative, particularly concerning sleep under habitual conditions and the role of environment, employed the observation technique and videorecordings. The recent development of ambulatory monitoring systems should also allow the use of electrophysiological information in field studies.

How much sleep and when to sleep

Sleep is the prevalent behaviour at birth: neonates spend more than half the 24-hour period sleeping[7]. The trend in the following weeks and months is for the amount of sleep in the 24-hour period to be reduced, reaching an average of 10–11 hours at the end of the first year of life[5]. Conversely, the waking period not only becomes longer but also shows new and differentiated characteristics[22]. Both trends (sleeping and waking) are clearly related to CNS maturation.

The change with age in the amount of sleep is paralleled by a different distribution of sleep over night and day. There is a significant diminution in the amount of sleep in the day-time and an increase in night-time sleep[5]. The preference for night-time sleep usually starts during the second month[11].

As is generally known, in early postnatal life, sleep is distributed over the 24-hour period in several episodes, i.e., there is a polyphasic rhythm of sleep. In the following weeks and months (up to the end of the first year of life), there is a tendency for both the total amount of sleep (see above) and the number of sleep episodes to decline. In particular, the number of sleep episodes diminishes at night[15], leading to consolidation in a long sleep period. With increasing age, the brief alternating periods of sleep and waking decrease in number and there is a growing ability to enjoy regular episodes of sleep and waking. During the day-time, a baby in the second semester of life still has about two episodes of sleep, which, however, are of short duration[15]. Day-time sleep episodes are also seen in older children: four-year-old children take one nap per day, but not every day of the week[13]. It should be noted that, at this age and even more so later, daytime sleep episodes already depend greatly on cultural and social factors.

The occurrence of sleep episodes of short duration during the daytime suggests that different factors regulate the propensity to fall asleep and the ability to maintain sleep.

Sleep states and their development

Sleep is not a homogeneous biological condition. From the early stages of development onward we may distinguish two types of sleep. It is interesting to note that though some distinctive features were identified and described in the literature a long time ago, the global description of the constituents of each state is of more recent date. Aserinsky and Kleitman[1] described, in infants, the alternation of periods of sleep with, and periods without, body movements. Subsequent studies investigated other characteristics of the two types of sleep, adding new elements useful for their

Giovanni Bellini (ca. 1430–1516)
Madonna del Prato
Oil on canvas, 67 × 86 cm
National Gallery, London

The eyes of the observer are drawn from the group of figures in the foreground to the distant mountains beneath a cloud-filled sky. The main figures are painted against a geometrically ordered background of horizontal strips of meadow and arable land, the animal pens and the seated shepherd, the hills and the city walls, and vertical elements such as the trees, the upright figure at the well and, in the background, the towers of the city. Dürer visited Venice twice in order to study perspective and proportion. He became friends with Giovanni Bellini, about whom he wrote when he returned to Nuremberg: 'He is very old but is still the best painter.' Here, the Venetian's choice of colours solemnly enhance the Holy Family. The blue, red and white of Mary's garments form a triangle around the unclothed body of the sleeping infant Jesus. Thus, Bellini, whose work spanned the transition from Gothic to Renaissance, succeeds in placing the holy in the midst of everyday life.

Paul Gauguin (1848–1903)
Where Do We Come From?
Who Are We? Where Are We Going?
1897–1898
Oil on canvas, 170 × 450 cm
The Museum of Fine Arts, Boston

Disgusted with the commercial culture of Paris, Gauguin settled in Tahiti in 1891. Amidst the native Maori of the South Sea island, and later on La Dominique, the artist Gauguin created his great masterpieces. As a human being, however, he was constantly at odds with the colonial establishment, drank and was often ill. He died a lonely man in the South Sea in 1903. Like a coded self-portrait, this magnificent painting poses the fundamental questions: Where do we come from? Who are we? Where are we going? The answers are concealed in the pictorial symbols which the artist has gleaned from Maori myths. Words fail here. The observer may understand the meaning intuitively – only if we are stirred deeply by what we see can we

comprehend it. Gauguin has incorporated all his life's experience in this powerful composition. In a typical South Sea landscape, before the raised image of a god, people – surrounded by animals – stroll about or stand still, whisper, are silent or listen. The contours of the figures twist and coil like creepers over the entire surface. The colours are beautifully heavy. We are aware of foreboding, melancholy and longing, but also of a presentiment of imminent danger. This representation of life in all its many facets can be read like a book of prophecies – from the old woman, the primal mother, crouching on the left to the sleeping child, the well of life and promise, in the right foreground.

identification and leading to multiple terminologies: quiet sleep – active sleep; state 1 – state 2; regular sleep – irregular sleep; deep sleep – light sleep; no eye-movement period – interval of ocular and body activity, etc.[14].

Before describing the characteristics and changes with age of the two types of sleep, we would like to emphasize that both share an important concept, that of 'state'. A state is a stable biological condition that takes several variables into account; the combination of the variables is fixed for each state, all the variables changing their characteristics while shifting from one state to the next. These points were stressed by Prechtl and his group[12] in their developmental studies. Using this framework, it is interesting to note that sleep states 'emerge' before birth around the 34th–36th week of gestational age[10]. At that time several variables (body movements, eye movements, respiratory rhythm), which, independently of each other, in the previous weeks showed some kind of fluctuation with time, start to fluctuate 'in concert' and constitute the first 'image' of the sleep states.

After birth, other behavioural and physiological variables can be detected and recorded, some of which may be included among the criteria used to identify sleep states. In line with several other authors, we have established the following criteria[19]: Paradoxical sleep: eyes closed (or alternately open and closed), eye movements and, in addition, body or limb movements, low-voltage EEG, chin muscle atonia, irregular respiration. Quiet sleep: eyes closed, no eye movements, diminished body movements, EEG with slow waves (and spindles) or 'tracé alternant', regular respiration.

In addition, we took into consideration those periods which include some of the paradoxical sleep and some of the quiet sleep characteristics, which we called ambiguous sleep. As we could see, some of the criteria used to define the sleep states are behavioural and could thus be expressed in pictorial terms. Even if a photograph or a picture cannot show the dynamics of the events occurring during sleep, it is possible to reveal the main behavioural characteristics of a state. This holds true in particular for quiet sleep, in which the face is relaxed, movements are absent and respiration is regular. We may guess that most of the infant sleeps illustrated in the pictures correspond to the state of quiet sleep.

Sleep states change both quantitatively and qualitatively with age. The amount of paradoxical sleep per 24 hours diminishes in the first year of life from an average of five hours to about two hours; the reduction takes place only in the daytime[5], which suggests that the daytime sleep of a one-year-old infant is 'quiet' most of the time.

Guido Reni (1575–1642)
Madonna and Child
Oil on canvas
Galleria Doria Pamphili, Rome

In his lifetime Guido Reni was more celebrated than he is today. His art stood for the movement away from ecstatic mannerism towards rigour of composition, clear harmonic lines and the use of a few clear colours. The consonance of blue, red and gold in the Madonna's gown and the flow around the naked infant of violet through salmon pink to grey are typical of Reni's cerebral style of painting which so fascinated his eminent patrons in the Church and aristocracy of Bologna and Rome. In the early baroque period, tangible physicality, as shown here in the hands held in prayer, and the figure of the sleeping child, was much admired.

Claude Monet (1840–1926)
The Artist's Son Asleep
Oil on canvas
Ny Carlsberg Glyptotek, Copenhagen

Virtually everyone photographs, films or video tapes their children so as to record their development for posterity. It is less common for people to paint or draw members of their family. But painters make a habit of it – Claude Monet, for instance, whose portrait of his son is reproduced here. The child, dressed in his daytime clothes, is lying in his cot having his afternoon nap. His right hand has fallen over the doll that he has insisted on taking to bed with him. Bright light, like sunlight shining through a window, outlines with the help of shading the round head and accentuates the clear forehead, the red nose and the full lips, chin and cheeks. Monet, one of the great Impressionists, set out to capture a happy moment – the result is this spontaneous sketch with its flowing lines.

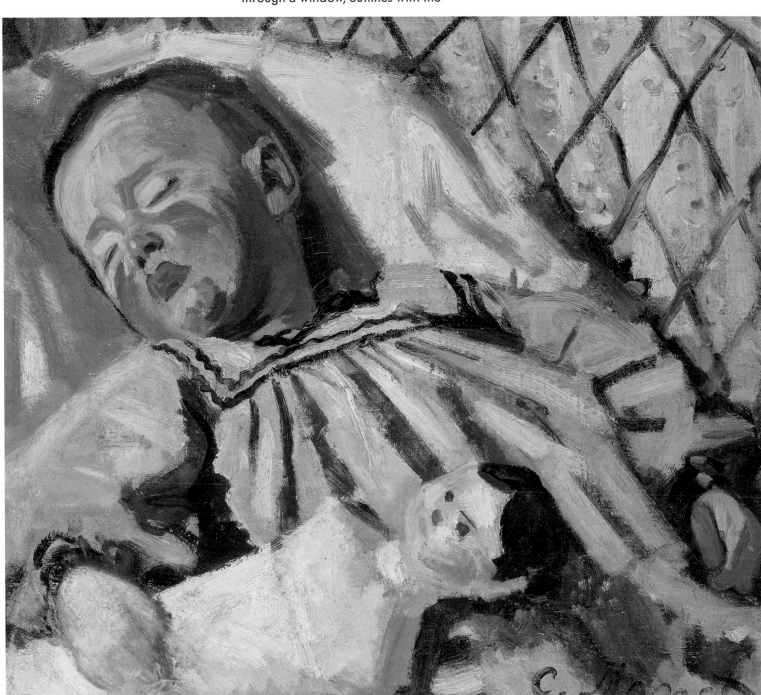

Jean Honoré Fragonard (1732—1806)
The Cradle
Musée de Picardie, Amiens

Fragonard was a remarkable person. Provençal by birth, a Parisian bourgeois by upbringing and education and a solicitor's clerk by training, he showed artistic talent and was accepted as an apprentice in the studio of the still-life painter Jean Baptiste Chardin. Although he had never attended the *Académie,* he won the coveted Prix de Rome in 1752 with a painting on a historical subject. He was in Italy between 1754 and 1761, staying in Rome and the Campagna and travelling to Naples and Venice. Years later, he visited Italy again, before going on to Vienna, Dresden and Strasbourg. This widely travelled man was taken under the wing of the distinguished painter François Boucher. But Fragonard was to break with the boudoir style of the 18th century, becoming, as it were, a precursor of Delacroix, who proclaimed that 'La peinture, c'est la couleur!' (painting is colour). The hallmarks of Fragonard's charming style of painting are his liberal palette, his spontaneous brushstrokes, the choreography in the sweep of his composition and, not least, the immediate, warm feeling for his subjects – like the youths in the present picture who have come upon a sleeping baby.

The amount of quiet sleep, which, at birth, is similar to that of paradoxical sleep, increases with age, particularly in the night-time period, while remaining the most important component of daytime sleep in a 12-month baby[16]. This means that, with age, infants spend most of their sleeptime in quiet sleep, a state characterized by a high level of homeostatic control[12, 23].

While both quiet sleep and paradoxical sleep continue with age to show the basic characteristics which contributed to their being defined as a 'state' (i.e., a stable biological condition), some aspects do change, for instance the changes in EEG activity, in particular during quiet sleep, with important steps in the first year of life[2, 17], the final step being the four stages of non-REM sleep habitually described in the adult.

What encompasses infant sleep?

While the effects of the environment on sleep have been extensively investigated in the adult, little is known about this aspect in relation to babies. Popular belief says that infants can fall asleep whatever the level of light and acoustic stimulation. However, mainly in the past, special care was given to protecting babies from external stimuli.

Few controlled investigations in natural conditions of the short-term effects of external stimuli on sleep initiation and/or maintenance have been performed. Some experiments performed in laboratory settings have suggested that sleep can be promoted by monotonous acoustic stimulation ('white noise'[20]) and by rocking[6]. To some extent, this kind of data furnishes experimental evidence to support a widely used (at least in the past, and even today in some cultures) mode of inducing sleep: the lullaby. Lullabies include the rocking of the infant in a cradle or in the mother's arms, and the melody, which is nearly always monotonous. It should, however, be pointed out that lullabies cannot be considered merely a stimulus that facilitates sleep. They form part of a complex relation between the mother and the child, and the passage from waking to sleep constitutes a 'privileged' moment of this relationship.

The study of the long-term effects of some external conditions is a different matter. This point is related mainly to the general question of the factors possibly involved in sleep regulation. Very few studies dealing with this perspective exist. The study performed by Martin du Pan[9] is well known. The author kept two infants in constant light for some weeks; in these conditions, they were able to sleep for consistent lengths of time, while their longest sleep episode occurred during the day rather than at night. When placed in normal environmental conditions, i.e., alternation of light and dark, the infants very rapidly started having their longest sleep episode at night. These results could be interpreted as an argument in favour of the

Schlaf, Kindchen, schlaf

Volksweise
Text: Aus ›Des Knaben Wunderhorn‹

1. Schlaf, Kind-chen, schlaf! Der Va-ter hüt't die Schaf, die Mut-ter schüttelt's Bäu-me-lein, da fällt her-ab ein Träu-me-lein. Schlaf, Kind-chen, schlaf!

2. Schlaf, Kindchen, schlaf!
Am Himmel ziehn die Schaf,
die Sternlein sind die Lämmerlein,
der Mond, der ist das Schäferlein.
Schlaf, Kindchen, schlaf!

Tomi Ungerer
Sleep, Little One, Sleep
From: *Das grosse Liederbuch*
Diogenes Verlag, Zurich

The Alsatian poet, painter and cartoonist has provided a rich set of illustrations for *Das grosse Liederbuch*, one in the series of *Diogenes Hausbücher. Schlaf, Kindchen, schlaf* (Sleep, little one, sleep) is one of the most popular German lullabies. Tongue in cheek, Ungerer has re-created the atmosphere of respectable petit-bourgeois family life. The full moon shines in through the window. A paraffin lamp stands on the bedside table. A pair of slippers lie on the bedside rug. The family's cat is asleep on the thick duvet. Underneath, father sleeps with his night-cap on. Mother is half-asleep beside him, rocking the child in the wooden cradle to sleep with her outstretched arm: 'Sleep, little one, sleep.'

role of light-dark alternation in the regulation of the temporal distribution of sleep and wake episodes.

Feeding has also long been thought to facilitate sleep: a baby sleeping after a meal is a popular image of restorative and peaceful sleep. However, Wolff[21] mentioned the possibility that sleep after a meal was more the result of the skin-to-skin contact between the mother and child than of the meal itself; infants being breast-fed fall asleep faster than infants being bottle-fed. The role of the rhythm of meals as a source of sleep-wake rhythm regulation has been called into question by results we obtained in continuously fed infants: the distribution of their sleep-wake episodes and of their sleep states was very similar to that of orally fed infants[4, 18, 19].

The role of afferent proprioceptive stimulation has been raised in some ethnological studies[3, 8]: infant swaddling seems to facilitate sleep.

Michelangelo Merisi da Caravaggio
(1573–1610)
Rest during the Flight into Egypt,
ca. 1586
Oil on canvas, 133 × 162 cm
Galleria Doria Pamphili, Rome

Caravaggio was named after his birth-place near Bergamo. He was a hot-tempered man who lived and duelled with men from the highest circles of the Church and the Order of the Knights of Malta. He was a vagrant, on the move between Milan, Venice, Rome, Malta, Sicily and Naples, often fleeing from his enemies; his talent was seldom appreciated. But his passionate nature was a fertile breeding ground for his art – an art that extolled beauty and tragedy. His way of seeing things was revolutionary. The precision with which he portrayed the reality of materials was combined with the movement

characteristic of *mannerist* composi-tion. The focal points of his scenes are illuminated as if by floodlight: Joseph holding the sheets of music; the young angel, around whose lovely body a white cloth is playfully draped; and Mary, who has nodded off from fatigue, with the sleeping infant Jesus on her lap. This way of portraying things was new. Its novelty and provo-cativeness, however, were to have an enormous influence on the development of painting right up to Rembrandt.

Rembrandt (1606–1669)
The Holy Family, ca. 1634
Oil on canvas, 183.5 × 123 cm
Bayerische Staatsgemäldesammlungen,
Alte Pinakothek, Munich

The portrayal of the Holy Family in
modest surroundings was very much in
line with the reformed religious thinking of the 17th century Dutch burghers.
Various tools of Joseph's trade, car-
pentry, hang on the back wall. Joseph
himself looks tenderly at his young wife
and child. Mary has lifted Jesus out of
the cradle and just finished nursing
him. The hunger of the chubby-cheeked
boy has been stilled and he now sleeps
blissfully. His mother holds him lightly in
her lap with her left arm, while she
warms his bare little feet with her right.
This scene is executed with the great
naturalness typical of Rembrandt,
whose strong Christian faith enabled
him on many occasions to render bibli-
cal subjects in such a way that they
could be understood by everybody.
And with what genius! The harmony of
the opaque colours set off by the light
is testimony to his art, not to mention
the apparently very natural but, in fact,
extremely skilful diagonal composition,
which incorporates the communicative
play of the hands in rhythmic fashion.

Andrea Mantegna (1431–1506)
Madonna and Child, ca. 1454
Oil on canvas, 42 × 32 cm
Nationalgalerie, Berlin

Mantegna, who was himself a collector of antiquities, embodied the spirit of early Humanism in the frescoes he painted in churches, chapels and palaces. The art of this North Italian merits the greatest respect. His achievements and the rigour and honesty with which he portrayed a new type of human being were a source of inspiration for the masters of the Renaissance that followed. Even Dürer wanted to visit him when he travelled from Venice to Mantua, but the Gonzaga family's court painter had just died. This delightful small-scale picture of the *Madonna and Child,* which Mantegna painted when he was barely 25 years old, possesses all the qualities that shaped his work: boldness of composition, as shown here in the severity which marks the Mother and Child's posture; the quasi-sculptural rendering of the human body through the use of a lateral light source that produces clear contours without illuminating the background, and the use of colour, which tends towards the monochrome. But this high art is imbued with the warmth and humanity of the contemplative young woman and the infant sleeping peacefully under her protective care.

Jean-François Millet (1785–1814)
Sleeping Child
Oil on canvas
The Chrysler Museum,
Norfolk, Virginia

Millet, the painter of country folk who was later to be so much admired by Van Gogh, was the son of simple peasants. However, his father recognized Jean-François's talent for drawing and helped him study the techniques of painting in Cherbourg. Millet later moved to Paris for further study. But because he did not feel at ease there, he and his young family left the city to go and live in Barbizon, where he made friends with people who shared his views, and painted the everyday life of the peasants in their cottages and on the fields. Millet and his friends saw the natural light shining over the countryside with new eyes and succeeded in capturing it in their paintings. Millet's works are imbued with a mild religiousness. In 1850 he painted *The Sower,* a picture that so impressed Van Gogh that he copied it towards the end of his life. *The Gleaners* of 1853 brought Millet recognition, and the *Angelus,* showing peasants at prayer after toil-

ing on the fields, irradiated by the evening light, made him famous. Our illustration is an image of simple household tasks. The father can be seen through the open window working in the garden. The room is barely furnished. The woman is doing some mending. She has drawn up her chair to the cradle, where the infant, carefully tucked in, is sleeping deeply. Its head is turned to the side, the mouth slightly open, the left hand resting on the cover and the right hanging over the edge of the cradle. The picture seems at first sight to capture spontaneously a moment in time. On closer scrutiny, however, the skill that underlies this simple composition is revealed by the interplay of diagonals of the window, the cradle and the woman, and by the sequence of colours – the blue, red and unifying brown tones.

Infant sleep in art

As we have previously remarked, the eye of the painter is a possible 'observer' of the sleeping child. At what epochs, for what reason and in what way was infant sleep represented in painting?

In ancient art, the choice of subject and the manner of executing it were often conditioned by the patron's wishes and by iconographic tradition. The mythological cupid asleep was frequently represented in Greek and Roman art as well as in the Neoclassicist period. He represented the peace of the senses. In Christian art, particularly in Northern Italian Renaissance paintings, the Christ Child is often depicted as sleeping near his mother. This sometimes suggests the death of the adult Christ: the posture of both may be very similar. In most Renaissance paintings, the representation of the sleeping child is an idealized image.

The *Cupid* of Caravaggio is a quiet different departure. The painter captures the realistic aspects of the sleeping body, such as the half-open mouth showing a glimpse of the teeth, and the sallow complexion.

The work depicting two small children in bed by Rubens offers a gentler, but nevertheless direct, image of reality. They are probably the artist's nephews, who usually served as models in Rubens's commissioned paintings. Rubens's purpose was clearly that of showing 'these' children in the state of sleep.

A similar attitude can be seen in the work of the Impressionists, for whom sleep represented an aspect of the human reality they were investigating.

It should be noted that, whatever the degree of realism involved, most of the representations of sleep correspond to the state of quiet sleep. The difficulty of representing movement rather than its absence could be an explanation of this tendency. Moreover, the social and cultural beliefs of the epoch may also play a role: until recently[1], sleep was believed to be a state of quietness and absence of activity. Finally, when artists started to portray infant sleep by taking their information from direct observation of children, they probably observed infant sleep during the daytime, when sleep is very often 'quiet'.

Peter Paul Rubens (1577–1640)
Sleeping Children
The National Museum of Western Art,
Tokyo

Rubens was a man of the world in the feudal age of the Baroque. As a courtier, he was accustomed to mixing in the highest circles. As a diplomat, he travelled often and widely on official missions. He was well paid, admired and pampered. His workshop was a meeting-place for devotees of his art and for princes and monarchs. He portrayed powerful rulers and beautiful women. His workshop, with its teams of countless assistants, executed all kinds of orders – altar paintings, historical canvases, scenes from mythology, allegories and even decorative work. The sketches provided by Rubens were masterly. Though many works were to a large extent executed by the assistants, they were always imbued with the sensuality of colour and vibrancy of form

that were Rubens's hallmarks. These qualities are particularly apparent in the intimate, small-scale works executed by the master himself. Our illustration is a case in point. This delightful study is the spontaneous product of an artistic perception that catches the finest nuances and captures them in flowing brushstrokes. The bedcovers and sheet are rendered with incomparable freedom. Bodies and heads, the *putti*-like chubby-cheeked children with their sun-drenched, sand-coloured curls, are rendered in more sculptural fashion. The child on the left is sleeping open-mouthed, while the other seems to be waking up.

Georges de La Tour (1593–1652)
Adoration of the Shepherds
Oil on canvas, 107×137 cm
Musée du Louvre, Paris

The composition is a central triangle with the tip pointing downwards and is designed solely to focus attention on the sleeping child. The painting style of the French artist Georges de La Tour is characterized by precision of drawing and the use of a few strong colour points which are incorporated into the picture in a precisely calculated manner. The work as a whole is reminiscent of a carefully composed group of sculptures. The burning candle in Joseph's right hand is the only source of the light that falls most brightly on the child in swaddling clothes, less brightly on Mary to the left (note the fascinating shadow cast by her hands) and in more subdued manner on the two shepherds and the lamb between them, and on the woman with the earthenware bowl. All eyes are on the child in the cradle. Reflections on the pupils of the worshippers' eyes bear witness to the light that becomes an inner light. Georges de La Tour is one of the last of the great painters of light – such as the Italian Michelangelo da Caravaggio (1573–1610) and the Dutch Gerard van Honthurst (1590–1656) – who practised their very particular art in the 17th century.

References

1. Aserinsky, E., Kleitman, N.: A motility cycle in sleeping infants as manifested by ocular and gross activity. *J Appl Physiol 8,* 11–18 (1955).

2. Bes, F., Baroncini, P., Dugovic, C., Fagioli, I., Schulz, H., Franc, B., Salzarulo, P.: Time course of night sleep EEG in the first year of life. *Electroencephalogr Clin Neurophysiol 69,* 501–507 (1988).

3. Chisholm, J.S., Richards, M.: Swaddling, cradleboards and the development of children. *Early Hum Dev 2/3,* 255–275 (1978).

4. Fagioli, I., Bes, F., Salzarulo, P.: 24-hour behavioural-states distribution in continuously fed infants. *Early Hum Dev 18,* 151–156 (1988).

5. Fagioli, I., Salzarulo, P.: Sleep-states development in the first year of life assessed through 24-hour recordings. *Early Hum Dev 6,* 215–228 (1982).

6. Frengut, R.H.: The effect of cradle rocking on the sleep pattern of neonates. Thesis, Yeshiva University, New York, 1977.

7. Kleitman, N.: *Sleep and wakefulness.* Chicago: University of Chicago Press, 1963.

8. Lipton, E.L., Steinschneider, A., Richmond, J.B.: Swaddling, a child-care practice: historical, cultural and experimental observations. *Pediatrics 35* (suppl.), 521–567 (1965).

9. Martin du Pan, R.: Le rôle du rythme circadien dans l'alimentation du nourrisson. *La femme et l'enfant 4,* 23–30 (1970).

10. Nijhuis, J.G., Prechtl, H.F.R., Martin, G.B. jr., Bots, R.S.: Are there behavioural states in human fetus? *Early Hum Dev 6,* 177–195 (1982).

11. Parmelee, A.H., Wenner, W.H., Schultz, H.R.: Infant sleep patterns from birth to 16 weeks of age. *J Pediatr 65,* 576–582 (1964).

12. Prechtl, H.F.R., O'Brien, M.: Behavioural states of the full-term newborn. The emergence of a concept; in: *Psychobiology of human newborn.* Ed. P. Stratton. New York: Wiley, 1982.

13. Reynolds, J., Mallay, H.: The sleep of children in a 24-hour nursery school. *J Gen Psychol 43,* 322–351 (1933).

14. Robinson, R.J. (Ed.): *Brain and early behaviour.* London, New York: Academic Press, 1969.

15. Salzarulo, P., Fagioli, I.: Sleep-wake rhythms and sleep structure in the first year of life; in: *Polyphasic and ultrashort sleep-wake patterns,* Ed. C. Stampi. Boston: Birkhäuser, in press.

16. Salzarulo, P., Fagioli, I.: Post-natal development of sleep organization in humans: searching for the emergence of 'S process'. *Neurophysiol Clin* (in press).

17. Salzarulo, P., Fagioli, I., Peirano, P., Bes, F., Schulz, H.: Levels of EEG background activity and sleep states in the first year of life; in: *Phasic events and dynamic organization of sleep,* pp. 53–63. Ed. M.G. Terzano, P.L. Halasz, A.C. Declerck. New York: Raven Press, 1991.

18. Salzarulo, P., Fagioli, I., Salomon, F., Duhamel, J.F., Ricpour, C.: Alimentation continue et rythme veille-sommeil chez l'enfant. *Arch Franç Pédiat 36* (suppl.), 26–32 (1979).

19. Salzarulo, P., Fagioli, I., Salomon, F., Ricpour, C., Raimbault, G., Ambrosi, S., Cicchi, O., Duhamel, J.F., Rigoard, M.T.: Sleep patterns in infants under continuous feeding from birth. *Electroencephalogr Clin Neurophysiol 49,* 330–336 (1980).

20. Wolff, P.: The causes, controls and organization of behaviour in the neonate. *Psychol Issues 1966/1,* 1–105.

21. Wolff, P.: Organization of behaviour in the first three months of life. *J Ass Res Nerv Ment Dis 51,* 132–153 (1973).

22. Wolff, P.: Discontinuous changes in human wakefulness around the end of the second month of life: a developmental perspective; in: *Continuity of neural functions from pre-natal to post-natal life.* Ed. H.F.R. Prechtl. Oxford: Blackwell, 1984.

23. Wolff, P.: *The behavioural states and the expression of the emotions in early infancy.* Chicago, London: The University of Chicago Press, 1987.

Francisco Goya (1746–1828)
Sleeping Woman,
Oil on canvas
The National Gallery of Ireland, Dublin

Among the most famous paintings of Goya in the Prado in Madrid are *The Clothed Maja* and *The Naked Maja.* Painted in 1797–1798, they were formerly in the possession of the Duchess of Alba, the wealthiest and most independent woman at the Spanish court. She was one of Goya's most devoted supporters on account of his genius as a painter and his spirit of critical independence. While convalescing after his serious illness in 1792, Goya lived for a time on her estate. He painted several portraits of the Duchess. It is said that Goya was a ladies' man – in his youth, he was known as 'El torero'. He was highly susceptible to female beauty, as is testified by the large number of fascinating paintings of women – famous, well-known and anonymous. His eye for the beauty of female form is probably at

the origin of this charming painting of a women asleep. Her body relaxed, she is lying with her rosy-cheeked face and her hair, a golden reflection, turned slightly to one side. Her bare shoulders are a cool, white flesh colour. Her high breasts and lightly draped body are covered with a fine cloth. The spontaneous, modern, almost impressionistic brushwork would suggest late Goya, were it not for the possibility that this canvas, like other paintings in the manner of Goya, could be ascribed to Eugenio Lucas, his best student, friend and imitator.

The subjective experience of sleep is as old as mankind, and the sight of sleeping organisms has never ceased to fascinate the human mind. Sleep was a source of inspiration to artists long before scientific study of its mysterious nature could be initiated.

The anatomical localization of sleep mechanisms is still poorly understood, but it appears to encompass almost the whole encephalon. Somnolence and insomnia have been associated by von Economo[6] with lesions of the caudal and rostral parts, respectively, of the hypothalamus. On the other hand, some events associated with sleep – such as atonia and myoclonic twitches – were shown by Jouvet[8] to be generated by structures located below the midbrain. From the functional viewpoint, it is indisputable that particularly the activity of the brain stem and the diencephalon underlies sleep phenomenology. However, all kinds of methodological approaches have clearly shown that sleep mechanisms involve not only bioelectrical processes but also subtle modulation by classic transmitters (acetylcholine, norepinephrine, serotonin, etc.) and humoral sleep factors. There are good reasons for avoiding controversial issues in this chapter and for approaching the physiology of sleep more directly by considering its functional events in greater detail.

The most striking subjective features of sleep are the cessation of environmental consciousness and the onset of oneiric consciousness. To the observer, the most striking feature is the motor and postural quiescence associated with the depression of reactivity to stimuli. This quiescence, however, conceals a variety of physiological events which have been ignored in the past because of the lack of adequate monitoring instruments. Scientific study of sleep phenomena has been possible only in this century. The development of electrophysiological techniques has provided adequate tools for discovering the existence of a great number of hidden variables that undergo important changes during sleep.

In particular, the registration of the bioelectrical activity of the human brain (electroencephalogram) by Berger[2] in 1929 stimulated the study of sleep. The electroencephalogram was then taken as the criterion for dividing sleep into different stages related to the level of vigilance (in humans, Stages I, II, III and IV of synchronized sleep, showing a progressive increase of low-frequency and high-amplitude waves in the electroencephalogram). Initially, the existence of a further sleep stage was overlooked and the electroencephalogram was considered the most important variable for unravelling the mystery of sleep. Desynchronization (high-frequency, low-amplitude waves) and synchronization (low-frequency, high-amplitude waves) of the electroencephalogram were practically synonyms for

Sleep Physiology
by Pier Luigi Parmeggiani

wakefulness and sleep among the community of sleep researchers. The discoveries of EEG-synchronizing and desynchronizing nervous structures in the diencephalon by Hess[7], and Dempsey and Morison[5], and in the brain stem by Moruzzi and Magoun[9] in the forties were major achievements of this period and demonstrated that specific mechanisms underlie sleep and wakefulness. However, the surprise can be imagined when, in 1953, Aserinsky and Kleitman[1] observed a stage of sleep that showed a desynchronized electroencephalogram as in wakefulness, but associated with skeletal muscle atonia, myoclonic twitches and rapid eye movements. This stage was variously designated REM sleep, desynchronized sleep, paradoxical sleep and active sleep. Particularly the term 'paradoxical' testifies to the surprise that was felt when the reductionist sleep paradigm based only on the bioelectrical dimension failed to match the reality.

Besides the electroencephalogram, a number of variables such as body temperature, cardiovascular and respiratory activities and hormone secretion need to be taken into account when studying sleep. This is the case when sleep with circadian polyphasic or monophasic rhythmicity is being investigated. State-dependent changes in the regulation of physiological

Philipp Otto Runge (1777–1810)
Lehrstunde der Nachtigall, 1802–1803
Kunsthalle, Hamburg

This drawing is a study for the large oil painting on the same subject in the Hamburg Kunsthalle. Runge studied at the Copenhagen Academy before going on to Dresden for further training. On his return journey, he spent some time in Weimar as a guest of Goethe. In 1803 he settled in Hamburg with his family. Runge became the leading representative of North German early romantic painting. He was a quiet, reflective man who specialized in figurative paintings. In addition, however, he took a particular interest in the theory of art and in the problems and principles of the visual arts in general. His studies on colour were rated so highly by Goethe that the latter used them in his essay on the theory of colour and published a detailed letter of Runge's on the subject. The rigour of Runge's artistic philosophy is evident in this subtle study. The winged Muse in the oaktree glade is instructing the nightingale on how to produce lovely flute-like tones – a romantic motif that is placed in the oval composition with great precision and executed very meticulously. A tender detail in the background is the curly-headed child sleeping peacefully on a cushion in the fork of a tree.

Correggio (Antonio Allegri)
(1489–1534)
Zeus and Antiope, 1528
Oil on canvas, 190 × 124 cm
Musée du Louvre, Paris

Correggio is one of the most idiosyn-
cratic of Italian Renaissance painters. In
his choice of composition and colour
he was quite at odds with contemporaries such as Michelangelo and
Raphael. His much admired art, with its
lively, curving lines, was the forerunner
of a new style that evolved from Mannerism to Baroque. Innovative perspectives and viewpoints, a strong sense of
movement and a predilection for
unusual lighting effects and colours
are the hallmarks of this art, which
found its apotheosis in dome frescoes,
religious paintings and, particularly,
scenes from mythology. This painting of
Zeus and Antiope, a masterpiece of
Correggio's maturity, is an important
example of the latter genre. According
to Greek legend, Zeus, disguised as a
satyr, took the young Antiope
(daugther of Nykleus, the ruler of
Thebes) by force. Correggio's painting
depicts the moment at which Zeus fur-
tively approaches Antiope. The composition is created around a diagonal:
above left, the lustful god, bending
forward; below, the small figure of
cupid asleep; and stretched out
between them, the lovely Antiope.
Tired by the hunt, she has lain down to
sleep, face covered, and wrapped in
her green cloak, at the forest's edge.
Her quiver is beside her, and her right
hand is touching the red bow. Zeus, in
the form of a satyr, clovenfooted and
hairy of thigh, approaches the sleeping girl. He uncovers Antiope's head,
revealing the long, golden ringlets and
full, red lips. A dire fate awaits the girl
thus awakened: she will be raped, vili-
fied, hunted down, enslaved and, ultimately, driven to madness. Her fate
was described by Euripides in his now
lost tragedy 'Antiope'.

functions during sleep are related to environmental adaptation (e.g., to light-dark periodicity for balancing energy input-output to meet the different needs of nocturnal or diurnal animals) and to other basic physiological needs, particularly of the nervous system itself (e.g., ontogenic maturation, information processing, recovery of transmitter functions). That sleep is a physiological necessity is demonstrated by the fact that sleep deprivation is followed by sleep recovery.

The classic principle of homeostasis, developed by Claude Bernard[3] and Cannon[4], is a very useful conceptual tool for understanding many aspects of sleep physiology. Homeostasis means the stability of variables directly underlying cellular life. Such stability is achieved by means of regulatory mechanisms which cope with disturbances arising in the body or in the environment. The functional adjustments are carried out by feedback loops. It is clear today that the activity of such mechanisms changes according to behavioural states. In other words, synchronized sleep is characterized by good homeostatic control of physiological variables, whereas homeostatic control is impaired in desynchronized sleep.

In all species, cardiovascular activity is decreased during synchronized sleep. It depends on the increase in parasympathetic tonic outflow and the decrease in sympathetic tonic outflow in relation to wakefulness: the drops in heart rate and output and in vascular resistance underlie a slight fall in systemic arterial pressure. As a rule, autonomic changes in synchronized sleep are consistent with the functional condition of motor and postural quiescence. In contrast, desynchronized sleep in all species is characterized by a great variety and variability of autonomic events. Heart rate and output, vascular resistance and systemic arterial pressure may increase or decrease in comparison with synchronized sleep, particularly in relation to the rapid eye movements and myoclonic twitches of desynchronized sleep. Also baroreceptive and chemoreceptive reflexes may be depressed or enhanced. This variability is of central origin and depends on phasic excitation and depression of sympathetic and parasympathetic neurons respectively.

Respiration is affected by sleep. In synchronized sleep, the automatic control of respiration is freed from volitional influences. Breathing is very regular in animals and in humans (Stages III and IV). Chemosensitivity to carbon dioxide is slightly depressed and ventilation is reduced in line with the decrease in general metabolic activity. Periodic apnea may occur in some individuals (overweight, malformation of upper airways) as a result of upper airway muscle hypotonia. The respiratory events of desynchronized sleep are the expression of a functional alteration in the automatic control of ventilation in mammalian species. The frequency and amplitude of breaths are irregular, particularly in the presence of rapid eye movements and myoclonic twitches. Upper airway resistance increases further and may induce prolonged apnea episodes in the adult. In neonates, intercostal muscle atonia may produce inspiratory collapse of the thorax as a result of diaphragmatic suction. Chemoreceptive and mechanoreceptive reflexes are altered in relation to age and species, particularly during rapid eye movements. Such functional disturbances are central in origin since they persist after deafferentation.

Thermoregulation is effective during synchronized sleep, which is characterized by a regulated decrease in central temperature. In contrast, thermoregulatory responses to thermal simuli are suppressed (shivering, panting, vasomotion, piloerection) or depressed (sweating) during desynchronized sleep. Such striking impairment of thermoregulation during this stage of sleep is the result of a state-dependent functional alteration of the hypothalamic-preoptic thermostat, as recent studies showing loss of thermosensitivity of the neurons of these structures have clearly demonstrated.

The global involvement of autonomic regulation in the phenomenology of sleep is one of the most important facts emerging from the analysis of the experimental evidence. The behavioural states of sleep are the result of systemic changes in the functional organization of the whole encephalon. Such systemic changes ought to be considered from the perspective of the morphofunctional organization of the central nervous system effected by phylogenic and ontogenic processes. In other words, the behavioural states are the expression of reversible permutations in the functional dominance ($>$) of the different parts of the encephalon. Three ranks of functional dominance ($I > II > III$) may be attributed to the telencephalon (T), the diencephalon (D) and the rhombencephalon (R) during wakefulness and sleep on the basis of effector phenomenology. Telencephalic dominance in wakefulness ($T > D > R$) underlies the appropriate relationship of the organism to the environment in terms of sensory-motor integration at a high transformation rate of energy. In contrast, synchronized sleep is characterized by stability of automatic functions at a low transformation rate of energy because of loss of the functional dominance of telencephalic structures ($D > R > T$). The impaired homeostatic regulation in desynchronized sleep is a result of the loss of diencephalic dominance of brain stem mechanisms ($R > T > D$) and is associated with great instability of effector functions. Moreover, this functional condition may be of relevance to the subjective experience of dreaming. As indicated above, the hierarchical ranks

Giorgione (ca. 1477–1510)
Sleeping Venus, 1510
Oil on canvas, 108 × 175 cm
Staatliche Kunstsammlungen, Dresden
Gallery of Old Masters

In this picture, sleep is revealed in its tranquillity and innocence. Except for the figure of Venus, the painting was unfinished when the master was carried off by the plague raging in Venice in 1510. Titian (1485–1577), who had been a student of Giovanni Bellini together with Giorgione, was so impressed by the perfection of this rendering of the sleeping goddess that he completed it in no less masterly fashion, adding the landscape which Giorgione had only started. With this painting of a sleeping nude, Giorgione created a genre that was to inspire many later painters down to Ingres (1780–1867). Giorgio da Castelfranco, known as Giorgione, was born in the province of Treviso and was active in Venice as of 1508. In his oil paintings, he developed a fluid style whose harmonious lines and warm colours evoke a lyrical mood. This Venus embodies the High Renaissance's ideal of beauty. Mankind and landscape are in perfect harmony. From the nearby bushes at the left, the landscape stretches to the blue mountains in the distance and to the sea just on the horizon. The sky is at first hazy, but then cumulus clouds gather, which draw to themselves the mild evening light. In the middle

ground, the countryside is tidy, with green fields, ochre-coloured roads and buildings nestling at the foot of a fortress. The trees lend rhythm and outline to the upper and lower parts of the painting. In the foreground of this cosmos (cosmos, after all, means order), close to the observer, lies the woman, her head resting on a red cushion; she is breathing lightly, stretched out on eggshell-coloured drapery. From her elbow at the left, the contours of the white body flow smoothly down to the legs; the right calf and right arm are covered. The fluid line of the right side contrasts with the folds of the cloth and is answered by the more restless line on the left side or the body which runs from the dark-haired head over the shoulder, breast, arm and thigh down to the tip of the toes. The modelling of the body is gentle, and Venus's hand preserves her modesty.

Félix Vallotton (1865–1925)
Baigneuse aux coquilles, 1921
Oil on canvas, 97 × 116 cm
Private collection, Switzerland
© Vallotton Gallery, Lausanne

As his success as a representative of
'art nouveau' grew in bourgeois
society at the end of the last century,
Félix Vallotton developed the habit of
depicting his nudes in an almost
unpleasantly dry manner. His style was
terse, and he liked to give his figures
symbolic attributes. This studio nude
– the modelling due to the strong light
is almost obtrusive – is lying on an
imaginary sandy beach. The large sailing ship on the horizon, the seashells
nearby, the yellow strands of hair – all
have an allegorical significance, but
any erotic impulse is suppressed and
extinguished. At the end of his life,
Vallotton the pessimist presents only
hard facts.

of desynchronized sleep (R>T>D) represent not only the impairment of homeostatic regulation, owing to the attainment of the lowest rank of functional dominance by the diencephalon, but also a higher level of telencephalic vigilance in comparison with synchronized sleep (D>R>T). In other words, this telencephalic arousal which lacks the behavioural motor correlates could be considered the first step in the ascent of the telencephalon from the lowest rank attained during synchronized sleep to the highest rank of wakefulness (T>D>R). The mechanisms that may underlie such hierarchical permutations are still unknown, although it may be surmised that diffuse influences on neuron populations exerted by the monoaminergic and peptidergic regulatory systems of the encephalon may play a fundamental role in such processes.

The previous considerations suggest that sleep entails a risk of failure in physiological regulation. In this respect, synchronized and desynchronized sleep correspond to two basically different functional states, as illustrated in the earlier description of the most important physiological events occurring during sleep. Problems arise in synchronized sleep only when the mechanisms underlying automatic regulation are impaired. The 'physiological risk' in synchronized sleep is, therefore, relative, for it depends on extrinsic factors and not upon the actual regulation paradigm of this stage of sleep. In contrast, desynchronized sleep entails a 'physiological risk' as a result of its normal regulation features. This risk is intrinsic and, therefore, absolute.

The changes in automatic functions in sleep, and particularly in desynchronized sleep, are so important that, as recent clinical evidence suggests, they may constitute an actual health risk. This fact has important practical implications for the diagnosis and treatment of pathological conditions in many branches of medical practice. In conclusion, oversimplified views of the phylogenic evolution of sleep as the result of perfect adaptation to the environment are conceptually unsatisfactory.

At present, the teleological significance of the 'physiological risk' of desynchronized sleep, i.e. of maintaining in the adult organism non-homeostatic functional processes rooted in early phylogenesis and still present in fetal life, ought to be considered only in terms of an unknown, but basic, functional need of the mammalian central nervous system.

References

1. Aserinsky, E., Kleitman, N.: Regularly occurring periods of eye motility, and concomitant phenomena during sleep. *Science 118,* 273–274 (1953).
2. Berger, H.: Über das Elektrenkephalogramm des Menschen. *Arch Psychiatr Nervenheilkd 87,* 527–570 (1929).
3. Bernard, C.: *Leçons sur les phénomènes de la vie communs aux animaux et aux végétaux,* Vol. 1, 2. Paris: Museum, 1878–1879.
4. Cannon, W. B.: Organization for physiological homeostasis. *Physiol Rev 9,* 399–431 (1929).
5. Dempsey, E. W., Morison, R. S.: The production of rhythmically recurrent cortical potentials after localized thalamic stimulation. *Am J Physiol 135,* 293–300 (1942).
6. Economo von, C.: Sleep as a problem of localization. *J Nerv Ment Dis 71,* 249–259 (1930).
7. Hess, W. R.: Das Schlafsyndrom als Folge dienzephaler Reizung. *Helv Physiol Pharmacol Acta 2,* 305–344 (1944).
8. Jouvet, M.: Recherches sur les structures nerveuses et les mécanismes responsables des différentes phases du sommeil physiologique. *Arch Ital Biol 100,* 125–206 (1962).
9. Moruzzi, G., Magoun, H. W.: Brainstem reticular formation and activation of the EEG. *Electroencephalogr Clin Neurophysiol 1,* 455–473 (1949).

Giotto (ca. 1266–1337)
The Dream of Joachim, 1303–1305
Fresco
Arena Chapel, Padua, Italy

The discussion between the contemporaries Dante and Giotto, the great poet and the great painter, in the Arena Chapel in Padua was one of the high points in Western culture. Dante had been banned from his native Florence in 1302 and came to Padua during his wanderings. At the time, Giotto was working on his powerful fresco cycle on the life of Mary and her Son, Jesus, a commission of the wealthy local patrician Enrico Scrovegni. This cycle

became the masterpiece of his mature period. The literary sources were the apocryphal gospels of Proto-James and Pseudo-Matthew in the Legenda Aurea. They tell of the childless marriage of the god-fearing Joachim and his wife Anna. Because Joachim had no children, he was not allowed to sacrifice in the Temple. Deeply shamed, he withdrew into the wilderness to live with the shepherds. This fresco shows an angel appearing to Joachim in a dream. The angel commands him to return to Anna, who will bear him a child. Giotto's manner is simple and calm and yet monumental. The drama is shown against a backdrop of moun-

tains, shepherds, sheep and a hut. Giotto, interweaving contours and colours, focuses on the sleeping figure of Joachim, who will awake from his dream full of confidence. He will go to meet his wife Anna, to whom an angel has brought the same good news, at the Golden Gate. Their child will be Mary, destined to be the mother of God's Son, Jesus.

The Dream in Art: Pictures and Symbols

by Silvia Evangelisti

In ancient culture the concept of the dream and the concept of prophecy were closely linked; at least the dream was considered a special place where predictions or revelations could be received from the gods. The idea that the dream was the preferred starting point for contact with divinity lives on into the Christian era, and in artistic representations we find innumerable examples of divine visions embodied in dream-like situations.

From the Middle Ages until the 18th century, the representation of the dream in the fine art of the west was, for artists generally, that 'place' in which they could describe what was by its nature indescribable; that is, the realm of the transcendental and celestial (as when describing visions or divine apparitions), or of the spiritual-ideal (the world of pure thought, Plato's Empyrean). Describing a dream event through pictures served to convey a religious or philosophical message, and therefore had to use a language understood by the target public, based on acquired and accepted traditions stemming from myths, religion and, at all events, a common cultural heritage. An example of a narrative language fully adapted to the religiosity of the 14th century (yet so new and revolutionary from an artistic viewpoint) is that used by Giotto in the Basilica of Saint Francis in Assisi or in the Capella degli Scrovegni in Padua, where the artist related the dream pictorially according to a definite division of space: Giotto put the sleeper and the events of the dream in separate places so as to leave no doubt that the two scenes had different sources – the first a realistic and the second a celestial one.

The 'educated' artists of the 16th century, with Raphael at their head, favoured a narrower and more intellectual treatment of this theme. Imbued with neo-Platonic and Ficinian theories, they regarded the source from which dreams are derived as the seat of the imagination, of philosophical thought and of the highest spirituality, which cannot be portrayed in pictures.

Attempts have been made elsewhere[3] to elucidate the relationship between art and dream using a number of examples which might represent an investigation of the analogies between the two spheres with respect to the inner mechanism and the form of expression. These examples extend from the Middle Ages to the present century like a pictorial meta-glossary. However, at this point we should like to turn to a discussion of scenes and symbols of the dream as portrayed by some post-1850 artists, with the help of a limited and purely illustrative selection of works of art.

85

Giotto (ca. 1266–1337)
The Dream of Pope Innocent III
Fresco
San Francesco, The Upper Church
Assisi, Italy

In *The Divine Comedy* (Canto XI, verses 94–96), Dante praises Giotto: 'Once, Cimabue thought to hold the field
In painting; Giotto's all the rage to-day;
The other's fame lies in the dust concealed.'*

Giotto ushered in a new epoch in the history of Western art. This great painter depicted in his fresco cycle in the Upper Church of San Francesco in Assisi the life of another great man, the holy beggar, St Francis of Assisi (1182–1226). The 28 frescoes capture the life, deeds and death of the saint known as 'il poverello'. The sixth scene shows Pope Innocent III (1198–1216) dreaming that St Francis is holding up the Church (symbolized as Rome's San Giovanni in Laterano), which is tottering at a precarious angle.

Giotto lived in an age of upheaval, and this is reflected in his art. In the Assisi frescoes (which date from around the turn of the century), proportions have an inner significance: St Francis is shown as larger than the porch of the church which is about to collapse; space is not yet captured in its depth. Giotto's frescoes of ca. 1305 in the Scrovegni (or Arena) Chapel in Padua (where Dante, fleeing from political persecution in Florence, came to visit him), marked the beginning of the modern, autonomous picture.

* Translation by Dorothy Sayers.

Domenikos Theotokopoulos, called El Greco (1541–1614)
The Dream of Philip II, ca. 1580
Oil on canvas, 140 × 110 cm
Escorial, Madrid

Oddly, in El Greco's tour de force of colouring and commitment not a single person is asleep: everyone is praying. The object of this general adoration is the radiant name Jesu, as IHS like a sun in the sky. Those who turn their back on this are damned to hell. This painting has a strange history. In about 1566 the Orthodox icon painter Domenikos moved from the Cretan village of Phodele to Venice, where Titian, Tintoretto and Veronese had embodied the golden age of Venetian painting. After the extremely gifted young man felt he had profited enough there, he stopped briefly in Rome and then moved to Toledo, the real centre of power in the Catholic Church. At that time, Spain and its empire were ruled by Philip II, an extraordinarily austere man. At the foot of the Guadarrama Mountains northwest of Madrid, far from Toledo, he built the Escorial, a complex containing a church, monastery, barracks and college. It needed to be decorated, and in the hope of contracts to paint religious scenes, the Cretan, now known as El Greco, submitted this small painting as a sample of his work. Initially, it seemed that the king liked it. But after seeing a second, larger painting, *The Martyrdom of St Maurice,* Philip lost all interest. Thereupon Greco started enjoying great success in clerical Toledo. He became Spain's greatest painter of religious scenes. Our picture refers to chapter 2, verse 10 of St Paul's letter to the Philippians, 'that at the name of Jesus every knee should bow, in heaven and on earth and under the earth'. Philip II is shown kneeling in black raiment, the Grand Inquisitor in an ermine cape, facing him Pope Gregory VIII. Above the worshippers are ranked the saints and the heavenly hosts, all kneeling around the Mother of God, as she gazes up at the celestial light. And that is how it should be: that is what the strictly orthodox, fanatical, black king of Spain demanded. El Greco expressed Philip's dream with the radiance of a great colourist. This justifies the title.

62.

José de Ribera (1588–1652)
Jacob's Dream
Oil on canvas, 179 × 233 cm
Prado, Madrid

The *Old Testament* (Genesis, Ch. 28) tells the story of Jacob's dream, and it has inspired many Christian painters from different countries and with different types.

In this painting, Jacob lies with his eyes closed and sees in his dream the full array of heavenly life. Worn out and weary, he is resting near a tree trunk by the roadside and has placed his head on a stone, which is covered with a cloak. The bright cloud bank behind him and the light on his spiritualized face vividly express the dreams Jacob is experiencing. The influence of the *chiaroscuro* style, popularized by the Italian Caravaggio (1573–1610), is evident, but the tonal relationships are entirely Spanish. The sombre mood of the picture is also typi-cally Spanish (and is absent from the religious painting of Italy and France). The intertwining of reality and inwardness, a typical feature of Ribera's work, is also Spanish. While Velázquez (1599–1660) served his king and friend Philip IV, Ribera (known as 'Lo Spagnoletto') graced the Spanish viceroy's court in Naples.

Since the Romantic period, artists have generally favoured an approach to the dream world that is linked to symbolism and the associations characteristic of dreams. These are ambiguous by nature and devoid of any logical connection with the generally understandable real world; they are the fruit of the artist's individual and unique imagination. 'In the waking state, every person has a common universe. In sleep, however, each turns to his own', wrote Heraclitus.

For the description of a dream (which is bound to the representation of dreamt visions), a new path therefore opens up which leads into the broad field of the artist's subjective imagination, treading the ground of the fantastic where images of the real are drawn in and often combined incongruously.

This is the dream dimension of the symbolist painters; they turn to the dream as the realm of the subjective, where the spirit of the individual — freed from the bounds of the logic which determines everyday reality — is able to cross the infinite fields of its own imagination and reach *another* reality which is no less real and immediate than everyday life and exists as a continuation and amplification of it. By using technically 'perfect', 'artificial' (sometimes to the point of illusion) painting (for examples one might think of Gustave Moreau, Franz von Stuck or Dante Gabriel Rossetti), or a restless and quivering drawing style that relies wholly on suggestive and indicative *chiaroscuro* (the graphic works of Alfred Kubin, Ferdinand Knopff and Odilon Redon are particular examples of this), symbolist painters describe this *other* world as something more real than reality itself.

In the realm of the dream the *other* reality reveals itself: the ambiguous and secret reality which exists in everyone's life and which is controlled by the pulsing of the senses; the realm of desire and of demons, immune to the guidance of reason, yet the unique and irreplaceable treasure-chamber of life's deepest secrets. 'Suggestive art is like irradiating things with dreams, where thought is also generated', observes Redon in his diary *A soi-même*[9].

Besides this interpretation of the dream as the realm of the surreal and of a secret and different reality, the realm of dream finds a further use in symbolist painting among those artists who have favoured its character as a mysterious place of unreality and mythical fantasy where they can rediscover the symbolic pictures of an ancient lost paradise, or which they can use as a place of refuge, remote from reality, for locating their own secret desires.

Freud always stressed that both our individual childhood and the childhood of our society remained permanently within us. The 'evolution' of

Dream and myth in symbolist painters

Alfred Kubin (1877–1959)
A Dream Visits us Every Night
Drawing on paper, 26 × 24 cm
Städtische Galerie im Lenbachhaus,
Munich

Kubin's real interest was not painting, but drawing: he was a highly original and gifted draughtsman. He left an apprenticeship in photography to study drawing at the Academy in Munich. Tired of life, he wanted to take his own on his mother's grave, but the revolver jammed. He had found his subject. Gauguin fled civilized Paris for the myths of the South Sea Maoris. In an age that believed technical progress was the answer to everything, the customs-officer Rousseau turned his fascination with botanical and zoological gardens into a dark poetic vision of the primal forest, the apocalypse and dreams. Redon, whom Kubin knew personally, secreted reality behind a veil of quiet symbolism. In his paintings of people, Ensor, whom Kubin admired, unmasked the constant self-delusion of the bourgeoisie. Klee, Kubin's friend since their time together in the *Blaue Reiter* group, painted pictures whose meaning only became apparent in the course of the artistic process, creating a world of optic poetry that, instead of reproducing what was already obvious, revealed what was not. In his graphic works, Kubin laid bare the dark, demonic and morbid worlds lurking behind the façade of everyday routine: there is no clear distinction between this façade and the dark side of man and life. Kubin's oeuvre comprises several thousand drawings. He also illustrated the poetic texts of writers who shared his view of the world, among them E.T.A. Hoffmann, E.A. Poe, G. de Nerval, G. Meyrink and F.M. Dostoevski. In his early work, Kubin was influenced by the Surrealists.

both the individual and the species constitutes progress, not victory, and history, even when forgotten, can at any time become a disturbing or an explanatory factor in the memory, even – indeed particularly – in the dream.

According to Freud, 'the original conditions of the mind can always be reproduced. The psychic origins are in the truest sense immortal[5].'

The reappearance of the past in the present is contained in the concept of 'repetition compulsion', and the *constantly recurring dream* is a prime example of subjective fulfilment. The concept has an anthropological basis in the repetitiveness of symbolic elements in the work of an artist or in art *in general*. This phenomenon is the basis for the theory developed by Jung concerning archetypes of the collective unconscious, which today more than ever represents an essential and important interface between psychoanalytical theory and other areas of knowledge. Among them is undoubtedly the history of art, particularly as regards the analysis of hidden elements in an artistic work.

Freud cites the phenomenon of *regression* as an essential feature of the dream, where it appears as a symbol. In the dream, the regression expresses itself as a hallucination, as defined by Freud. This is a hallucination which can be put into a topical concept and assist psychoanalysis to find its bearings in the dark maze of the unconscious. But it is also of value to all who wish to trace dream-regression in works of art. The formal arrangement of symbolic elements in relation to their arrangement in a context reveals the correspondence between the two significant areas of distraction from the concept of reality (namely artistic representation and 'dream work').

In this sense the evocation of myth can be seen as a regression to the archetypal roots of human history, a kind of dream-memory which by its 'distraction from the concept of reality' provides the present with a primordial insight. 'By means of culture-related dreams the history of mankind speaks in the first person and recalls – through myth, metaphor and ritual – everything that remains hidden from the conscious while in the waking state. Between history and the unhistorical, there extends the realm of fantasy which binds together day and night, the ordinary and the extraordinary, man and his gods and demons[10].'

The German post-romantic painters, 'dreamy and profound' as Arnold Böcklin declared, speaking of himself, sought this 'distraction' from reality in the dimension of myth as a timeless realm devoid of history, where things meet and coexist according to inner, autonomous rules, ignoring the laws of rationality and the concepts of time and space. Myth – a univer-

sally and eternally inalterable *reality* which can be understood only through symbols, represents the *other*, inner world hiding behind visible reality; the key to this reality is symbolized by dreaming, which is 'our usual source of mythological representation' as Edward C. Whitmond writes in *The Symbolic Quest: Basic Concepts of Analytical Psychology*[12].

For artists like Arnold Böcklin (1827–1901) and his pupil Max Klinger (1857–1920), an engraver, painter and sculptor with more marked symbolist traits, the realm of dream melts into the magical realm of myth and symbol, as the instrument of understanding. Through the images of myth and its symbols, they try to reach and touch the profound secret meaning of nature, 'the darker side of life'.

In contrast with Böcklin's 'dream', which sought the profound truths about the mysterious pulsing of the natural universe in the world of myth, there stands the vision of those artists who strive in the dream for a utopian, ideal and harmonious reality and use the dream as a safe refuge, protected from the menacing blows of earthly fate. In the work of these artists, dreaming expresses a longing for a flight from reality and becomes a medium which allows entry to a yearned-for, mysterious world of bliss. Thus, the dream becomes utopia and paradisiacal illusion. The utopian dream with a 'metahistorical' character is exemplified by *The Architect's Dream* by Thomas Cole (1801–1848), an outstanding representative of American romanticism and founder of the Hudson River school.

The French painter Pierre Puvis de Chavannes (1824–1898) on the other hand looks for his Garden of Eden outside time and history. For him, the dream is a faraway place, a world on its own, foreign and isolated. Even time, which in his pictures appears to be suspended, has no relation to real time, but like the frozen, honey-coloured light, belongs to a dimension of longed-for bliss in a place of unending dreams.

The dream seems here to be an allegory of a magical, enchanted happiness with a vision similar to that of Puvis de Chavannes's contemporary, Edward Burne-Jones (1833–1898), 'the last Pre-Raphaelite'. The protagonists in his pictures are allegorical figures taken from classical mythology, medieval legends or Christian tradition, portrayed in coy poses graceful to the point of *affectedness*. While they express a deceptive and unshakeable sensibility and are placed in idyllic landscapes belonging to the world of dreams, they seem to be estranged from the whole environment and all worldly passions. A totally different mood — albeit equally masterly in its execution — surrounds the women's figures 'dreamed' by their creator Dante Gabriel Rossetti (1828–1882): they are the erotic expression of an intense overpowering passion which the artist tries to keep in check by styl-

Arnold Böcklin (1827–1901)
Waldlandschaft mit ruhendem Pan, ca. 1855
Oil on canvas, 90×77.5 cm
Kunstmuseum, Basel

The 19th century is, quite rightly, considered to be the century of France's great painters: from Ingres, Delacroix and Corot to Manet, Monet and Renoir and to Gauguin and Cézanne. However, Britain, Germany and Switzerland also had painters whose distinctiveness is gaining critical recognition. One of the most important was Arnold Böcklin from Basel. He draws on a subject matter which is familiar to the educated middle classes. Unlike the city-bred Corot, who painted his light-shimmering Ile de France landscapes outside, or the country-bred Courbet, who tried to conquer Paris with his unabashed realism, Böcklin, who had trained in Düsseldorf and married a Roman, carefully composed his mythical scenes within his studio walls. Böcklin is a dreamer in his feelings, a classicist in his thoughts and a pedantic and yet inspired portrayer of nature in his pictorial idiom. The goat-footed Pan is lying on the ground, half in the shade, transported to a forest in the Jura. He has put down his flute and is daydreaming. Pan embodies unrestrained sensuality, the source of the unconscious and hidden side of every person, yet Pan is also calm, dreamy yearning.

Max Klinger (1857–1920)
Träume, 1884
Etching, 30.3 × 17.7 cm
Print Collection, Albertina, Vienna

At the age of seventeen, Klinger, the
son of a Leipzig soapmaker, enrolled at
the Academy of Arts in Karlsruhe. From
1877 to 1883 he lived in Berlin, where,
among other things, he worked in
Böcklin's studio. But he turned his back
on Neo-classicism to pursue, with great
discipline, his own vision of art. This
laid the basis for his graphic work,
which, with time, became increasingly
expressive, and was to occupy him for
the rest of his life. He is famous for his
cycles on sleep and dreams and their
mysterious causes, which de Chirico
wrote about and the Surrealists
admired. Our print *(Dreams)* is the third
sheet in the series *A Life.* It is obvious
that Klinger admired Goya's *Caprichos,* which lay bare the dark aspects
of human life. Through his technical
control of line and the interplay of
chiaroscuro, Klinger achieves a fluid
form of oppressive intensity, which
imparts an immediacy of presence to
the individual faces: the sleeping young
man, the pensive young woman, and
the nightmarish visages that beset and
crowd the pair.

94

Max Klinger (1857–1920)
Der Traum, 1878
Pen and ink on paper,
11 × 19 cm
Staatliche Graphische Sammlung,
Munich

It is hardly possible to do justice to Max
Klinger, that exceptional figure among
the masters of German art around
the turn of the century. He was a sculptor, painter, etcher and graphic artist.
In 1891 he published his *Malerei und
Zeichnung* (Painting and drawing), in
which he emphasizes the importance of
pencil, crayon and brush in ordering,
outlining and defining. A sojourn in
Italy set him on the path away from the
naturalism of his beginnings towards
the idealistic treatment of the historical,
philosophical, religious and mythological themes that characterize his mature
art, which displays marked Art Nouveau features. This pen-and-ink drawing, which Klinger produced when he
was twenty-four, depicts a woman fast
asleep in bed. We see only her face;
it emerges from layers of shading, the
modelled product of pure lines that
quiver across the white page. The
dream girl is borne aloft by a bird. The
dream within the sleeper's soul is set
off by an arrow shaft decorated with
a peacock feather and the symbolic
peacock's eye.

Thomas Cole (1801–1848)
The Architect's Dream, 1840
Oil on canvas, 134.7 × 213.6 cm
The Toledo Museum of Art,
Toledo (Ohio), USA

In 1832 William Dunlap, painter and museum director, published his account of the origin and progress of the fine arts in the United States. This first ever book on American art was an expres sion of the 'American dream', and was imbued with the conviction that the new American society, for which every-thing seemed possible, was also going to achieve unsuspected greatness in the arts. And Dunlap, an American Vasari, regarded Thomas Cole as an artist of greatness. Cole had left Britain for Ohio at the age of seventeen, and later moved to New York. His landscape paintings of New England inspired the artists of the important Hudson River school. In 1829 Cole returned to

Europe for three years. Claude Lorrain (1600–1682) became his exemplar; the visions of William Turner (1775–1851) fascinated him, as did the buildings of classical antiquity. These inspired him to produce great, visionary paintings on returning to America.

One of the most significant of these works is *The Architect's Dream.* The curtain of a magnificent stage has been drawn back. To the left, the spire of a church surrounded by solemnly sombre cypresses rises against the rays of the morning sun. In the foreground, the golden light of day is reflected in the waters of a harbour. On the far shore, we see the most glorious sacred build-ings ever created by humanity: the obelisques and pylons of Ancient Egyp-tian temples, the colossal hypostyle of the temple at Karnak, the ambulatories of the Athenian agora, classical Greek colonnaded temples, a Roman rotunda, an aqueduct and, rising heavenwards

and transcending all, the Great Pyramid of Cheops – that mountain of the gods created by human hand. The architect, surrounded by books and plans, contemplates all this from his vantage point on a column. Putting his faith in divine providence, he dreams that he, too, will be permitted to create such magnificent works of the human spirit and art for his country and fellow countrymen.

Pierre Puvis de Chavannes (1824–1898)
Le rêve
Oil on canvas
Musée d'Orsay, Paris

It was Puvis de Chavannes who said that 'art perfects what nature has sketched'. Proud words from a proud artist. In his time – when somebody like Gauguin lived in poverty – the greatest honours were heaped on him; today – perhaps unjustly – he is almost forgotten. The scion of an old and wealthy family in Burgundy, he wanted to become an engineer like his father but had to abandon his studies on account of illness. He decided to become a painter while travelling in Italy, where he was inspired by classical antiquity and Christianity. He became the most important fresco painter of the 19th century in France. His works in the Mairie of Poitiers, the museum in Marseille, the Pantheon in Paris and the Public Library of Boston (USA) bear witness to his desire to paint scenes mainly of a historical, religious and allegorical nature. At the height of impressionism, he championed the

highly structured, narrative composition, typical of Ferdinand Hodler's highly symbolic paintings. In his canvases, which are fewer in number, Puvis de Chavannes was a lyrical symbolist. Our picture *(Le rêve)* is a fine embodiment of this tendency. Weary, the traveller has laid aside his staff and his pack and has stretched out to sleep under a tree at the foot of a hill. A waning moon can be seen in the transparently blue, starlit heavens. The man – is he perhaps a misunderstood poet? – is dreaming that three genii are gliding by, strewing flowers and stars, and placing a golden laurel wreath on his head.

Dante Gabriel Rossetti (1828–1882)
Daydream, ca. 1880
Study, pastel, 104.9 × 76.8 cm
Ashmolean Museum, Oxford

izing the women into alarming, mysterious and unapproachable virgins to whom only the dream-world will secure access.

In reality, one should speak of 'rêverie' rather than dreaming in referring to Rossetti (*Rêverie* is indeed the title of one of his well-known works, of which he made a number of replicas), or one might speak of fantasizing by which the artist can release himself from the fatiguing and desperate everyday constraints of space and time and forget an unloved reality, replacing it with the vision of an imaginary and personal world where he alone sets the rules and frontiers. For the artist, eluding the dimension of time means finding eternity in the dream or in the attempt to regain peace in the solitude of a world visible to him alone, in which the agonizing obsessions and fantasies of Eros, as well as life and death, come under control. As the artist said, he does not lose himself in his imaginings, but rather they transport him – willy-nilly – out of this world. And Maria Teresa Benedetti adds: 'He lives his true and only life in that faraway dream-world represented by his idealized portraits of women: a dream which is often disturbed and which can become a veritable nightmare[1].'

The reality that is described in precise pictures evaporates increasingly in his portraits of women, which both resemble the models and are idealized. His models seem to have withdrawn into a distant and restricted space hovering between dream and reality, a clear sign of the artist's desire to seek solace in the individualistic dimension of the dream, in the melancholy restriction of his desperate but lucid vision, which was further intensified by his use of the drug chloral. According to the artist, people told him that dreaming contained many dreams, but he had found the whole of life to be nothing more than a single dream. His dream is one of love and death, where the picture of the woman – that is, the picture of the soul – which for the artist is a veritable obsession, reflects his feeling of unease and lack of fulfilment.

His painting 'always arises from a kind of creative *trance,* through a mixture of sensory and supernatural elements as in a dream or in the mood between dream and the waking state'[1].

Ambivalence of this kind has its precise counterpart both in pictorial reproduction and in the choice of symbols which fill the pictures – true figurative metaphors taken from a unique and confusing 'culture' of myths and legends from antiquity and the Middle Ages.

The middle of the 19th century was, in intellectual and artistic terms, like a patchwork quilt. Revolution was followed by restoration. Industrialization brought forth unrestrained capitalism and this was followed by the birth of Marxism. Narrow, feudal arrogance gave way all across Europe to nationalism, which generated new wars. The revolutions of 1830 and 1848 opened up new political perspectives. The proletariat grew in strength; intellectuals expressed their demands; artists, poets and musicians appeared on the scene, heralding a new era in art. Unlike the emerging impressionists, some artists longed for the past. The German 'Nazarenes' in Rome dedicated themselves to a renewal of religious art. In Britain the Pre-Raphaelite Brotherhood sought to rediscover forms and ideas which they believed to have existed in the period before Raphael. Rossetti, the leading light of the movement, and his companions Holman Hunt and John Everett Millais, created their poetry or painting from the depth of the soul, from an inner and very personal communion. Nature was to be more than a model; it was to provide impulses for art. This esoteric view was a substitute for religious art. Man must listen to the voice of his soul. Rossetti's study for *Daydream* draws on these ideas. A beautiful woman is sitting in a grove, as if she were part of the sycamore tree. For the ancient Egyptians, the sycamore was the tree of life. The young woman holds a flower in her narrow hand. If the calyx were facing upwards, it would signify the receipt of divine gifts; facing downwards, it is a symbol of death. The white of the woman's robe is also ambiguous: white can mean purity but also the absolution of death. Looking up from her book, the woman is lost in a daydream. Her eyes are gazing elegiacally at inner scenes. This approach to art and to life was a precursor of *Jugendstil* and *Art nouveau.*

Henri Rousseau (1844–1910)
Le rêve, 1910
Oil on canvas, 204.5 × 298.5 cm
The Museum of Modern Art, New York

We know a lot about Henri Rousseau, the man and his life – that he was physically small, had only limited schooling, that his wife was an unassuming soul and that both led simple lives. But how this self-taught scion of the lower middle classes was able to create paintings of such exquisite poetry remains a mystery. His achievement is an astonishing one. Aged around forty, he retired on a minor government official's pension in order to have more time for himself – for walking in the botanical and zoological gardens, but especially, of course, for his painting. For many in the Paris art scene, Rousseau – who termed himself a 'realist' – was not taken seriously. But Braque and Picasso admired him, and Jean Cocteau praised him as a great and original artist. Rousseau's works are veritable poems in paint with a tonality that is unmistakeably their own. *Le rêve* (The dream) depicts a primeval forest in which exotic, verdant vegetation of a fantastic nature proliferates. The forest is home to tropical birds, elephants, tigers, lions and snakes. The scene is lit by a full moon. A dark guru plays a flute. All of nature appears to be bewitched. At the centre, a voluptuous, naked woman reclines on a red divan resembling the one in the painter's studio. And yet her allure has a coolness about it. Does this scene represent the painter's dreams? Rousseau himself supplies an explanation couched in poetic terms: 'Cette femme endormie sur le divan rêve qu'elle a été transportée dans la forêt; elle écoute les sons de l'instrument de l'enchanteur.' (This woman asleep on the divan is dreaming that she has been transported to the forest; she listens to the sounds of the enchanter's instrument.) At the time, the artist was in love with Jadwiga, a young Polish girl. But whatever the droll Rousseau's source of inspiration for this painting, it is a masterpiece.

A truly unique case in the art history of the last century is Henri Rousseau (1844–1910), a self-taught 'naive' painter apparently foreign to the visual culture of his time, but in reality an indispensable member of the fascinating and extremely lively artistic movement known as the 'historical avant-garde'. A number of the key figures in this artistic development which revolutionized fine art at the beginning of this century, among them Picasso, Matisse, Derain and de Chirico, took note of his simple style which, disregarding academic rules, with its elementary drawing and flattening perspective, amazed both public and critics.

An enchanted feeling of happiness seems to emanate from Henri Rousseau's pictures, with their landscapes full of dream symbols which take absolute precedence over any connection with reality.

From among Rousseau's paintings we have chosen two representative ones, an example from the decisive years of his artistic experience and another from the final period of his creativity in which the artist concerned himself deeply with the subject of dreaming: the mysterious picture *The Dream* and the unusual painting *The Sleeping Gipsy*, a work which according to Robert Melville seems to hold the 'key to the riddle in painting'[8, 13]. *The Sleeping Gipsy* was especially valued by the Surrealists, who discovered it in 1924. In 1926, Jean Cocteau dedicated a poem to it in which he stressed the picture's ambiguity and suggested a number of possible interpretations: is the vision of a lion beside a sleeping gipsy in the desert the portrayal of a real event or the representation of what the gipsy is dreaming, asked Cocteau; or is the picture perhaps one of the artist's dreams? (It is known that Rousseau had the habit of keeping his working materials constantly by his bed so that, as he told Apollinaire, 'quand je me réveille, je peux faire risette à mes tableaux'. (When I wake up, I can smile at my pictures.)

We are in no position to find precise answers to these questions. However, the surrealists were not so much intrigued by the possible answers as by the capacity of the work to raise such questions by conjuring up an unreal and enchanted world in which light is nothing out of the ordinary, but simply a sourceless irradiation, and people and things cast no shadows.

In Jungian theory, the shadow represents the 'Alter ego'. According to Jung, shadow appears in almost all dreams in which we make use of a human being (often also an animal or an object), so that symbolic tasks or actions which cause us anxiety can be assigned to it. In this way we divide ourselves in order to save our self-image, which means much to us and which is indispensable if our feeling of our own worth is to remain undam-

Dream symbols in the enchanted landscapes of Henri Rousseau

aged; in symbolic 'danger situations' we put a kind of counterpart in our place. This phenomenon is also frequently met in folk tales, especially in situations where the young hero must undergo initiation rites for his emancipation, symbolized by the break with home and thus with childhood. At this moment the mother usually dies (as in Tom Thumb, Hansel and Gretel, Snow-White and so on), and a stepmother, functioning as a shadow, takes her place and assumes the unpleasant part of child-rearing with its rejection, trials and separation, so that the image of the original mother, who personified goodness and protection, can remain intact. In reality, however, the mother figure is one and the same.

Thus the presence of the shadow, despite its complexity and ambivalence, guarantees the integrity of the person: Barrie's Peter Pan, recently presented by Walt Disney in a somewhat different light, is simply a symbol of the refusal to step into real life, to remain in the life of dreams as an archetype of the 'puer aeternus'; he loses his shadow, and Wendy, in love but a genuine and corporeal child-wife, manages to reunite Peter's two 'souls'.

There are no shadows in Rousseau's pictures; objects and people — sharply delineated by clear outlines and 'single-toned colours without nuances or chiaroscuro' — are regularly and brightly lit, without however having any duplicate in the form of a shadow. We may believe with Jung that in truth there is nothing but shadows in Rousseau's painting, that nothing of what is portrayed can be attributed to reality; rather, the pictures are to be seen solely as the artist's dream landscape in which each object can only be interpreted symbolically. Even the very frequent appearance of animals permits a symbolic interpretation: animals enable us to see our consciousness, or in the sense of Laurens van der Post, our reflecting consciousness, and we may thank them for fire, language and symbol, for animals are the mirror-image of ourselves. We cannot know ourselves without looking at ourselves in the mirror[7].

Henri Rousseau (1844–1910)
La tzigane endormie, 1897
Oil on canvas, 129.5 × 200.7 cm
The Museum of Modern Art,
New York

This painting radiates tranquillity and poetry. It would be quite inaccurate to describe it as 'peinture naïve'. Henri Rousseau, whose position as a minor official at the Paris municipal customs house earned him the epithet of 'le Douanier', was certainly a strange man. But he was also a highly gifted painter who, despite being self-taught, came to be associated with the great outpouring of art that characterized the Paris of the turn of the century. Simple though they were in their execu-tion, his paintings – whether large or small in format – were products of an inner vision. Such great moments have been seldom enough in human history; at almost the same time, the Paris-based Romanian sculptor Brancusi (1876–1957) was creating works that were compressed in masterly fashion to render the essential – his *Muse endormie* is spiritually related to this picture of Rousseau's, with its depiction of sleep. In *La tzigane endormie,* we see the barefoot, dark gipsy girl in the foreground, her right hand still clutch-ing her staff. Her left arm is covered with a brightly coloured shawl and supports her head. She is wearing a headscarf as protection against the coolness of the night. Next to her is a mandoline, an instrument that, like Orpheus's lyre, symbolizes sleep, dreaming and enchantment. The finely modelled clay pitcher on the extreme right is also symbolic: a sacred vessel that contains secrets – including the dreams of whoever is sleeping next to it. The full moon exerts a massive presence in the star-spangled night sky. The landscape is hilly and barren. A lion has padded silently up to the sleeper and is inspecting her. The crea-ture's sulphurous-yellow eyes have a fixed expression; its tail is raised. Does danger threaten the sleeper? But noth-ing will happen – it is as if the world were hypnotized. Is the lion, that symbol of dominant power, passing through the gipsy's dream?

Giorgio de Chirico (1888–1978)
Nostalgia del poeta, 1914
Oil on canvas, 89 × 40 cm
Peggy Guggenheim Collection, Venice
(The Solomon R. Guggenheim
Foundation)

De Chirico's Sicilian father was an
engineer whose work took him to
Volos, Greece, where the artist was
born. De Chirico later attended the
Athens polytechnic and then studied
painting in Rome, where he died
after a long life. The influence of
antiquity in his work is unmistakeable.
He spent the period 1906–1909 at the
Munich academy, where he was
strongly and lastingly influenced by the
mythological paintings of Arnold
Böcklin (1827–1901). In Paris, where de
Chirico lived from 1911 to 1915,
he enjoyed a close and spiritual friend-
ship with the poet Guillaume Apollinaire (1880–1918) and his group of
young fantasts, whose visions of creative activity fuelled by the automatism
of dreams were soon to take shape in
surrealism. During these years, when
the shadow of impending war was
lengthening, de Chirico developed a
hypnotic style of painting that was
inspired by classical and mythological
themes and is now termed 'pittura
metafisica'. Objects from the real world
that are defined with exaggerated
clarity are improbably combined with
detached fragments of other objects to
produce scenes suffused with an unreal
light. These scenes incorporate architectural elements and are inhabited by
figures frozen for eternity. One of these
magical paintings is *Nostalgia del
poeta.* An obelisque looms up against
an ominous, greenish-blue sky;
attached to the obelisque, which bears
a linear hieroglyph, is a doughy, fish-
shaped object. A tailor's dummy has its
back turned to us. The stone bust of a
bald man – representing Guillaume
Apollinaire – is shown side-on, the eye
covered by a round, black lens. What
does it all mean? Is there a comprehen-
sible answer to its riddles? All is
enveloped in an impenetrable silence.

Henri Rousseau's painting fascinated the Surrealists to a high degree, not only because of the suggestion of the possible symbolic interpretation of his pictures, but also because of that characteristic in the Douanier's work of representing the dream with 'too much' realism and thus anticipating the surrealist concept of dream as the true *reality*. The magical, mysterious and continually *surprising* atmosphere of Rousseau's pictures drew Giorgio de Chirico (1888–1978) under their spell and set him on the search for 'the demon that hides in everything'; he found in Rousseau's pictures elements surprisingly related to his own strivings for self-expression.

De Chirico, whose artistic training had been shared between the 'idealistic' Florence of Giovanni Papini and the 'classical' Munich of Arnold Böcklin, was also very familiar with the Douanier's work, both through the article that Ardengo Soffici wrote in 1910 in *La Voce* (a magazine widely circulated at that time among Italian artists and intellectuals) and also through Uhde's monograph of 1911, among the illustrations to which was *Le rêve*. Guillaume Apollinaire wrote: 'Je ne sais à qui comparer Giorgio de Chirico. La première fois que j'ai vu ses tableaux, j'ai pensé instinctivement au Douanier.' (I don't know who to compare Giorgio de Chirico with. The first time I saw his paintings I instinctively thought of the Douanier.)

Apart from the profusion of symbolic elements which have in part been described above, the unreal dimensions of the objects portrayed, the compact and *absolute* colours, the diffuse light and the unmeasurable time, blocked as it were in the rigidity of a dream, must have especially fascinated the Italian painter.

Certainly the dreamlike dimension in de Chirico's painting is more intellectual and, as one might say, more conscious than in the work of Rousseau the 'naive'; they clearly contain references to Freudian theories of the dream such as those of the confusion and alienation of objects in reality, in which de Chirico – like Rousseau – was an unchallenged master, a recognized forerunner of surrealism.

His melancholy views of Italian squares – which reflect pictorially 'that strong and secretive feeling on reading Nietzsche: the melancholy of lovely autumn afternoons in Italian towns', as the artist wrote – rest in a sort of unreal atmosphere which makes one think of a dream world. They are pictures showing no sign of life, in stationary time, as if eternally waiting for an event which nevertheless seems just about to occur, and from this there arises a feeling of unrest and indecision. These architectural landscapes have been estranged from history and consist of distorted, prolonged perspectives in an artificial calm. On their stage, everyday objects have been

Max Ernst (1891–1976)
2 enfants sont menacés par un rossignol, 1924
Oil on wood with wooden elements,
69.8 × 57.1 × 11.4 cm
The Museum of Modern Art, New York

In the autobiographical notes Max Ernst published in 1942 there is a reference to a feverish dream he had as a six year old. Perhaps it inspired this fantastic assemblage. Throughout his life this Surrealist drew on his dreams for his collages, frottages, assemblages, drawings, paintings and sculptures. The son of a teacher and painter, Ernst studied philosophy and taught himself to paint. In 1914 he made friends with the later Dadaist Jean Arp, and in 1921 joined the circle of Surrealists in Paris. His art has its own unmistakeable poetry, in which demonic nature, and in it, birds – and ever more birds – play a powerful role. Everything is determined by instinct, oppressively so. Man cannot escape his sexual drive. Accordingly, in our work, the song of the nightingale singing against the clear sky is the siren's corruptive call. The faceless father flees with one child over the roof of the hut, in an effort to reach a large, protruding knob, which, hurriedly turned, would enable him to vanish through the door into the unknown. In the meadow an older girl is lying where she has sunk to the grass. Her mother is rushing towards her, brandishing a knife to frighten off the singing nightingale. Within reach, a lattice wicket at the front edge of the picture grants a view down the length of the meadow to the gateway and the large, mosque-like building: an impression of depth that draws the viewer hypnotically into the dream scenery, the depiction of an early dream taken form.

placed and carefully described and yet they remain alienated, disproportionate and standing in relations to each other which have nothing to do with the logic of waking reality but 'function' according to a dream-like mechanism in which contrasting contexts are combined and various levels of reality exist side-by-side.

In de Chirico's pictures the silent and deceptive presence of objects with their own independent and recognizable meaning conveys the vision of a two-fold reality, of the objects' second identity, which communicates the obscure messages of restlessness and anxiety and puts forward a riddle without an answer. In his monograph *On metaphysical art,* de Chirico theorized that 'all things have two aspects: a commonplace one, which people in general always recognize, and a ghostly or metaphysical aspect which only a few people in moments of clairvoyance and metaphysical abstraction can see'[2].

The surrealists made generous use of de Chirico's extraordinary metaphysical 'theatre', fascinated as they were by the possibility of using art as an instrument for expressing pictures from dreams. Although de Chirico never wanted to join the movement, Italian painters accorded him a kind of official paternity, which is attested by the publication of his monograph 'Un rêve' in the first number of the magazine *La Révolution Surréaliste,* founded in 1924, the year in which André Breton's manifesto appeared.

In the works of Max Ernst (1891–1976) and René Magritte (1898–1967), the dream becomes a real place where man's deepest and most secret drives, suppressed in the waking state – are set free. Every object in the pictures has a strong symbolic value even if it is often consciously inexplicable. The constant use of the technique of estrangement and illogical and inappropriate juxtaposition of everyday objects serves to portray a further mysterious and sometimes disquieting dimension. The central role in this is played by the effort to place objects in relation to each other rather than the choice of the objects themselves. This can be seen in Ernst's pictures from the 1920's, for example in *Oedipus Rex* of 1922, *The Swinging Woman* of 1925 and in the well-known work *Two Children Threatened by a Nightingale* of 1924; also in the works of Magritte (*The False Mirror, The Wind and the Song, The Key of the Dreams, Human Fate,* all painted between 1928 and 1934), which have their most important source of inspiration in de Chirico's pictorial oeuvre. Besides these works we could mention illustratively one of the surrealist period's masterpieces by Joan Miró, *The Poetic Object* of 1936, now in the Museum of Modern Art in New York, in which the artist portrays the dream dimension (three-dimensionally) as a kind of container of totally different and unconnected pictures which could only 'logically'

2 enfants sont menacés par un rossignol /M. ernst

René Magritte (1898–1967)
Eloge de la dialectique, 1937
Watercolour on paper
Musée d'Ixelles, Brussels

The young Magritte's lower middle-class upbringing in small Belgian towns was a sheltered one until his mother committed suicide when the boy was only fourteen years old. After attending the *Académie des Beaux-Arts* in Brussels, Magritte married and started designing carpets for a living. In 1927, he had his first contacts with the Paris Surrealists, becoming a friend of Paul Eluard and André Breton. The theorizing of the Surrealists was too cerebral for Magritte, however. In 1930, weary of the hothouse atmosphere of Paris, he returned to Brussels and remained there until his death in 1967. Attempts at painting in the expressionist manner were unsatisfactory. Magritte was to remain true to the heritage of the early Flemish masters, using local colours to portray reality with a precision that dispelled any hint of the picturesque. But reality is double-edged and contradictory. The present work – 'In praise of dialectic' – depicts a scene abounding in contradiction. We see a realistically painted house with walls, windows, eaves and a slate roof in a setting that we cannot place. Everything is suffused with a clear light. Through open windows with white curtains we look into a spacious room with a white plaster ceiling – but the room contains a two-storey house with closed windows and front door. So are we looking in or out? We see from within and without at the same time. Life means thinking in contradictions. What is truth?

René Magritte (1898–1967)
La vie secrète, 1928
Oil on canvas, 73 × 54.5 cm
Kunsthaus, Zurich

A huge ball hovers, free and immobile, in an empty room. Everything seems to be turned on its head. Among painters, Magritte, who lived no differently from any other honest citizen, was a craftsman. Though considered a surrealist,

he is in fact a fantastical realist, quite different from Delvaux, Dalí or Ernst. In an autobiographical sketch, Magritte wrote: 'From his cradle M. saw helmeted men wearing the shroud of a stranded balloon on the roof of their family residence.' Magritte never painted this picture, but it is a Magritte picture. He once painted with meticulous accuracy a tobacco pipe, under which he wrote the words 'Ceci n'est pas une pipe.' He called the picture *La trahison des images* (1928–1929). Magritte's fantasy combines fantasy with the craftsman-like skill of a master copyist, presenting it as something ordinary without any personal signature. He slyly paints the most everyday

objects slightly out of kilter, thus creating a new reality. An easel in front of a window bears a painting with the same landscape as can be seen through the window, but just slightly different. He called the painting *La condition humaine* (1933). This tiny shift is the unexpected, uncanny, irritating and surreal element we encounter in everyday life but which is hidden to the eye. Magritte does not paint for the sake of painting. He invents pictures in order to show the truth. The interior of this bare room exists, the heavy ball also exists. But it can only hover freely in space in its imaginary life. The writer Karl Kraus defined an artist as 'somebody who can make a riddle out of a solution'.

Joan Miró (1893–1983)
The Poetic Object, 1936
Material composition, 81 × 30 × 26 cm
The Museum of Modern Art, New York

Pierre Matisse, the son of the Fauves
master, and his wife donated this
assemblage to the Museum in recognition of one of the greatest Spanish
artists of our time. It is the tangible
expression of a naive, yet ingenious
man's dream, of an artist whose work
in all phases of his career, from the
earliest realistic paintings, through the
surreal transformation to the colour-
fully melodious, childlike late works, is
characterized by an exceptionally
powerful poetic vividness. To do justice
to such objects, the viewer must be
willing to accept the work as the
expression of a creative play that is the
product of inspirational fantasy in the
manner of the Surrealists' program-
matic 'réalisation automatique'. By putting this into practice, Miró, who also
behaved like this with people, realized
his naive dreams in his works with the
playfulness of a person who has
remained a child and never quite
grown up. It is only right that his stage
sets, costumes, pottery, paintings and
sculptures should have made him
famous in a very technical world.

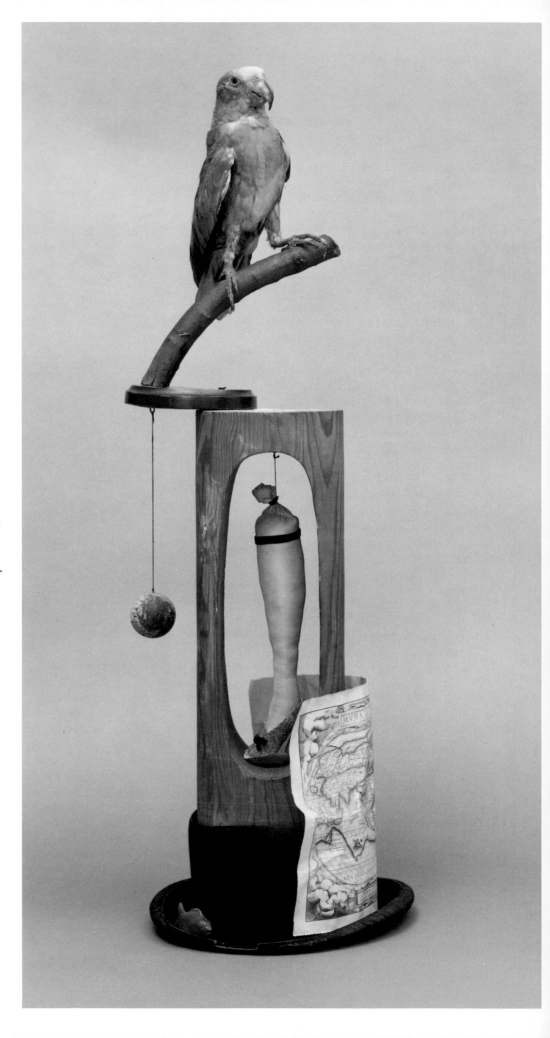

belong together in a dream: a woman's leg hanging up, a parrot on a stand, a ball and a page torn from a book arranged above a hat to illustrate the dreams of the man who is lost in thought beneath the hat.

The Dream
by Arturo Martini

We close this short consideration of the scenes and symbols of the dream with one final example, a further small element in the profusion of pictures which form a multiple and colourful mosaic of the iconography of the dream.

In 1931 the sculptor Arturo Martini (1889–1947) created a delicate lyrical panel with the title *The Dream,* a favourite work of the artist who, always critical and dissatisfied despite his self-assurance, stated that he was content with hardly any of his works apart from this one, 'my chief work'.

From the end of the twenties, after an initial period of symbolist and expressionist tendencies, Martini developed a mature and sculpturally differentiated form of expression in full harmony with the artistic climate of the time, which throughout Europe was governed by a 'return to order' after the breakneck experimentation of the avant-garde. The revived need for solidity and compactness of shape and volume and, consequently, for renewed attention to the architectural and constructional values of the work, gained ground in the Europe of the twenties, shaken as it was by the dramatic experiences of war. With his compact and 'antique' sculpture, reminiscent of the mysterious realism of Etruscan culture and the restrained power of medieval sculpture, and therefore more marked by a certain three-dimensional 'archaism' than by actual 'classicism', Arturo Martini contributed substantially to the altered artistic climate, with its return to classical values and the great tradition of Italian art.

In his search for a pure form of expression, the sculptor in fact undertook an expedition into the history of art until he reached the pre-classical sources of ancient sculpture, in which the mystery and poetic wonder of creation are still untarnished. The tranquillity and perfect harmony of the proportions seen in ancient sculpture made the longed-for flight from everyday mediocrity possible for Martini, and opened up to him the doors of a dreamed-of world at the threshold of the Empyrean which nevertheless remained in constant balance between experienced reality and imagined desires, hovering as it were between heaven and earth. 'Heaven and earth',

writes Umberto Galimberti, 'are separated by an intermediate zone which Plato calls "metaxy". . . . Metaxy equally describes the space between two different realities and their common ground[6].'

In his panel *The Dream*, Martini seems to describe not so much the dream itself or the dream-like dimension, but something that comes very close to the Platonic concept of metaxy, namely the dividing moment between dream and reality, between the inner and the outer, suggested by that mysterious small window which can be seen above the form of the sleeping girl. This window in the work of art symbolizes the dimensions of immanence and transcendence and is half open, as if to suggest some osmosis, a crossing from one dimension to the other. The mouth of the sleeping girl is also half open, as if to indicate that breath is flowing through it; yet breath symbolizes the soul, another type of *transitory relationship* between the inner and the outer. The Christian religion, the jealous guardian of the soul, closes the mouth and eyes of the dead, whereas among the Indians it was the tradition to leave their dead exposed to the weather so that the soul, which left the body through the mouth, could be re-united with the 'whole' of nature.

'All the poetry in this sculpture', wrote Martini, 'lies in the half open window: so that the wind may come, that night may draw in, the fear that a hand may approach and be able to touch this creature.' The dog which is sleeping at the girl's feet seems also to be watching over her sleep; the oldest mythical function of the dog, familiar to all anthropologies and documented everywhere, is that of *Psychopompos,* the liberator of the deceased's soul. In today's society the dog is guide to the blind, man's companion and guide in the hunt and, after being his life-long companion, his escort at death; Anubis, Cerberus, Thot, Hecate and Hermes all had the appearance and qualities of dogs.

Martini's work illustrates the difficult relationship which, as already mentioned, the artist had with everyday life: mistrust and anxiety towards the real world, a place of uncertainty, worry and threats. The sense of anxiety cast over the whole scene by the small window does not affect the girl's sleep, but it does affect her dreaming and thus not the physical, but the intangible, security of the soul or of the spirit which finds repose in sleep and is symbolized by the gentle tranquillity of the feminine posture, as we find it in other of Martini's works such as *The Sleeping Woman* (or *Sleep*), a sculpture pervaded by a soothing sense of peace. Conscious in the unconsciousness of the dream, the girl holds fast to her dream with the determination of one who, for fear of daily life, sleeps late and tries by dreaming to prolong her defence against the danger of a renewed confron-

Arturo Martini (1889–1947)
Il sogno, 1931
Bronze
Collezione Achille e Ida Maramotti
Castello di Albinea, Reggio Emilia,
Italy

Arturo Martini's rectangular sculpture of a woman asleep in a bedroom typifies the artist's distinctive grasp of space. After studying at the Faenza school of ceramics, Martini spent the period 1909–1911 in Munich with the then influential sculptor Adolf Hildebrand (1847–1921), whose example enabled him to find his own sense of balanced, tranquil form. In 1918, after a stay in Paris, Martini moved to Rome where he became associated with the 'Valori plastici' group. Growing recognition of his work brought him many commissions, for instance at Milan's palace of justice. Martini was a sculptor in the classical tradition with a strong feeling for the tectonics of his figures. In *Il sogno (The Dream),* the sleeper's bed is accommodated with meticulous precision in the space provided. The window shutter on the rear wall is an echo of the overall composition; the beam supporting the ceiling and the dog sleeping at the foot of the bed reinforce the impression of depth, as does the positioning of the arms. The woman, covered only lightly by a fold of the sheet, is rendered all the more lifelike by the severity of the spatial coordinates.

Arturo Martini (1889–1947)
Il sonno
Stone
Private collection, Milan

It is the artist's gift that enables him to fashion a living figure from stone that, for countless eons, was part of the primeval matter of the earth. Martini's lightly covered young woman lies face down on the ground before us, sleeping, her head supported by the fold of her arm. We almost imagine that we can follow her dreams.

tation with everyday problems; this behaviour is characteristic of young people and adults in especially difficult and anxiety-provoking situations in life.

In all his works, Martini seems to seek a dimension other than that of everyday reality, in which he can 'create' a place of bliss, and sleep (that is, the state which permits dreaming) is that place.

Myth, fairy tale and the dream (not the dimension of the dream) are for Martini the means of liberating himself from the mediocrity of daily life, raising himself above the banal and expressing his own deep need to create freely. Metaphor is the means by which the painter's imagination and thinking can be communicated by artistic means.

References

1. Benedetti, M.T.: *Dante Gabriel Rossetti,* p. 8. Florence: Sansoni, 1984.
2. De Chirico, G.: *Sull'arte metafisica,* p. 16. Rome: Valori Plastici, 1919.
3. Evangelisti, S.: Sogno e arti visive; in: *Sogni: figli d'un cervello ozioso,* pp. 46–61. Ed. M. Bosinelli, P.C. Cicogna. Turin: Bollati Boringhieri, 1991.
4. Fagiolo dell'Arco, M.: *L'opera completa di de Chirico,* p. 89. Milan: Rizzoli, 1908–1924.
5. Freud, S.: Zeitgemässes über Krieg und Tod; in: *Gesammelte Werke,* Vol. 10. London: Imago, 1915.
6. Galimberti, U.: *Gli equivoci dell'anima,* p. 82. Milan: Feltrinelli, 1991.
7. Hillmann, J.: *Gli animali del sogno,* p. 48. Milan: Raffaello Cortina, 1991.
8. Melville, R.: Rousseau and de Chirico; in: *Scottish Arts and Letters,* Vol. 1, p. 33, 1944.
9. Redon, O.: *A soi-même,* p. 26. Paris: José Corti, 1985.
10. Resnik, S.: Pensiero visivo, rito e pensiero oniroco; in: *I linguaggi del sogno,* p. 41. Ed. V. Branca, C. Ossola, S. Resnik. Florence: Sansoni, 1984.
11. Rubin, W.S.: *L'arte dada e surrealista,* pp. 127–129. Milan: Rizzoli, 1972.
12. Whitmond, E.C.: *The Symbolic Quest. Basic Concepts of Analytical Psychology.* Princeton: Princeton University Press, 1969.
13. *Le Douanier Rousseau,* p. 254. Catalogue of the exhibition held in the Grand Palais, Paris, and in the Museum of Modern Art, New York, 1984–1985. Paris: Editions de la Réunion des musées nationaux, 1984.

Michelangelo (1475–1564)
The Night, 1525–1531
Marble
San Lorenzo, Florence

In 1521, Cardinal Giulio de' Medici, who was to be Pope Clement VII, commissioned Michelangelo to design a chapel for the tombs of the Medici family. The times were tumultuous, and the work was delayed for years by war, sieges of Florence and political upheavals. Michelangelo was both the architect and the sculptor of the Medici Chapel, a work which exemplifies the spirit and art of the Florentine Renaissance. The marble effigy of Giuliano de' Medici, Duke of Nemours, who died in 1516, is placed in a wall decorated with niches, engaged columns and friezes. On the curved lid of the sarcophage in front of the wall, lies the naked male figure – 'non finito' – of *Day* on the right and the female figure of *Night* on the left. The art historian Jakob Burckhardt (1818–1879) wrote in his *Cicerone:* 'Michelangelo was driven more than any other artist by the desire to create from within himself every conceivable aspect of the living, preferably the naked, human body, providing this did not clash with higher stylistic canons ... He had two spirits fighting within his breast: one strove, through ceaseless anatomical studies, to probe the causes and manifestations of human form and movement and to lend the statue the most life-like perfection; the other, however, sought what is beyond human life.' Michelangelo's *Night* is lying on drapery and cushions, her right hand raised to her deeply bowed head and her left arm draped over a mask, which appears to be a kind of a sentinel. Her left leg is bent, and below the knee an owl looks out; this bird of the night sees all. The woman's body is strong. The convex and concave forms of the muscles, folds and breasts reflect the sculptor's delight in the three-dimensional form. Michelangelo used to go to the quarries of Carrara himself to seek out the blocks of marble in which he saw, with his artist's vision, the body's form inhabiting the marble. As the observer's eye wanders over the sculpture, he sees the choreography of the living form which has been hewn out of the stone. The woman, symbol of the night, is fast asleep.

Full of admiration, the young Florentine Giovanni Strozzi placed this epigram below the figure of the *Night:*

'La Notte, che tu vedi in sì dolci atti dormir, fu da un Angelo scolpita in questo sasso, e perchè dorme ha vita. Destala, se nol credi, e parleratti.'

Michelangelo, in his epigram *Night,* allowed the statue to give her own answer:

'Caro m'è 'l sonno, e più l'esser di sasso, mentre che 'l danno e la vergogna dura, non veder, non sentir, m'è gran ventura: però non mi destar, deh! parla basso.'

Part of the greatness of two contrasting statues, Michelangelo's *Night* from the Tomb of Giuliano de' Medici and Donatello's penitent Mary Magdalene in the Baptistry of San Giovanni, Florence, lies in the direct experience of untroubled sleep and peace, sleepless anguish with anxiety. Our ideas about sleep owe as much to art and poetry as to science although most of what we know about sleep disorders has been learnt since 1953, when REM sleep was first recognized. Major developments since then have included the discovery of sleep apnea (initially by Henri Gastaut in 1965 in a Marseilles sleep laboratory), the development of benzodiazepines and hypnotic drugs, the birth of a molecular biology of sleep following the recognition of the unexpected association between human leukocyte antigens and narcolepsy by Yotaka Honda in Japan, and the cloning of the first two clock genes, one from a fruit fly and one from a fungus[17].

Sleep disorders are common. Napoleon, after the Battle of Aspern, the first battle which the Emperor lost after 17 victories, was so overcome that he slept for 36 hours without awakening, and his suite feared for his life. He usually slept very little, only four or five hours. Lady Macbeth was a sleepwalker. Edgar Allan Poe, who may have suffered from sleep paralysis himself, described the fear of this condition in *The Premature Burial*. Melville described narcolepsy in *Moby Dick*, and the hero of George Eliot's novel, *Silas Marner*, was paralyzed with surprise. The English Lakeland poet Wordsworth was an insomniac who wrote:

'A flock of sheep that leisurely passes by
One after one; the sound of rain, and bees
murmuring: the fall of rivers, winds and seas,
smooth fields, white sheets of water, and pure sky;
I thought of all by turns and still I lie sleepless.'

Sleep Disorders
by David Parkes

Night
Michelangelo

St Mary Magdalene
Donatello

At both extremes of life, infancy and old age, day sleep is normal, not abnormal; as with the Holy Infant on His parents' dangerous flight into Egypt, and with the elderly Joseph in the wonderful painting by Mantegna of the *Adoration of the Shepherds.*

Between 12 and 15% of all people living in industrialized countries have sleep problems although many of these are trivial. Insomnia is the commonest complaint, respiratory distress during sleep the most serious. Excessive daytime sleepiness is a problem for well over 100,000 Americans, and parasomnias such as night terrors and sleep-walking take a further toll. The personal, social and political consequences of sleep disorders are considerable. *Encephalitis lethargica* may have been responsible for the rise of National Socialism in Germany, with the rage, violence and aggression of Adolf Hitler, and shift-work patterns resulting in lowered work-time vigilance may have caused many industrial disasters, including that at the Chernobyl nuclear power station. Loss of sleep before the departure from Zermatt may have been partly responsible for one of the greatest disasters of mountaineering history, the fall from the Matterhorn after Whymper's first successful assault[22].

Circadian rhythms

Man shares the same time world as oak trees, marine algae, Antarctic penguins and fruit flies. All living organisms show regular cycles of rest and activity under the influence of the rotation of the world and internal time clocks. Surely no map of the Old World – and its creator – is more supreme than that of the Creation in the Duomo of Monreale, Sicily, although the new Mappa Mundi, that of the human genome, which may include a DNA sequence in common with that which determines time clock activity in both *Drosophila* and *Neurospora,* may prove to be its equal.

Flight into Egypt
Michelangelo

Creation mosaic
Monreale

Mosaic (1180–1190)
The Creation
Monreale, Sicily

The cycle of mosaics in the Cathedral of Monreale near Palermo is one of the most magnificent and richest *bibliae pauperum* that has survived from the High Middle Ages down to the present day. Byzantine mosaic masters executed this splendid pictorial bible in Norman-ruled Sicily shortly before the birth of the last great Emperor of the West, Frederick II. Countless small pieces of natural stone of different hues, and glass cubes shot through with gold combine to form a rich succession of iridescent, coloured images. All the columns, walls, vaults and apses of the cathedral are covered in mosaics. Our picture shows a scene from the story of the creation. God in all his majesty is creating the sun, the moon and the stars in the firmament of the heavens on the fourth day of creation (Genesis 1, 14–19).

Adam and Eve
Blake

Circadian biology was born when the French astronomer, Jean-Jacques D'Ortous de Mairan, discovered in 1729 that a heliotropic plant which regularly opens its leaves in the morning light and closes them at dusk, continued this cycle for a while when the plant was placed in darkness in his closet. The Swiss botanist Alphonse de Candolle added a second important piece of evidence when he showed, in 1832, that the precise period of daily leaf movements in a flowering plant was not exactly 24 hours, but nearer to 26, with a progressive phase advance of about two hours each day [14]. William Blake, when he drew Adam and Eve peacefully asleep in the Garden of Eden before the Fall to illustrate Milton's *Paradise Lost*, could not have foreseen that the intrinsic time clock period of Eve was a little shorter than that of Adam.

Much of our knowledge of biological clocks in man has come from experiments in caves in the French Alps, hospital cellars or isolation laboratories in Munich or the Bronx. The search for the clock ended in 1972 when a timing mechanism in the paired small suprachiasmatic nuclei of the hypothalamus was discovered. Retinal stimulation by light acts as the winder of the clock, which in turn regulates the clock hands – the pineal hormone melatonin [1].

William Blake (1757–1827)
Adam and Eve Sleeping, 1805
Etching/watercolour/paper,
49.2 × 38.7 cm
The Museum of Fine Arts, Boston

This picture is a poet's vision re-worked by a visionary painter. In the twelve books of his epic poem *Paradise Lost* (1667), the blind poet John Milton (1608–1674) described his religious vision of man, before his fall from grace, in God's creation. The poet's vision was later expressed pictorially by an artist of comparable power, William Blake, whose ideas were close to those of the Swedish 'ghost-seer' (Kant) and mystic, Emanuel Swedenborg (1688–1772). In an essay on Blake written in 1920, T.S. Eliot wrote that 'he was naked, and saw man naked, and from the center of his own crystal'. This coloured etching is of crystalline transparency. Blake, the son of a hosier, was a trained engraver, and put his faith in the pre-eminence of line, defining contours with it and yet creating compelling points of reference from its inception to its end-point. He then coloured the page lightly with watercolour to allow light and shadow to accentuate the corporeal in the modelling of the figures. In a catalogue of 1808, Blake described his highly individual art as 'visionary and imaginative'. Milton's vision of Adam and Eve lost in innocent slumber well before their fall from grace, is portrayed like an unfolding song: the figures, created in God's image, lie on billowing cushions in a paradisiacal landscape under a starlit sky and waxing moon. Two angels hover soundlessly above them, but their faces are grave and sorrowful. One angel has a hand raised questioningly, while the other points down to the toad crouching near Eve. What fate awaits the sleepers?

Time, the central clock, the changing seasons and the procession of life succeeded by the great reaper, Death, are the subjects of Galle's 1574 engraving, *The Triumph of Time*, thought to be from one of the lost works of Pieter Bruegel the Elder.

Many human sleep and wake problems result from failure of the internal brain clock to measure the time of day with any precision, or failure to synchronize ('entrain') the outside world, dawn and dusk, with the inside clock. Jules Verne's hero sensibly took 80 days to travel round the world in 1878, whilst, in 1965, American astronauts circled the earth in 88 minutes.

The Triumph of Time
Galle

Philip Galle (1537–1612)
The Triumph of Time, 1574
Copperplate

William Blake (1757–1827)
Satan Smiting Job with Sore Boils,
1825–1826
Tempera on wood, 32 × 43 cm
Tate Gallery, London

William Blake was virtually ignored by the public of his day. It was not until shortly before his death that a circle of young admirers formed around him, and the reclusive drawer, engraver and painter would have endured even more embitterment and hardship had he not had the support of a small number of patrons. In 1818, he met the landscape artist, John Linnell (1792–1882), who commissioned two series of illustrations from him for Dante's *Divine Comedy* and the Book of Job. Blake conveys in a very particular manner his preoccupation with questions such as the meaning of life, the force of evil and the significance of suffering. This painting, outstanding for the expressive power of its drawing and the dramatic contrasts of its colours, illustrates the sixth verse of the second chapter of the Book of Job.

The Lord – in order to test pious Job's faith in God – puts him into Satan's hands: 'Behold, he is in your power; only spare his life.' Then Satan, towering over Job, afflicts him with 'loathsome sores from the sole of his foot to the crown of his head'. His wife is on her knees in despair. But Job, 'receiving the evil', opens his hands and raises his eyes to the heavens. This is no dream; it is reality. Suffering makes the righteous man.

Insomnia

The English composer Vaughan Williams responded wholeheartedly to the language of the Bible. He set two great religious parables to music, the Old Testament story *Job*, and the morality dream of the Bedford tinker, John Bunyan, *The Pilgrim's Progress from this World to that which is to Come*. In the fourth movement of *Job*, the Patriarch is smitten with sore boils by Satan and moans his fate.

'When I lie down I say, when shall I arise and the night be gone? and I am full of tossings to and fro, until the dawning of the day.'   *Job 7, 4*

Hippocrates knew that insomnia was connected with sorrow. Loss of sleep may be due to very many causes including anxiety, despair, alcoholism, pain, loneliness, worry about money or health, physical ailments, intestinal worms or AIDS. Drugs, alcohol abuse and many medical disorders including hypertension, Parkinson's disease, asthma and head injury may be to blame. Cigarette smoking close to bedtime, starvation and, in infants, food allergy, all lead to insomnia.

Insomnia may be familial. Recently Emilio Lugaresi and his colleagues have described an Italian family with a genetic form of fatal insomnia, associated with thalamic degeneration, involvement of the autonomic and motor systems, and eventual death [12].

The 'healthy life' approach to insomnia has been practised for centuries. The ideal book at bedtime must be Virgil's *Georgics* with Blake's magical woodcuts to promote country thoughts, followed by sleep. Horace, in his *Satires*, follows the advice of the Roman lawyer, Trebatius, who advises swimming the Tiber three times and also saturating the body with wine from within before sleep. In 19th century Paris, Gélineau substituted the Seine and specified the vintage; not surprisingly that grown around his own Bordeaux estate at the castle of Saint-Luce La Tour. Country air, mountaineering – compared to drinking champagne without the bad effects –, sea bathing, massage and, in particular, the cold bath were all common remedies, founded on practical experience.

In England the old Malvern gas bath was popular, in which the bather sat on a wooden chair, surrounded by several thick blankets securely fastened round his neck, a safety spirit lamp lighted under the chair. The lamented death of Dr Carpenter from an accident arising out of an arrangement of this kind did not pass unnoticed.

Virgil's Georgics – woodcuts
Blake

Portable, winged altarpiece showing scenes from the life of Christ (detail), ca. 1330
Oak,
middle panel 65 × 48 cm,
wings 65 × 24 cm
Ferdinand Franz Wallraf Collection,
Wallraf-Richartz-Museum, Cologne

The scenes depicted on this small altarpiece are five of the church's main feasts. The left wing shows the birth of Jesus and the adoration of the Three Kings, the middle panel the Crucifixion and the right wing Christ's Ascension and Whitsuntide. The frames have been set with imitation precious stones (rectangular for the blue glass and round for the red). The large rectangular wells were originally covered by glass or horn plates and used to display relics. The figures are depicted against a background of richly ornamental embossed gold leaf, representing the visible, transcendental light of God. The delicacy with which the anonymous artist has coloured the figures brings to mind the illustrated manuscripts of the period. Our scene is framed, below, by the earth-coloured ox and donkey next to the crib and, above, the angel's hosanna. The angel's wings are green. The glad tidings it brings are written on a banner. The shepherd, seated amidst a green landscape, has been playing the bagpipes; now he raises his eyes in astonishment. A ram – the animal used as a burnt offering instead of Jacob and hence the symbol of Christ's sacrificial death – is climbing a tree, which must therefore be the new Tree of Life. The shepherd's cloak is a vivid red. But the Holy Family is the focal point of the picture. Fair-haired Mary, Mother of God, wears a bright red cloak over a long blue gown. Joseph, asleep on his long staff, is wearing a dark red cap, grey robe and green cloak. All these colours are symbolic: green stands for the Old Testament, blue for pregnancy and red for the incarnation of the divine plan that can be sensed in the radiant gold of the star. This exquisite altarpiece was produced at a time of intense Rhenish mysticism centred on Meister Eckhart (d. 1326). The mystic, Heinrich Seuse, became his pupil in Cologne in 1324. Their wider circle included Johann Frankom, the reading master of the Dominicans in Cologne, and another Cologne Dominican, Giselher von Slatheim. It is in this world of intense piety that our small altarpiece has its roots. Judging by its size and nature, it probably stood in a private chapel or monastery cell.

Hypnos (4th century BC)
Bronze
The British Museum, London

This fragment, the head of the god Hypnos, is a rare bronze from the late classical period in Greece. The god of sleep is a beautiful youth. Shown in full length on vase paintings, he has wings on his back, like his twin brother Thanatos, the dark god of death. Hypnos is sometimes shown holding poppy stems in his hands, proof that the ancients were aware of this plant's opiate properties. Dioscorides, a Greek physician living during the reign of the Roman emperor Vespasian, wrote in his five-volume work, *De Materia Medica,* the foremost textbook of pharmacology until well into the Middle Ages, that the opium obtained from the poppy was used to make sleeping potions and other therapeutic drugs. Hypnos is depicted pouring his gift of welcome sleep from a horn. The head, with wings attached at the temples, radiates a sense of gentleness and calm.

Real progress in the treatment of insomnia only came with the introduction of the first hypnotic, chloral, in 1868, the synthesis of benzodiazepines by Leo Sternbach in 1933, and the introduction of chlordiazepoxide in 1960/61. The search continues for a natural arousal-reducing, sleep-promoting compound.

Hypersomnia

One of the most lovely eternally sleeping girls is that of Auguste Rodin.

Le sommeil
Rodin

The joint record for prolonged sleep or trance is held by the Cretan poet, Epimenides, who allegedly slept for 57 years in a cave, and the 78-year-old Italian village saint, Alfonso Cottini[24]. Other examples of prolonged sleep that have been described illustrate the borderland between coma, akinetic mutism and functional trance states rather than deep sleep, and 'familial' rather than 'organic' disorders.

African sleeping sickness

African sleeping sickness extends in tropical Western Central Africa from the Sahara to the Kalahari desert, and east to the Rift Valley, and is found in East Africa from Ethiopia in the north to Botswana in the south. Approximately four million square miles in Africa are not populated because of the impossibility of keeping animals in sites where tsetse flies are infected with trypanosomes.

'At the commencement of the disease, the patient has commonly a ravenous appetite, eating twice the quantity of food he is accustomed to take when in health, and becoming very fat. When the disease has continued some time the appetite declines, and the patient gradually wastes away... The disposition to sleep is so strong, as scarcely to leave a sufficient respite for the taking of food; even the repeated application of a whip, a remedy which has been frequently used, is hardly sufficient to keep the poor wretch awake[23].'

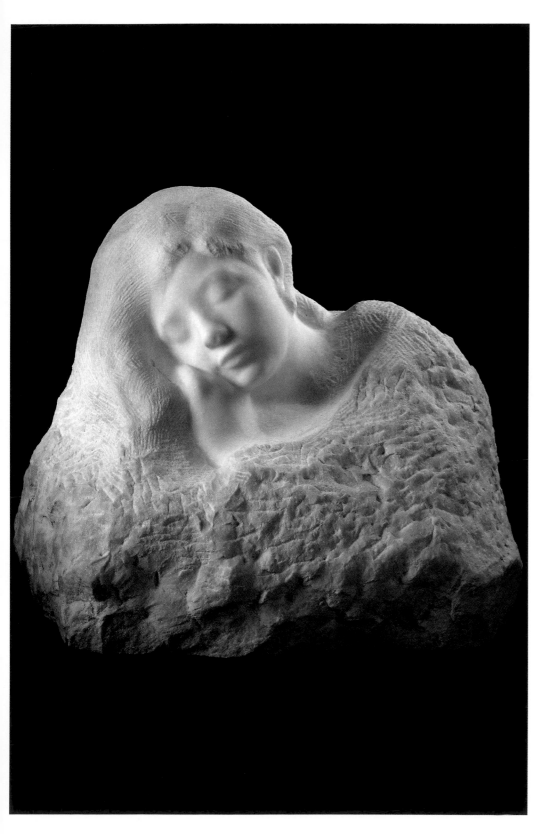

Auguste Rodin (1840–1917)
Le sommeil
Marble, 48.4 × 56 × 47.5 cm,
Inv. S. 1004
Musée Rodin, Paris

In the beginning is a block of marble.
Then the artist comes with his chisel
and liberates the figure that is present
in the stone, waiting to be given a form
and existence of its own. The inspiration of Michelangelo (1475–1564), the
greatest sculptor of the Italian Renaissance, is evident in this work by the
Frenchman Rodin, the 19th century's
greatest sculptor. Rodin was born in
Paris and trained at the *Ecole des
Beaux-Arts.* As a stone-mason, he
learned to observe, to see into the
stone and, above all, to use the chisel,
and as an artist he learned how to
sense the inner contours of stone. In
1875, he travelled through Italy. In
1878, he settled in Paris for ever, and
from then on never stopped working:
'J'ai eu, jusqu'à cinquante ans, tous les
ennuis de la pauvreté: j'ai toujours
vécu comme un ouvrier, mais le bon-
heur de travailler m'a fait tout suppor-
ter.' Enduring fame came only with the
Exposition Universelle in Paris in 1900.
But this had no effect on the principles
– observe, draw, model, hew – that
governed Rodin's work.

In his testament, he stated that 'drawing from all angles is the formula for
evoking the sculpture that will cause the
spirit to enter the stone'. In this piece,
light flows over the white stone in chiselled streams, revealing all gradations
of the figure that has been released
from the stone and rendering it tangible
to the exploring hand. The material
conveys all grades of consistency from
hard to soft, from the solidity of matter
compressed into stone in the primordial
ocean to the satin sheen of the young
sleeper's skin. The figure – now freed
from its confinement – seems about to
wake up, imbued with animate life.

Progress in African colonization required the introduction of measures of public health and hygiene. The welfare of the native became paramount and at the same time religious and philanthropic sentiments were responsible for much of the propagation of Western medicine in these areas of the world. Makerere was the first hospital of Uganda, where there were appalling outbreaks of trypanosomiasis; it was opened in 1897 by a missionary doctor, Sir Albert Cook. This dreaded plague of cattle and men was first understood when Major-General Sir David Bruce, a military physician, posted to Zululand with a commission of inquiry into disease in cattle in 1894, succeeded in finding in the blood of sick animals a flagella which he named *Trypanosoma brucei*. The same organism was later found in the carrier of sleeping sickness, the tsetse fly as well as in the blood of man.

To date, the cause of drowsiness in sleeping sickness is unknown. Sleep centres of the brain may be damaged by the parasite, which colonizes the choroid plexus and neighbouring brain. Alternatively, the trypanosome itself or the immune response caused by infection may be the cause. Polysomnographic studies show that sleep stages become unrecognizable in the illness, which has still not been completely eradicated.

Gélineau and the narcoleptic syndrome

Jean Baptiste Edouard Gélineau, born at Blaye near Bordeaux in December, 1828, came of a family of businessmen and farmers. Always a man of wide interests, he was a Member of the *Société de Médecine,* the *Société de Hypnologie* and many other scientific academies. He retired in 1900 at the age of 72 to devote his energies to viniculture. He was amply rewarded for his Bordeaux wine with a gold medal at the Anvers exhibition, a diploma of excellence in Amsterdam and a great gold medal at the Paris Universal Exhibition of 1900 [15].

In the *Gazette des Hôpitaux* for 1880, Gélineau described a wine dealer who, at the age of 36 and following an unhappy love affair, had as many as 200 sudden sleep attacks a day, particularly near the monkey cage in the *Jardin des Plantes*. The sight of a grotesque person, or excitement at being dealt a good hand at cards made him weak with laughter or expectation, and caused him to fall, a symptom Gélineau named *astasie*. Gélineau distinguished narcolepsy from phobias, and in his monograph, *De la narcolepsie*, published in 1881, analysed 14 cases [7, 8].

Narcolepsy is now recognized to be about as frequent as multiple sclerosis or myasthenia gravis with perhaps 100,000 cases in Europe. The exact prevalence in different countries and ethnic groups is unknown but there may be large regional differences. For example, very few cases have been recorded in the Israeli population in contrast to a prevalence rate of 2–3 cases per 10,000 in the former Czechoslovakia and 5–7 per 10,000 in the San Francisco area.

In 1941 John Burton Dynes and Knox H. Findley applied the electroencephalograph to the diagnosis of narcolepsy, and in 1960 Gerald Vogel described sleep-onset REM periods which characterized the illness[21]. In addition to the sleep attacks, the episodes of loss of muscle tone, sleep paralysis and vivid dreaming before sleep onset have been attributed to a disorder of REM sleep. The muscle atonia and dreams of this sleep stage occur separately and also when the subject is awake.

A genetic basis for narcolepsy was finally established in 1984 by Honda and his colleagues, who discovered the surprisingly high (98–100%) association between the narcoleptic syndrome and the human leukocyte antigen DR2[9]. This discovery opened the way to the molecular biology of sleep and also focused attention on the relationship between HLA systems, cytokines, and sleep 'juices' or 'hypnotoxins' as well as upon the connection between infection, fever, temperature, rhythms and sleep.

The modern era of treatment of narcolepsy commenced in 1931 when ephedrine and later amphetamine were used. A great number of central stimulant drugs are now known and the WHO Committee on Drug Dependence considered 28 amphetamine-related substances in 1985. The effects of amphetamine and related compounds on alertness, mood, behaviour and the sympathetic nervous system have proved difficult to differentiate, and, because of the euphoria produced by these compounds, widespread abuse has occurred although not by subjects with narcolepsy.

Imipramine, followed by clomipramine, was first used to treat cataplexy (Gélineau's astasie). The neuropharmacology of clomipramine and other anticataplectic drugs as well as central stimulant drugs has been investigated in detail in the colony of narcoleptic dogs at Stanford, California[5], the equivalent of the NOD mouse model of diabetes.

Rámáyana

Willi Kleine and Max Levin

The Kleine-Levin syndrome is the most dramatic example of a number of unusual and infrequent cyclical sleep-wake disturbances, although rare disorders are never as rare as they seem. During the florid phase of this strange malady, the patient's life is largely dominated by food, sleep and sex – apparently a reversion to a primitive form of existence. In the Indian mythological epic, Rámáyana, there is a graphic account of a possible case of the Kleine-Levin syndrome – Kumbhakarna, the younger brother of the demon king Ravana, used to sleep six months at a stretch, getting up for a short period in which he ate up herds and herds of people and animals, and drank an enormous quantity of wine. At this rate, according to the epic, he would have consumed all three worlds within a short period, were he not to be overcome by another long spell of sleep[16].

In 1925, a Frankfurt psychiatrist, Willi Kleine, described five similar examples of episodic somnolence separated by long intervals of normal health. In 1927, Max Levin, a New York psychiatrist, described a 19-year-old patient with pathological hunger accompanied by attacks of sleep. Up to now about 250 cases, mostly male, with typical features of the syndrome have been described. The cause is still completely unknown with no post-mortem studies and no long-term follow-up. Unusually for sleep disorders, there have been no cases of two members of the same family diagnosed with the Kleine-Levin syndrome.

The unusual interest of the Kleine-Levin syndrome lies in its cyclical nature and in the combination of 12–14 hours of sleep each day with compulsive eating behaviour, feelings of irritability, unreality and confusion with sexual disinhibition. In up to half of all patients, these symptoms may start following fever, drunkenness, sea-sickness or a physical blow to the head.

The Sleeping Demon Kumbhakarna
The British Library
Oriental and India Office
Collections, London

This picture is taken from an illustrated version of the *Rámáyana*. This great Indian epic was composed by the poet Valmiki in the second century AD and, among the faithful, is probably the most popular of all the epics. It vividly evokes the life and suffering of the mythical hero Rama and his exploits in the struggle for the moon-eyed Sita against the demon-king of Sri Lanka, Ravana. Rama is the eternal embodiment of God, radiating majesty and beauty. Incarnated in human form and accompanied by the goddess Shakti in the guise of his loving wife, he travels the world as an example to mankind. When Sita is abducted to Sri Lanka with the help of demons, Rama – with the assistance of the great monkey-general Hanuman – sets out to rescue her unharmed. Our picture was executed by a 19th century Indian artist and illustrates a scene from the sixth book of the *Rámáyana*. Ravana, the villainous abductor of Sita, has ordered his demon-minions to waken the giant demon Kumbhakarna from his deep sleep so that he can engage in combat with Rama. According to the text: 'They gazed upon the awesome giant as he lay there in sleep, like a mountain ... They seized sticks, cudgels, clubs, whips and thorns; they drove elephants over his body and tried in every possible way to waken him with their blows and cries.' When Kumbhakarna eventually rose and entered the fray, he was defeated by the divine Rama. 'Then the earth and the mountains trembled, and the entire heavens cried out for joy.' This epic poem has always enjoyed immense popularity. The story of Rama can be seen, chiselled in stone reliefs, in the temples of Vishnu and Shiva, whether in India, Sri Lanka or Java, and it is brought to life again in the shadow play of the Javanese and in the monkey dance performed on Bali.

Von Economo and encephalitis lethargica

Constantin Baron Economo von Sans Serff was born of aristocratic Greek parentage in Rumania. Many members of his family had taken holy orders and occupied high positions; several were bishops of the ancient Macedonian capital, Vodena. He was not only a scientist in the best sense of the word, but peerless as a man and it is not without interest that Vodena — known since the liberation of Macedonia from the Turkish yoke in 1912 by its ancient Greek name Edessa — was the birthplace of Alexander the Great. In 1920 he married a daughter of the Austrian general, Prince Alois von Schönberg-Hartenstein. Von Economo, as well as a fearless balloonist and aviator, was a brilliant clinician and neuropathologist.

In the winter of 1916/17, in a land suffering from the devastations of war, he described a new disease, encephalitis lethargica. The epidemic spread without warning, and by its strange, novel features puzzled those who first encountered it. It disappeared in 1927 as mysteriously as it had commenced. The initial picture was that of a violent encephalitic illness, with constant eye muscle disturbances, accompanied or followed by changes in movement, behaviour and sleep. A wide range of psychotic disturbances including hypomania, dream-like syndromes and conditions reminiscent of Korsakow's psychosis sometimes led to a mistaken diagnosis of psychiatric disease. The most common sleep problem was hypersomnia. From his clinical and pathological observations, von Economo deduced the areas of the brain important for sleep[4].

The Land of Cockaigne
Bruegel
(see article 'Sleep and Dreams in Myths')

The Harvesters

In Bruegel's pictures *The Land of Cockaigne* and the Metropolitan Museum's *The Harvesters* there is a contrast between the sleeping peasants, exhausted by gluttony or labour, and the extraordinary landscape world cornfield and fairyland, although one picture celebrates a hot August day whilst the other is obviously intended as a condemnation of the sins of gluttony and sloth. The circumstances in both pictures could easily give rise to obstructive sleep apnea, described by Hartmut Schulz in his article on 'Day Sleep'.

The Pickwickian syndrome

The modern history of sleep apnea syndromes started in 1965, when Gastaut and his colleagues, and Jung and Kuhlo [6, 10], studied the neurophysiology of sleep and breathing in the Pickwickian syndrome, and recognized various forms of apnea. All respiratory disorders are worse during sleep, owing to reduced central ventilatory drive, sleep atonia, reduced vital capacity with an elevated diaphragm as compared with the erect posture. It was soon recognized that sleep apnea could occur in many conditions, not only in the so-called Pickwickian syndrome of obesity, alveolar hypoventilation, polycythemia, right heart failure and somnolence.

Another sleep-related breathing disorder, without snoring or obesity, called 'Ondine's curse' was described by John W. Severinghaus and Robert A. Mitchell in 1962, and named after the water nymph in Giraudoux's play *Ondine* [19]. Ondine is a Scandinavian water fairy and Hans is her human lover:

'Ondine: Try to live Hans, you will forget.

Hans: Try to live! That's easy to say, isn't it. If only I cared about living! Since you went away, I've had to force my body to do things it should do automatically... If I relax my vigilance for one moment, I may forget to hear or breathe. He died, they'll say, because he could no longer bother to breath.'

(Giraudoux, J., *Ondine*, English adaptation by Maurice Valency, New York, Random House, 1954)

The Posthumous Papers of the Pickwick Club
Dickens

Ondine
Giraudoux

Mary and the Fat Boy Joe
From: *The Posthumous Papers of the Pickwick Club*
by Charles Dickens (1812–1870)

Obstructive sleep apnea usually develops as a result of passive collapse of a narrowed hypotonic oropharynx during sleep in response to the negative pressure developed by respiratory muscles. It is a common condition, particularly in men over 40, and the reported incidence in the elderly is surprisingly high. Some old people die in their sleep as a consequence of sleep apnea, and a 30% increase in mortality rates for all causes during the usual hours of sleep can be partly accounted for by sudden respiratory failure. This may be a common reason why old people die quietly and peacefully, and without distress, in their sleep. Central sleep apnea, as with Hans in Ondine, is not nearly so common.

The central problem of sleep apnea is that of sleep atonia, loss of muscle tone or failure of respiratory motor neuron output to the upper airways during sleep, resulting in airway collapse. The Roman poet Titus Lucretius Carus (around 50 BC) wrote, in a poem entitled *De rerum naturae*, about the loss of central control that leads to loss of peripheral muscle control and relaxation, the foundation of a neural theory of sleep that took two millennia to be expanded upon.

'And since there is nothing which can, as it were, support the limbs, the body grows feeble, and all the limbs are slackened. Arms and eyelids drop, and the hams, even as you lie down, often give way, and relax their strength.' Freud

Why should muscle tone be lost during sleep? Freud recognized that this prevented the acting out of dreams. Animal physiologists have speculated that sleep atonia may conserve energy, human physiologists that it may permit learning of motor plans without their execution.

Catatonia

Catalepsy, in contrast to cataplexy, is a state of heightened, not reduced, muscle tone, initially associated with mental illness, in which the peculiar rigidity makes the patient behave very much like a statue, or maintain one posture like a mummy. It is accompanied by a state of dull stupor, daydreaming and lack of concentration, sometimes with parrot-like repetition of words or actions.

No selective respiratory stimulant drug which would increase respiration without preventing sleep has been discovered and most treatments for obstructive sleep apnea use mechanical means to splint the airway, not drugs. Tracheostomy, which has been performed since the time of Asclepiades in the first century BC, was used by Wolfgang Kuhlo and Erich Doll in 1972 to relieve obstructive sleep apnea. It has now been largely replaced by nasal continuous positive airway pressure, introduced by Colin Sullivan[20].

The parasomnias

In 1664, Thomas Willis (1621–1675) published *Anatome Cerebri*, then probably the most thorough summary of the nervous system. The book was illustrated by Christopher Wren, architect of St Paul's in London. Willis's anatomical and physiological studies led to the use of his name in connection with the circle of arteries at the base of the brain. He comes into this book for his place in describing sleep myoclonus:

'Wherefore to some, on being abed, they be taken themselves to sleep, presently in the arms and legs leapings and contractions of the tendons, and so great a restlessness and tossings of their members ensue that the diseased are no more able to sleep than if they were in a place of the greatest torture.'

The association of a number of common complaints, restless legs, leg jerking during sleep and severe leg discomfort was clearly defined in Ekbom's thesis of 1945. Ekbom's syndrome is familial in up to a third of cases. An Italian family has been described which was followed closely for over 20 years. The propositus was a 68-year-old monk whose leg restlessness started at the age of 15 and gradually got worse, causing severe insomnia and sensory disturbances in the legs by the age of 48[13].

Sleep paralysis

The American Edgar Allan Poe, author of *Premature Burial,* and the Swiss composer Othmar Schoeck, who wrote a song cycle entitled *Buried Alive,* must have known sleep paralysis first-hand to describe it so vividly. Sleep paralysis, like Ekbom's syndrome, is sometimes familial. The French terms *'crise à l'état de veille'* and *'cataplexie du réveil'* stress the time of occurrence of sleep paralysis and its similarity to cataplexy. Night nurses' paralysis is probably an example of the same phenomenon, with flaccid paralysis of the skeletal muscles similar to that of REM sleep although the extra-ocular muscles and diaphragm may be spared.

La Sonnambula
Bellini

Sleep-walking

Sleep-walking was known to the composer Bellini, who wrote an opera *La Sonnambula* about it. Our illustration shows the heroine, Amina, treading her way across a perilous bridge whilst her friends anxiously watch. Sleep-walking is most common in children and up to 30% of healthy children and 1% of adults sleep-walk.

The *Glasgow Medical Journal* for 1878 (p. 371) describes a 27-year-old man who, on being put on trial for the murder of his child, pleaded somnambulism in defence.

'At the time of the murder of his child, in a somnambulistic attack, he imagined that he saw a wild beast rise up from the floor and fly at his child, a babe of 18 months. He sprang at the beast and dashed it to the ground, and when awakened, to his horror and overwhelming grief he found that he had killed his beloved baby.'

The decision as to whether somnambulism is a sane or insane automatism has perplexed the English judiciary with important forensic consequences for, if a crime is committed by the insane, the sentence is one of incarceration in a mental asylum, while the sane automatist goes free[2]. (*The Lancet,* 9th August, 1991)

La sonnambula
Lithograph
Royal Opera House,
Covent Garden, London

The Sicilian composer Vincenzo Bellini (1801–1835) completed the opera *La Sonnambula* in Milan in 1831. Gioacchino Rossini (1792–1868) was his inspiration and Gaetano Donizetti (1797–1848) his friend. These three composers dominated the operatic stage for a whole generation. Our picture, which is taken from an opera programme, shows a scene from *La Sonnambula* (The sleep-walker), as recorded by an unknown lithographer in the popular style of the time. Amina has climbed out of the window and is 'sleep-walking' along a narrow beam that links the romantic old mill to the mansion. The local inhabitants who have hurried to the scene are afraid she will fall. Amina's young lover is eager to come to her aid, but he is held back – for as long as the sleep-walker does not awake, she will survive the danger unharmed.

Ferdinand Georg Waldmüller
(1793–1865)
Die erschöpfte Kraft
(Strength exhausted), 1854
Oil on canvas
Österreichische Galerie, Vienna

It is nighttime. Black curtains drape the window of the simple living-room. Everyday objects lie around on the chair, on the floor, waiting to be cleared away. A table lamp casts its light on the cradle in which the infant is sleeping. The light also falls on the basket and a piece of sewing just begun, and on the floor, where a woman is lying, probably the child's mother. Exhausted by her day's toil, she has fallen asleep. This painting exemplifies the uncompromising realism that Wald-

müller expected of art. He was unrelenting in the demands he made on himself and on others. Himself fatherless, he had experienced the harshness of life at first hand. His mother had hoped that her talented son would become a priest, but at the age of only fourteen he ran away from home to become a painter. He kept himself alive and paid for his training by painting pictures for boxes of confectionery. He became a drawing instructor, painter of theatre backdrops, copyist and portraitist, eventually acquiring the title of Academic Councillor. But because he was critical of the official art world, he called for the abolition of the Academy. From then on, he was an outcast in his Austrian homeland, until he was rehabilitated shortly before his death.

Waldmüller was as opposed to classicism as he was to the ideas of the Nazarene group, and he despised the regurgitation of existing art and social historicism. According to Waldmüller, 'It is our own times, our own customs, that we have to show.' Such was the attitude that generated this socially critical picture.

Sleep-walking, night terrors and confusional arousals in childhood share many features in common and have all been considered as arousal disorders, awakening from deep slow wave sleep[3]. The night terror or visit from the night hag, so vividly illustrated by the Swiss artist Fuseli, is sometimes familial, having been recorded as occurring in twins and in three generations of one family. Night terrors, in contrast to nightmares, are arousals from NREM, not REM, sleep with extreme autonomic activity. The child awakes but is only partially aroused, exhibiting intense fear, screaming, widely dilated pupils, tachycardia and sweating, lasting up to 30 minutes.

Much of the normal physiology of sleep remains unexplained and the reason for many of the parasomnias, which occur in children more often than adults, is unknown. Although these are not psychiatric disorders, the church still attempts to banish incubi, or terrors-by-night, with prayer, and there is no doubt that behavioural therapy is sometimes effective in preventing arousal disorders. However, psychotherapeutic intervention is not useful in most cases. Benzodiazepines and other hypnotics which reduce the amount of stage 3–4 sleep, and may also limit the degree of arousal from sleep, are often more successful.

The Nightmare
Fuseli

Henry Fuseli (Johann Heinrich Füssli) (1741–1825)
The Nightmare, 1781
Oil on canvas
The Detroit Institute of Arts, Detroit

Zurich-born Johann Heinrich Füssli, a friend of the physiognomist Caspar Lavater, had been producing drawings from his youth onwards. At his father's wish, however, he studied theology. After being ordained in 1761, he preached in a number of churches in Zurich. But his too liberal views made him politically unpopular and he was forced to flee the city in 1763. He settled a year later in London, which was to become his adopted home up to his death in 1825 and where he came to be called Henry Fuseli. A meeting with the great English artist, Sir Joshua Reynolds, was instrumental in his decision to become a painter. He then travelled to Italy, where he stayed for eight years studying his chosen métier. Returning to London in 1778, he attracted attention with his wash drawings and highly original oil paintings, which portrayed scenes from the Bible and the poetry of Homer, Milton and, above all, Shakespeare. They are executed with great technical skill and have a baroque sense of drama.
The Nightmare is one of Fuseli's masterpieces. A slender woman is sleeping, her head and arms dangling over the top of the bed. A wave-like movement, reinforced by the white nightgown and hanging covers, seems to be generated from the tip of her right foot to her head and arms. The background is masked with dark drapes through which a horse's head terrifyingly emerges, its eyes glittering. Terror itself, a sprite, crouches on the chest of the frail woman: the sleeper's nightmare has been rendered visible.

Sleeping cat

A well-fed domesticated cat has a very different sleep-wake pattern from man (see article 'Sleep in animals') and studies of sleep in cats may not be directly relevant to man. However, one parasomnia caused by large bilateral brainstem lesions that damage the locus coeruleus in cats has its counterpart in man where motor dream activity occurs without atonia. This new REM sleep behavioural disorder was described by Carlos Schenck in 1986; it usually occurs in elderly males and is associated with dramatic and potentially violent motor behaviour, jerking, sleep talking and yelling, sometimes resulting in self-injury [18].

REM sleep is sometimes lost altogether. The clearest documentation so far available of an exactly localized brainstem lesion with near total loss of REM sleep was in a 33-year-old lawyer who sustained a shrapnel injury at the age of 20. Despite almost complete absence of REM sleep and a mild degree of hyposomnia, the patient led a relatively normal life [11].

The greatest mystery of sleep remains the mystery of dreaming. Most of us enjoy our dreams, and the idea of a life without dreaming is very unattractive. Many believe that much that we honour in literature and art is the direct result of mental work during sleep and is due to unconscious cerebral activity. The great Danish storyteller, Isak Dinesen, longed to escape from the waking pain of syphilitic arachnoiditis and from the tragic loss of her coffee plantation to the fantasy world of her dreams.

Jacob's ladder
Lambeth Bible

The Three Wise Men
Gislebertus

Two of the most wonderful dream pictures I know come from early Medieval art: the page from the English 12th Century Lambeth Bible showing the dream of Jacob with a ladder between earth and heaven; and the sculpture in the Cathedral at Autun of the three magi all asleep in one bed and dreaming of the angel warning them to flee from Herod.

Jacob's Dream
Lambeth Bible
The Archbishop of Canterbury and the
Trustees of the Lambeth Palace Library

This illustrated page from the *Lambeth Bible,* a 12th century English manuscript, portrays three scenes from the Old Testament. Above right, Abraham, submitting to God's test of his faith, prepares to sacrifice his son Isaac as a burnt offering. But as he raises his knife, the angel of the Lord stops him. Abraham has passed the test, and instead of his son, he is told to sacrifice a ram caught in a thicket by its horns (Genesis 22, 1–14). The other two scenes concern Isaac's son, Jacob. During Jacob's flight to Haran (Genesis 28, 10–22), he lies down and sleeps with a stone as his pillow. He dreams that he sees angels ascending and descending a ladder reaching up to heaven. When he wakes up, Jacob knows that God has just announced his presence to him in that place. And so he takes the stone, sets it up as a pillar, and calls the name of the place Bethel, the 'house of God'. When Jacob later returns to this place (Genesis 35, 14), he pours oil on the pillar of stone: this is portrayed in the scene on the left margin of the picture. The dream has transformed Jacob's life. Strength comes from the Lord, the God of Abraham and Isaac and Jacob, and He is shown in the divine circle in all His might, with a banner announcing His words: *Ego sum Deus.*

The Three Wise Men Asleep
Cathédrale Saint-Lazare Autun,
Burgundy

In the Middle Ages, Autun (the once celebrated Roman city of Augustodunum) in the duchy of Burgundy was an important episcopal seat. The magnificent Romanesque cathedral is particularly rich in figure capitals dating back to ca. 1130. This particular example is famous. Originally located in the nave of the church, it is now kept in the tower chamber and is attributed to Gislebertus, the master mentioned in the tympanum. It shows the Three Wise Men from the East who had come to Bethlehem to worship the newborn child (Matthew 2, 1–12). An angel appears to them in a dream, warning them not to inform Herod but to return to their own country. The star that guided them to the Son of God is standing over them and will show them the way home. The Three Wise Men – each of them wearing a crown – are lying under one cover, as was usual in the

Middle Ages. They are sleeping, but their eyes are open because they see what the angel is commanding them to do. A delicate detail: God's messenger is touching the youngest of the Three Wise Men with his right index finger.

Master Heinrich of Constance
John, Lying Close to the Breast of Jesus,
ca. 1320
Wood, painted
Mayer van den Bergh Museum,
Antwerp

For secular society, the Gothic epoch meant the culture of the minnesinger, but for the faithful – particularly in the regions along the Rhine – it was an age of mysticism. The pursuit of the contemplative life, the striving after an inwardness stemming from the force of prayer and meditation, found an apt reflection in the sacred art of the period. This *unio mystica* created a demand for devotional images. Old subjects such as the crucifixion and the *pietà,* the *mater dolorosa* with the Son of God lifeless in her lap, found fresh expression in new, more vibrantly emotional forms. And new subjects which satisfied the desire for mystical experience were also popular, for instance the two figures of Jesus and His young, favourite disciple John lying close to His breast. The group is derived from the Gospel of St John 13, 23: 'One of his disciples, whom Jesus loved, was lying close to the breast of Jesus.' In accordance with Greek custom, the apostles and Jesus were lying on benches around the table, and therefore John's head could have lain close to Jesus's breast. But the Gothic woodcarver imagined the group seated round the table. He solved the problem by having Jesus and John sitting very close together and holding hands, while John – with intense feeling – inclines his head towards Jesus's breast. John is not asleep; he is – in this hour of parting – filled with sorrow. Such representations of the apostle John were almost all the products of Swabian sacred art in the first three decades of the 14th century. Most of them were commissioned by convents, as was probably the case with this fine group produced by the Constance master, Heinrich.

The Interrupted Sleep
Boucher

I shall end this chapter with one of my favourite images of sleep, in the make-believe world of François Boucher. Two courtiers in fancy dress play at being a shepherd and shepherdess, in a landscape where it never rains.

François Boucher (1703–1770)
Interrupted Sleep, 1750
Oil on canvas, 75 × 64.8 cm
The Metropolitan Museum of Art,
New York
The Jules Bache Collection

The wealthy, jaded society of 18th century France considered theirs to be the best of all possible worlds, created free of problems for the *beati possidentes* by divine intervention. The grinding poverty of the lower orders was simply ignored. The harsh life of the rural population was transformed into a pastoral idyll, as in our picture with its feast of seductive colours and forms, gay, well-modulated feelings, and teasing artifice. Even a cage with a songbird hangs in a tree. The flock of sheep and the sheepdog (more suited for the drawing-room) coexist in tranquil harmony. The lovely shepherdess has been gathering pretty flowers which she has put in a basket decorated with a charming ribbon. Now she has fallen asleep by a babbling brook. She is barefoot but over her skirt she is wearing an apron of silver-striped damask with a pink border. She lies there innocently, her white breasts visible over her tightly laced bodice. A fresh-faced youth approaches her and tries to wake her so that he can engage her in amorous dalliance. He tickles the graceful neck of the lovely, slumbering shepherdess with a straw.

References

1. Arendt, J.: The third eye and the biological clock. Inaugural Lecture, University of Surrey, 28 November 1990, p. 7.
2. Brahams, D.: Sleepwalking – 'disease of the mind'? *Lancet 338,* 375–376 (1991).
3. Broughton, R.J.: Sleep disorders – disorders of arousal? *Science 159,* 1070–1078 (1968).
4. von Economo, C.: *Encephalitis lethargica, its sequelae and treatment,* p. 200. K.D. Newman. London: Oxford University Press, 1931.
5. Foutz, A.S., Mitler, M.M., Cavalli-Sforza, L.L., Dement, W.C.: Genetic factors in canine narcolepsy. *Sleep 1,* 413–421 (1979).
6. Gastaut, H., Tessinari, C.A., Divon, B.: Etudes polygraphiques des manifestations épisodiques (hypniques et respiratoires) du syndrome de Pickwick. *Rev Neurol 112,* 568–579 (1965).
7. Gélineau, J.B.E.: *De la narcolepsie,* p. 63. Paris: Société d'éditions scientifiques, 1881.
8. Gélineau, J.B.E.: De la narcolepsie. *Gaz Hôp (Paris) 1880,* 626–628, 635–637.
9. Honda, Y., Doi, Y., Juji, T., Satake, M.: Narcolepsy and HLA: Positive DR2 are a prerequisite for the development of narcolepsy. *Folia Psychiatr Neurol Jpn 38,* 360 (1984).
10. Jung, R., Kuhlo, W.: Neurophysiological studies of abnormal night sleep and the Pickwickian syndrome; in: *Sleep mechanisms,* Vol. T8, pp. 140–159. Ed. K. Albert, C. Bally, K.P. Stradling. Amsterdam: Elsevier, 1965.
11. Lavie, P., Pratt, H., Scharf, B., Peled, R., Brown, J.: Localised pontine lesions: nearly total absence of REM sleep. *Neurology (Cleveland) 34,* 118–120 (1984).
12. Lugaresi, E., Medori, R., Montagna, P., et al.: Fatal familial insomnia and dysautonomia with selective degeneration of thalamic nuclei. *N Engl J Med 315,* 997–1003 (1986).
13. Montagna, P., Coccagna, G., Cirignotta, F., Lugaresi, E.: Familial restless leg syndrome; in: *Sleep/wake disorders: natural history, epidemiology and long-term evolution,* pp. 231–235. Ed. C. Guilleminault, E. Lugaresi. New York: Raven Press, 1983.
14. Moore-Ede, M.C., Czeisler, C.A., Richardson, G.S.: Circadian timekeeping in health and disease: basic properties of circadian timekeepers. *New Engl J Med 309,* 469–476 (1983).
15. Passouant, P.: Historical note: Doctor Gélineau (1828–1906): Narcolepsy Centennial. *Sleep 3,* 241–246 (1981).
16. Prebhakaran, N., Murthy, G.K., Mallya, U.L.: A case of Kleine-Levin syndrome in India. *Brit J Psychiat 117,* 517–519 (1970).
17. Rochbach, M., Hall, J.C.: The molecular biology of circadian rhythms. *Newon 3,* 387–398 (1989).
18. Schenck, C.H., Bundie, S.R., Ettinger, M.G., Mahawold, M.W.: Chronic behavioural disorders of human REM sleep: a new category of parasomnia. *Sleep 9,* 293–308 (1968).
19. Severinghaus, J., Mitchell, P.: Failure of respiratory centre automoticity while awake. *Clin Res 10,* 122–127 (1962).
20. Sullivan, C.E., Berthon Jones M., Issa, F.G.: Nocturnal nasal-airway pressure for sleep apnoea. *New Engl J Med 309,* 112 (1983).
21. Vogel G.: Studies in psychophysiology of dreams, III. The dreams of narcolepsy. *Arch Gen Psychiat 43,* 421–428 (1960).
22. Whymper, E.: *Scrambles on the alps.*
23. Winterbottom, T.: *An account of the native Africans in the neighbourhood of Sierra Leone,* p. 29. London: Hatchard and Maxman, 1803.
24. *Sunday Times,* 8 November 1980, p. 9.

John Souch
Sir Thomas Ashton at His Wife's Deathbed, 1635
City Art Gallery, Manchester

This picture was intended to record, as a fitting farewell tribute, the extraordinary event of this death. Though no easy task, it was accomplished with great decorum by the English master of the miniature, John Souch. The work is filled with detail. The observer looks down onto the scene, as if watching actors on a stage. The focal point of the entire composition is the death's head above the black pall which covers the basket. The two daughters are placed on either side, and both they and their father are wearing court mourning dress. Above this scene hangs the family coat of arms, while the globe in the background on the left symbolizes worldliness. Maintaining his bearing and with a solemn expression, Sir Thomas places his left hand on the death's head. With his right hand, aided by his youngest daughter, he holds the wooden cross which will be inserted into the burial mound. In this way, the husband expresses his acceptance as a Christian of the finality of what has occurred. The deceased lies in bed as if she had just fallen asleep. She is wearing a bonnet and dress, both of which are trimmed with costly lace, as was common in court circles at the time.

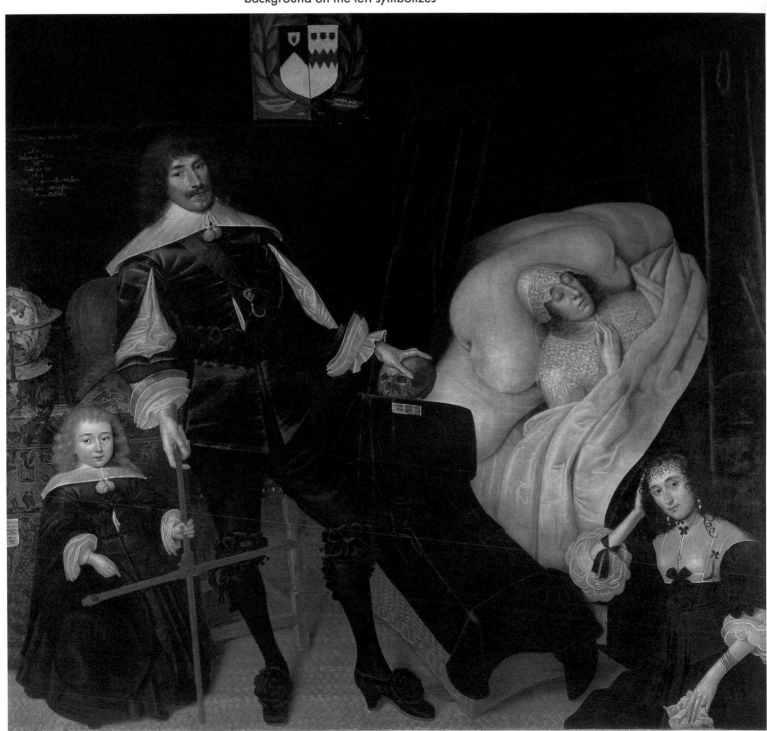

In Federico Fellini's film 'La dolce vita' (1959), the world famous star 'Silvia' declares in an interview that 'I sleep between two drops of perfume', thus making it clear to everyone that this woman with the seductive air (as played by Anita Ekberg) sleeps naked in bed. In the fifties, the tabloid press probably attributed just such remarks to real film stars. What at that time was thought to be somewhat scandalous was a matter of course in the Europe of six hundred years earlier. Many people slept naked between the bedclothes, wearing only a bonnet. This nakedness was not considered offensive, nor was it – as is claimed in certain versions of popular history – a sign of permanent readiness for sexual intercourse.

There are few pre-16th century references to clothes worn in bed. Daytime clothing, however, was strictly regulated. Numerous decrees on clothing in the late Middle Ages show that the inhabitants of a city were obliged under threat of punishment to clothe themselves in accordance with their rank. The custome of each rank was of extreme importance in society. During the daytime, it provided a means of recognition, but, since this was of no importance at night, clothing was often dispensed with completely in bed. In addition, before the introduction of mechanized cotton mills in England in the 18th century, cloth was worth far more than it is today. Particularly valuable textiles served as investments in the same way as jewellery or gold coins. Each household often produced its own linen from flax, and individual items of clothing were worn for years or for a lifetime, sometimes even being handed down to the next generation. Clothes were probably removed at night to reduce wear-and-tear on the material. As late as the 19th century it was said of miserly women that, in order to save on cloth, they sat at the spinning wheel with their bare backside on the chair. There was also the joke about the farmer who would beat his wife in bed so as not to damage the only valuable thing about her, her dress.

The first accounts of night attire come from the nobility. It is known that women wore nightdresses embellished with lace and other expensive trimmings in the 15th century. Nightshirts were listed among the bills for the wardrobe of King Henry VIII of England (1491–1547) and, in 1556, Queen Mary received a New Year's gift of two nightshirts decorated with black silk. Queen Elizabeth I also received a New Year's gift of an exquisitely finished nightshirt in 1589. During her reign (1558–1603), heavily perfumed cambric shirts were very popular. Their design was based on that of the shirts worn during the day and they would certainly have been very costly items of clothing.

From the end of the 16th century onwards, it became usual in courtly circles in France to change one's shirt every morning and evening. A mas-

Night Attire
by Katharina Eder Matt

Manesse manuscript (ca. 1330)
Meister Heinrich Teschler
Folio 281 v 25×35 cm
University Library, Heidelberg

The great art of the *minnesang* (minstrelsy) was already in decline when the family of the Zurich patrician Rüdiger Manesse established its collection of *Minnelieder* (love songs) between 1300 and 1340. This *Manesse Codex* is now kept in Heidelberg University Library. It comprises 426 sheets of parchment on which about 5400 verses, the love songs of 137 minnesingers (minstrels) are written. Each poet is introduced by means of a 'Portrait of the artist'. The high format of the composition, the expressive strength of the drawing, and the strong natural colours produce a very fresh effect. These illuminated manuscripts demonstrate the cultural importance of the Minnesang and provide an attractive picture of courtly life in the Gothic period. The first composers of these ardent love songs were emperors and the high nobility and, later, specially gifted citizens. The Minnesang was a form of idealized ritual courtship of an unattainable married woman. In the whole of this splendid piece, the work of four painters can be distinguished. It is not known which one painted this particular portrait. Meister Teschler was perhaps a member of the Zurich nobility. He was a town councillor for many years, and in 1275 he is mentioned as the canon of the choir. Here, in a green cloak, he has forced his way into the bed chamber of his beloved. A page and lady-in-waiting are witnesses. The noble lady is sitting rather than lying in her bed, her back supported by cushions. She is wearing a garland around her head scarf. With a stern face, she rejects the singer who is begging for audience. With her left hand she is trying to draw up the bedclothes to cover her nakedness.

ter of the hunt at the court of King Henry IV (1553–1610), following an audience with the King in Olainville, declined an invitation to remain the night because he had with him neither a fresh change of clothes nor a nightshirt. It is claimed that the Sun King, Louis XIV, even changed his shirt twice a night because he sweated heavily. This 'new fashion' was related to contemporary ideas about hygiene. It was thought that clean underwear cleaned the body. Washing with water, by contrast, was considered unhealthy. There was, however, little difference between shirts for day and night wear, while night attire, which included bonnets and night jackets, was of no particular significance compared with daytime dress. For a long time, the wearing of special night attire remained the preserve of the upper classes. However, in the general population, the use of undershirts which were kept on during the day as well as overnight became common.

It was not until after the French Revolution that the practice of wearing special shirts, bonnets and sleeping jackets became widespread among the urban population. With the dismantling of the guild regulations governing clothing habits, fashion began to dictate clothing behaviour even outside court circles. Although clothes designers were very active in creating house coats and morning gowns, they were not particularly interested in nightshirts because these were still accorded little importance within society. In the 19th century, however, nightdresses formed part of the trousseau of women of the middle classes. They were classified as 'body-linen' and were often made by the bride-to-be herself. With the spread of industrialized processing of the raw materials and mechanized manufacturing of cloth, the cost of these items began to fall. Although various trimmings such as lace and embroidery were used to give a decorative touch to women's bonnets, jackets and dresses, elegance of night attire was not in tune with the prudish mentality of the time. Even in mid-century — with industrialization spreading rapidly — a night-dress which had been decorated with lace to make it more attractive was still regarded as a sign of depravity by older English people. Hence, throughout the entire 19th century, fashion in this area showed little change. Any changes that did occur were based invariably on the undershirts that were worn during the day, while the basic design remained more or less the same. Pockets in men's shirts were introduced to England from the United States in the 1870's. Around the turn of the century, the younger generation in particular stopped wearing bonnets at night.

Although the theme of sleep was a favourite subject of art, in the 19th century the portrayal of people in everyday night clothes was one of the more unusual subjects, even in the genre painting so popular at the time.

Honoré Daumier (1808–1879)
Lithograph

The widespread idea in European culture that people in night-shirts look foolish has provided caricaturists with a rich source of material. The satirical lithographs which Daumier produced for the Paris newspaper *Caricature* (1831–1835) and, for many decades from 1832 onwards, for *Le Charivari,* are famous. Daumier was an exceptionally gifted painter, but his reputation was made by his lithographic opus which comprises more than 3400 pieces. Executed with a rapid but sure hand in lithographic chalk, enhanced to a vivid *chiaroscuro* composition, his caricatures castigated bourgeois and political life in France. In the series *'Croquis d'expression'* he contrasted two distinct types of physiognomy and exposed all the latent humour of the situation, as in this picture showing a concerned wife spreading warm talc on her husband's nose as a cure for his cold.

Honoré Daumier (1808–1879)
Journée du célibataire
(A day in the life of a bachelor)
Lithograph

A Daumier series from 1839 is entitled *'Journée du célibataire'*. Marriage being too expensive and risky a proposition, the miserly bachelor makes do with the company of small animals. Thus dogs, cats and birds are omnipresent in his life. They accompany him while he rises in the morning, during his dutiful period of exercise in the street, even during his midday meal in the restaurant and, especially, as shown here, when he goes to bed at *'9 heures du soir'*. Monsieur Coquelet lies in bed with his dog and cat on the bedspread. He has his night-cap on his head and smiles contentedly as he extinguishes the candle on his bedside table.

Honoré Daumier (1808–1879)
Professeurs et moutards
(Teachers and brats)
Lithograph

The 30-page series *'Professeurs et moutards'* published in 1845/46 was very critical of the principles of education practised at the time. Even the captions are ironical. This lithograph from the February 3, 1846 edition of *Le Charivari,* executed in the soft chalk strokes of the artist's mature style, is entitled *'Le dortoir d'un pensionnat bien tenu'* (The dormitory of a well-run boarding school). This dormitory has all the appearances of a training ground. The teacher is beating time and – one, two, three – the pupils, dressed in long shirts, with knees drawn up and all their night-caps arranged in the same way, have to lie down, close their eyes and go to sleep.

Votive picture 'Maria, hilf!' 18th century
Oil on canvas, 21 × 27 cm
S. Maria del Buon Consiglio
Cureglia, Ticino, Switzerland

In all cultures, the practice of showing gratitude for help received in fulfilment of a request made in one's hour of need is widespread. In Christian folk-culture, votive plaques are especially popular. These offerings of a pious people are important historical documents which reflect everyday events. This small picture is one of many votive offerings to be found in the pilgrim chapel of 'S. Maria del Buon Consiglio'. It is signed 'G.R.' and was probably painted by the petitioner himself. In a clumsy yet expressive way, it shows how the sick person lying in bed

implores the Mother of God, hanging as an icon on the wall of the room, for help. He is wearing a night-cap and the usual white linen shirt, which was normally kept on both during the day and at night.

By contrast, the figure in night clothes was extensively caricatured, given the widespread belief that people, and especially men, seldom appear more ridiculous than when they are standing there with only their shirts on, a situation which removes all social distinctions. The dishevelled, unshaven character in his nightshirt and night-cap has remained a favourite figure of fun in pictures up to the present day. Even today, the trick of imagining someone we are afraid of standing in their shirt-tails is still one of the general mechanisms for coping with the trials of daily life. During the carnival period, many communities in the Baden region of South Germany are still visited by the *Hemmliglunggi,* who wear long white shirts and night-caps. It is obvious whom they are caricaturing.

At the start of the 20th century, one hundred years after fashion had triumphed over the regulations that used to link clothing to guild and rank, night-clothes began to attract designers. This was seen initially in the introduction of men's pyjamas, a form of clothing modelled on Far Eastern designs and, to begin with, mostly worn when travelling, i.e. in situations where it was not possible to have complete privacy during sleep. In the course of time, pyjamas became the standard night attire for men, but never completely replaced the night-shirt, which is again being recommended today as a particularly healthy type of (night) dress for men. Pyjamas for women were first introduced in about 1920 by Garçonne-Mode as clothing to be worn around the house and at night. The Paris couturier Lucien Lelong (1919–1948) designed two-piece pyjama suits in crêpe de Chine which could also be worn around the house with high heels. This novelty was not immediately accepted. In 1925, the *Berliner Illustrierte* criticized this 'embarrassing lapse' and demanded that 'healthy male taste should abjure such vile fashions'.

Full-length, women's night-dresses closed at the neck now had to slowly give way to more fashionable designs which emphasized the female form. The increasing sexual freedom in this area is most clearly evident from the mail order catalogues. In their spring/summer catalogue of 1895, Montgomery Ward & Co (which claimed to be the biggest mail order firm in the USA at the time) offered in the 'white linen and cotton' section a selection of two cambric and twelve muslin night-dresses for ladies (cheaper by the dozen). They are shown folded so that the collars and sleeves can be clearly seen, since this is where the main differences between them were to be found. In 1890, the Zurich department store Jelmoli advertised not only folded nigth-dresses but also pictures of three being worn by models ('Anna', 'Isabella' and 'Helene'). Here too, the main feature was the decorative element, with lace and embroidered trimmings, in addition to

Pieter Bruegel the Elder
(1525/30–1569)
Yawning Man
Oil on canvas
Musées Royaux des Beaux-Arts, Brussels

Bruegel's reputation as the finest northern painter of the late 16th century is well merited. His works are the creative testimony to a new way of viewing ordinary people. In earlier courtly times, a picture such as this would not have been possible. Someone is yawning. It could be a yawn before going to bed. Or it could be a yawn in the early morning, in anticipation of the day's work which is about to begin. The latter interpretation is the more likely since the man is still wearing a simple nightshirt. He has not yet had enough sleep; the red nose could be a clue – perhaps he had too much to drink the evening before. Whatever the situation depicted: free and unobserved, his eyes mere slits, the man opens his mouth wide and yawns uninhibitedly.

For a long time, fashion designers showed little interest in the night-dress. It was not until the beginning of the 20th century that the designs began to be based on contemporary trends. Five examples from fashion mail-order catalogues show developments in styles of women's night-dresses during the first half of this century (1890–1961).

a) Montgomery Ward & Co (USA), Spring/Summer, 1895
b) Jelmoli (Zurich), 1890
c) Jelmoli (Zurich), Winter 1931/32
d) Jelmoli (Zurich), Winter 1946/47
e) Jelmoli (Zurich), Summer 1961

Night Dresses—Continued.

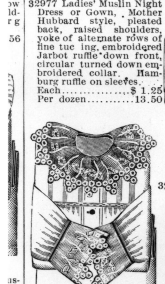

32977 Ladies' Muslin Night Dress or Gown, . Mother Hubbard style, pleated back, raised shoulders, yoke of alternate rows of fine tuc ing, embroidered Jarbot ruffle down front, circular turned down embroidered collar. Hamburg ruffle on sleeves.
Each................$ 1.25
Per dozen..........13.50

32981 Ladies' Muslin Night Dress or Gown; Mother Hubbard style, raised shoulders, yoke of 6 alternate rows of fine tucks and herringbone t r i m m i n g, handsome embroidered ruffle collar and 5 inch edging on sleeves.
Each........... ....$ 1.40
Per dozen..........15.12

32984 L a d í e s' Cambric Night Dress or G o w n, Mother Hubbard back, raised shoulders, circular shaped yoke trimmed fine

Ladies'
Cotton

Weight of l
is 8 to 1

32995 La
Muslin S
ing of 3
5½-in c h
ruffle at b
Each.....
Per dozen

32999 L
Muslin S
tucks f
bottom t
5¼-inch
ng. Eac
Per dozen

a

Damen-Wäsche.
Lingerie pour dames.

Coupe excellente et façon irréprochable

Isabella Damen-Nachthemde aus feinst. Baumwolltuch, Säumchen und Stickerei garniert Fr. **6.25** in hocheleganter Ausführung „ 14.25

Isabelle. Chemises de nuit pour dames en toile de coton extra fine, avec garniture à petits plis et broderie, la pièce . . . . Frs. 6.25 en plus élégant modèle riche . . . . . „ 14.25

Helene Damen-Nachthemde aus prima Batistgeweb. m. St. Gall. **21.—** Stickerei, hochelegant . . . . Fr. in einfacherer Ausführung . . „ 12.50

Hélène. Chemises de nuit pour dames en tissu batiste, avec broderie de St-Gall, modèle élegant . . . . Frs. 21.— en plus simple . . . . „ 12.50

ndigem
.50
. 40
. 90

e coton .
6.40
4.90

b

| Pyjama pour dames, flanellette unie, confection soignée
Grandeur 40—48
No. D 18932   Fr. 9.80 | Pyjama pour dames, Flanellette avec jolie rayure moderne
Grandeur 42—48
No. D 18931   Fr. 11.50 |

BARCHENT

FLANELLETTE

FLANELLA

Damen-Nachthemd aus Croisé-Barchent, schön verarbeitet, mit modischer Stickerei garniert und Manschetten zum Oeffnen.
Grössen: 40, 42, 44, 46,
Länge 130 cm,
lachs   No. 3040,449
hellblau No. 3040,450   18.50

Mollig warmes Damen-Nachthemd aus unifarbiger Flanellette, mit Reverskragen hübsch garniert.
Grössen: 40, 42, 44, 46, Länge 130 cm,
rosa   No. 3040,451
hellblau   No. 3040,452   Fr. 18.50

Dito, extra-weit für starke Figuren,
Grössen: 48, 50, Länge 130 cm,
rosa   No. 3040,453
hellblau   No. 3040,454   Fr. 19.50

Mol
Nac
rein
aufg
sche
G
lach
hell
frais

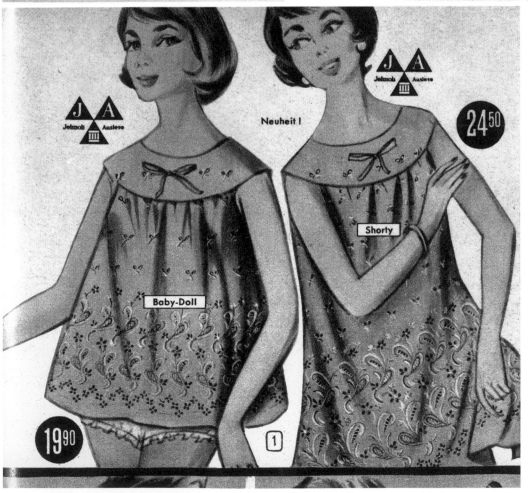

J A Jelmoli Auslese III

Neuheit!

24.50

Baby-Doll

Shorty

19.90

①

Albrecht Dürer (1471–1528)
On Courting at Night, 1494
Woodcut, 17 × 14 cm
Kupferstichkabinett, Basel

At the start of the 16th century, the Christian world was in turmoil. Albrecht Dürer expressed his fears in this magnificent apocalyptic wood cutting. Erasmus of Rotterdam (1469–1536), in his essay *In Praise of Folly* dedicated to the English Chancellor, Thomas More, had exposed the whole world – both men and women of noble birth and the ordinary people, both the learned and the illiterate – as willing servants of the Goddess of Folly. Sebastian Brant from Strasbourg (1458–1521) was a professor in the faculty of law of the University of Basel, the episcopal city on the Rhine which at that time was a magnet for printers, illustrators and book publishers. It was here that he published his *Ship of Fools,* which portrayed the world as a rocking boat filled with fools. They are sailing to Narragonia, the Land of Fools, and their journey is luridly described in over seven thousand rhyming verses. This illustrated satire was very successful and was quickly translated from German into Dutch, English and French. Albrecht Dürer, who at that time was working as an illustrator in Basel, drew and cut 75 of the total of 116 woodcuts. Our illustration is taken from the sixty-second chapter which is entitled 'On courting at night'. The waning moon is in the sky. Foolish minstrels serenade their beloved with flute, lute and song. But the woman who has been so rudely awakened from sleep is not in the least interested. Naked but for her bonnet, she empties the contents of her chamber pot over the unwanted suitors.

quality of material, taking pride of place. The 1931/32 winter catalogue of the same mail order firm advertised two sets of lady's pyjamas shown in typical fashion drawings of the time: two women posing in page-boy hair-styles and with accessories in the form of powder-puffs and high-heeled shoes. It appeared by this time that fashionable night-dresses were finally here to stay, though conventional designs were, of course, still retained. With the growing awareness of style in everyday living, a need for style in the bedroom also began to make itself felt. As a result, night attire became designer objects. Great emphasis was placed not only on elegance, but also on comfort. Frills, lace and the dream of sleeping in silk were incorporated into the fashions of night attire. Just after the Second World War, body-hugging shapes were very popular. Synthetic materials began to be used not long after. In the fifties, many forms of behaviour and styles in clothing were based on Hollywood films, and night attire for women also followed this trend. One remarkable feature in the history of the night-dress was the appearance of the 'Baby Doll' style, which was named after the film of the same name by Elia Kazan (1956) with Carroll Baker in the title role. In one scene which was condemned for its shamelessness, the actress wore a short-sleeved night-dress and short baggy pants. These became all the rage among teenagers and young women in the late 1950's and 1960's.

Even though fashion and dress are the subject of wide-ranging investigation and analysis in all branches of the cultural sciences and undoubtedly reflect an important aspect of human behaviour, very little attention has been paid to night attire, despite the fact that we wear such garments every day (or rather every night), and generally spend a third of our lives in them.

References

1. Cunnington, P., Willet, C.: *The history of underclothes,* 2nd edition. London, Boston: Faber and Faber, 1981.
2. Junker, A., Stille, E.: Die zweite Haut. *Kleine Schr Hist Mus Frankfurt a.M. 39* (1988).
3. Loschek, I.: *Mode im 20. Jahrhundert, eine Kulturgeschichte unserer Zeit.* Munich: Bruckmann, 1988.
4. Vigarello, G.: *Wasser und Seife – Puder und Parfüm, Geschichte der Körperhygiene seit dem Mittelalter.* Frankfurt a.M., New York: Campus, 1988.
5. Widmann, M., et al.: *Anziehungskräfte – Variété de la mode 1786–1986.* Munich: Carl Hanser, 1986.

Gentle sleep. You come like purest bliss, most willingly when unasked, unsought. You loosen the knots of rigorous thought, you blend all images of joy and of pain ..., enfolded in exquisite chimera we sink, and cease to be.

Johann Wolfgang von Goethe (Egmont)

The World's Sleep
by Annemarie Seiler-Baldinger

Sleep is a basic need, yet man the world over is ambivalent about it. Sleep has been variously perceived as 'nature's soft nurse' (Shakespeare, *Henry IV,* Part 2), 'most exquisite invention' (Heine, *William Ratcliff*) and as a form of madness, as 'savoured death' (Hebbel, *Epigramme II*).

In sleep, man loses control of himself and his 'spirit', and becomes vulnerable. He tries to protect himself against this fragile and hazardous state by fitting out his bed with devices to ward off any evil. His bed (human beings generally lie down to sleep; we sleep in the sitting or standing position only unwillingly or from exhaustion) affords not only protection against the powers of evil, but also an opportunity to display magnificence and demonstrate membership of a specific culture or social class. The actual positions in which man sleeps (on his back, stomach or side) and the bed itself, offer few variants. Sleep is possible on the floor or ground (if need be, lying on the bare ground, but preferably with something underneath) or raised up from the floor but connected with it by means of a frame (a bed) or suspended in mid-air in a net, i.e. a hammock.

Throughout the world, the majority of people sleep on the floor or on a bed. Sleeping in a hammock is a special case, the hammock being an invention of the South American Indians. In contrast, the equipment needed for sleeping on the floor or in mid-air is closest to the basic concept of furniture, i.e. movables. As a rule, the greater the division of labour and class distinctions in a society, the more limited, i.e. specific, is its use of furniture. The variety of uses to which a single object can be put is typical of 'aboriginal' peoples and, for that matter, of rural areas in Europe. Mats, for instance, are used not only for sleeping on, but also for sitting, eating and working. Beds are used for resting, but also as tables and storage areas. Chests can be slept on, besides being used for storing clothes and bedding.

If we consider the three basic forms of 'bed' historically and geographically, sleeping on the floor or the ground (on a groundsheet) is certainly the oldest and most widespread. Sleeping while raised above the floor or ground is a more recent development and more likely to be encountered in hierarchical than egalitarian societies.

Herr Hug von Werbenwag, ca. 1300
Codex Manesse, 25 × 35 cm
Heidelberg University Library

Herr Hug (or Hugo) von Werbenwag came from a noble family originating in the upper Danube valley. He was one of the tradition-bound, Swabian minnesingers at the court of the Emperor Henry VI. Hugo's songs, however, are surprisingly modern, and his portrait in the *Codex Manesse* is bolder than is usually the case. The minnesinger sits with his beloved on the wooden edge of a bed which fills the entire picture. Herr Hug is shown in a tender embrace, cheek to cheek, fondling the hands of his 'frouwe' and seeking an approving glance in her eyes. The man is wearing a blue cloak, the woman is clothed in a red shawl. A blanket with a striped patterns and fur lining lies on the bed. Two cushions, one blue and the other red, each with gold dots, have been made ready. The whole bed is covered by a curtain held in place by rings on a frame, gathered together in four places and falling down at the sides. This is an elegant bed such as was customary in courtly circles at the time.

The primeval bed: the ground . . .

The circumstances surrounding archeological discoveries are such that the existence of some kind of groundsheet for sleeping on is hard to demonstrate unequivocally from the archeological context. Sleeping on the 'bare' ground, unless it consisted of grass, moss or fine-grained sand, was probably an emergency solution at all times in history. As a rule, the use of soft, warm mats that protect against damp has been favoured.

In the paleolithic and mesolithic eras, man slept on leaves, brushwood, grass, straw, hides, pelts and so on, depending on the geographical region and climate, with hides also serving as blankets and, during the day, as clothing to keep out the cold. In cold parts of the world (Arctic and Antarctic regions, mountainous areas), people still wear hides to keep themselves warm. They sometimes made do with hollowed-out tree trunks for sleeping in, like the Tasmanians and the African bushmen at the turn of the century and, even nowadays, some Indians of South and Central America who sleep in their canoes when they are on the move.

The earliest known textile groundsheets in the form of woven matting as well as felt and bark-cloth date back no later than neolithic times.

Mats are still a very popular form of bedding in warm or temperate climates. The earliest samples are from North America, particularly the Great Basin (USA), where woven mats dating back to the ninth millenium BC have been found.

In the ancient world, the earliest clay imprints of matting were found in Jarmo (Iraq) and date from between 5270 and 4630 BC. Soft matting and weft-twined fabrics were used in Central Europe as bedding until the emergence of weaving. The significance of the mat as bedding can still be seen in the German word 'ermattet', meaning 'tired, weary'.

Compared with woven textiles, matting was, and still is, considered cheap. As a consequence, it is widely used, for instance by many Indian tribes in North, Central and South America (northwest coast of North America, Mexico, Central Brazil), most of the inhabitants of Oceania and Indonesia and large numbers of Africans and Asians (matting is still used in Japan, for instance). Mats are easy to transport and take up little room, for they can be rolled up and stacked away if they are not to be used for sitting on, or as wall hangings and floor carpets or room dividers. In addition, they can be made from a variety of unprocessed plant material using every possible technique of interlacing, often in ad hoc combinations. In comparison, mats or covers made from bark and felt depend on certain raw materials – certain types of tree for bark and certain animals for felt. Bark-based materials *(tapas)* are used particularly in the South Sea islands and in North, Central and South America, while felt is popular with the

Félix Vallotton (1865–1925)
Le sommeil, 1908
Oil on canvas, 113.5 × 162.5 cm
Musée d'Art et d'Histoire, Geneva

As a youth, Félix Vallotton's ambition to become a painter was reinforced by the cultured atmosphere prevailing in his old-established Lausanne family. At the age of seventeen, he went to study painting at the *Académie Julian* in Paris. He was only twenty-one when he exhibited for the first time at the *Salon Officiel.* Like his contemporary, Henri Matisse, Vallotton knew that he represented a new generation of painters and he turned his back on impressionism. He played a leading role in the 'Nabis' group ('nabis' means prophet), whose members were fascinated by the solid colour surfaces of Gauguin; yet Vallotton was at the same time a master of black and white

woodcuts. Rejecting impressionism, which bathed everything in colour-based luminosity, Vallotton sought an expressively static colour-based form. His artistic programme is reflected in his statement 'I dream of painting which is free of any image drawn direct from nature.' Much thought went into composing – our picture of a sleeping woman. The scene is viewed from above, moving the focus to the foreground of the painting, which has been intentionally built up around the strong skin colour of the body, accentuated by the even more pronounced blue and red. The conscious choice of a yellow-bound book in the lower left hand corner creates a further formal contrast.

Ravinder Reddy
Couple, 1988
102 × 186 × 45.5 cm
Fibreglass
National Gallery of Modern Art,
New Delhi

Though Indian art was synonymous with religious art for thousands of years, the sacred books, the Vedas, are rich in images which elevate scenes from everyday life to the holy world of the deities. One such subject – procreation as a creative act – is also frequently handled by 20th century artists. Ravinder Reddy is one of the outstanding and most respected artists of our time. The figures shown here – a couple sleeping under a blanket – are a sublimated expression of Indian writings on love that are so vividly illus-

trated in the friezes of the temples of Kajuraho. Just as the figures of married couples on Etruscan sarcophagi were created in praise of the life that goes on weaving its threads, the lovers shown here also breathe, imbued with the vitality of their love.

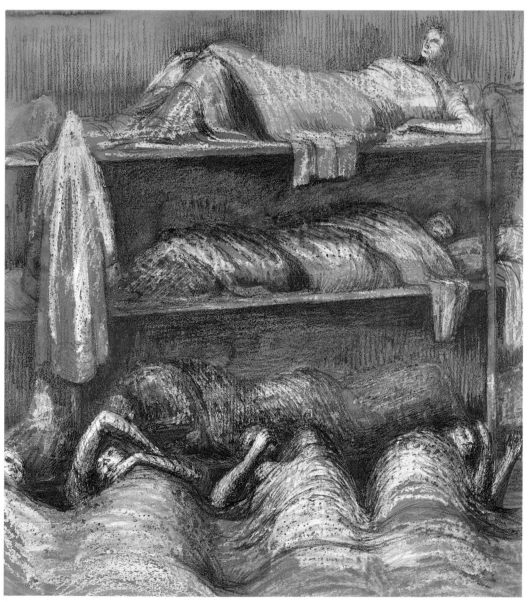

Henry Moore (1898–1986)
Pink and Green Sleepers, 1941
Bunks and Sleepers, 1941
both 38.1×55.9 cm
Pen, ink, chalk, pencil, watercolours
Tate Gallery, London
By courtesy of the
Henry Moore Foundation

Henry Moore, who died in August 1941, was Britain's first great sculptor. His rich artistic legacy has gained worldwide recognition on account of his very personal language. Henry Moore was born near Leeds, the son of a coalminer, and first became a school-teacher. During World War I, he was injured by poison gas, an event that left a lasting psychological effect. A grant enabled him to study at the Leeds School of Art from 1919 to 1921. Later, he taught at the Chelsea School of Art in London. In 1940, he was appointed a 'war artist' and commissioned to draw scenes from the blitz. His 'shelter scenes' show Londoners seeking refuge in the air-raid shelters and stations of the London Underground. These carefully observed scenes were the basis for Moore's later large-scale sculptures. The sparsely applied colours under the soft chalk lines convey the impression of dusk. The sleepers are lying on bunks and the floor. The blankets which keep them warm seem to evoke slowly breaking waves. Details bring the overall composition to life: the position of the arms, the spreading of the fingers, the open mouth, a person turning over to make himself more comfortable in bed.

Henri de Toulouse-Lautrec (1864–1901)
Le lit, ca. 1892
Oil on cardboard, 53×70 cm
Musée d'Orsay, Paris

Toulouse-Lautrec was from an old aristocratic family in the South of France. As the result of a bone disease – the effects of which were exacerbated by riding accidents – his legs atrophied and he became a cripple. However, thanks to his powerful intellect and creative energy, he was able to overcome his handicap with supreme accomplishment. He found his métier as a drawer and painter, and his posters of dancers and singers made him famous. No one knew and understood better than he did the Parisian nightclubs, dance halls, the-atres, cabarets and other such establishments, as well as their denizens and clientele. He became the confidant of the demi-monde. His ability to perceive the realities – suffused with a gentle irony, as if for protection – enabled him to depict not only the glitter but also the more humdrum sides of Parisian life. The series includes the work reproduced here. It is a fine, spontaneous study of two people in bed, snug under the blankets but not yet asleep.

nomads of Asia and in Eastern Europe for making yurts, blankets and groundsheets. Like papyrus and paper, both these 'materials' are produced in similar fashion (beating, maceration).

Though the mat did not lose its function as a groundsheet through the advent of weaving, it ceased to be used as a blanket since most woven cloths were softer and warmer. It was now possible to spread cloth over straw, leaves or grass, which made for greater comfort, or to sew bags which could be stuffed with soft material – the mattress (from the medieval Latin *matratrium;* see section on 'Bedding') was born!

Kelim carpets have been known in Anatolia since the 6th century BC. Woven or knotted carpets have since provided comfortable bedding for the pastoral tribes of the Middle East and North Africa.

Mattresses, blankets, carpets and mats, in other words all movable bedding, are of course, used not only for sleeping on the floor but also for resting on a bed.

In cultures in which sleeping in beds or raised above the floor is the rule, sleeping on the floor or ground reflects the sleeper's position on the socioeconomic scale. The homeless children of Bogotá, the clochards of Paris and the subway dwellers of New York do not sleep 'willingly' on newspapers or in cardboard boxes or wrapped up in their clothes on the ground; they do so out of pure necessity – like the farmers of the Andes, whose poncho is both overcoat, blanket and mattress.

In hierarchical societies, sleeping on the ground is a sign of submission and humility. The Inca sun virgins who served in the temple of the supreme deity slept on the floor.

Sleeping raised above the ground or floor is a habit of savanna country and colder regions. The simplest form of such beds is a block bed or clay-built platform, usually around the fireplace or, in Alpine regions, the tiled stove. Such beds do not differ fundamentally from sleeping arrangements on the floor or ground. They are not furniture (i.e. not movable goods) but part of the architecture.

In contrast, beds and cots are, depending on the material used, relatively mobile. There is almost no end to the variety and design of beds found around the world – from the simplest of wooden frames in Africa to the boards of the Eastern slopes of the Andes and the magnificently ornamented beds of Asia and Europe.

As you make your bed, so you must lie on it . . .

The Greeks and Romans adopted their beds from the Middle East, replacing the footboard with a board at the head of the bed. Turned legs on beds were fashionable in Greece in the 7th century BC. The Greeks, and more particularly the Romans, developed a distinct bed culture, as is evident from the countless Latin words for reclining, which vary according to the function intended. The Romans helped introduce the bed into other parts of Europe, particularly Gaul, while the Germanic tribes continued to sleep on the ground or on benches. The bed did not become established in the rest of Europe until the 12th century. But possession of one's own bed was for a long time the privilege of the upper classes, as it still is in countries of the Third and Fourth Worlds. The 'common people' slept in communal beds (if in beds at all), with men and women and old and young all together and scantily dressed, very much to the displeasure of the church. The medieval bed consisted of a massive wooden frame, with boards or straps on which mattresses, bags of leaves or 'down-beds' – depending on the region and the owner's wealth – were placed.

Beds varied greatly in size from narrow, Spartan boards to beds four metres long and four wide, the sumptuous beds of the Renaissance, the enormous four-posters of the 16th and 17th centuries and the canopied beds of the *Empire*. The number of beds in each household and their size and fittings continued to reflect the owner's standing and wealth. Since the Baroque period, the bed (for instance, the bed of state) – has acquired a significance similar to what it had in Roman times – indeed, the Roman Empire was deliberately evoked.

In the 19th century, the Orient was a fruitful source of ideas and also provided the names. This was the age of the ottoman and sofa, pouf, borne, turquoise and divan (Persian for meeting, company, council) and the advent of the first upholstered furniture. The second half of the 19th century also saw the invention of patented furniture in the industrialized countries of Great Britain and the United States. Such articles could be folded up and used for different purposes. Sometimes they had metal springs instead of upholstery – marking a return to the simple wired bedstead. They were, however, not intended for the household but for hospitals, prisons, and later for steamships and railway sleeping-cars. But they very soon found their way into the residences of the middle classes eager to enjoy some comfort in their confined urban surroundings. Once again, lack of space underscored the importance of multifunctional furniture. That item going back to ancient times, the folding chair, was transformed into a bed.

Beds were designed which could be converted into cupboards or tables (our pull-out sofa beds are a relic of this period, as are the fittings of the railway sleeping car and the caravan). 'The article of furniture that most intrigued inventors between 1850 and 1890 was the bed that could be transformed into something else' (Gideon[6], p. 477). A US patent dated 1869 refers to a piano that could be converted into a bedroom suite without 'the qualities of the piano as a musical instrument being in any way impaired' (Gideon[6], p. 490).

In short, everything 'was collapsible, foldable, reversible, pull-out-able and combinable' (Gideon[6], p. 465). This development, with its extravagant swings from one extreme to another, was confined to Europe.

In India, for instance, the bed – as in the Middle East – is one of the oldest articles of furniture. The charpoys (literally 'four feet') are simply bed-frames with matting stretched over them, of the type also encountered in the Middle East and Africa. Like beds in ancient times, they were also decorated with animals' feet and carvings.

Divans first appeared in the time of the Moguls. They were used mainly by the nobility, while the common people continued to sleep on charpoys (Pahari illustrations). During the day, both divans and charpoys were used for sitting and resting on. Chests and swings, which enjoyed great popularity from the 7th century on, were also converted into beds at night (Dongerkery[3], pp. 40 ff.).

In Africa, block beds coexisted with beds and mats, often within the same ethnic group. Among the Tiv in the Cameroon grasslands, beds were a status symbol for chieftains, while their subjects slept on the ground on mats. In Sudan, the bedstead sprung with straps was extremely popular on the coast and in the tropical forest region, while beds carved from a block of wood were used in the savanna regions of the hinterland.

Sleeping on beds does not seem to have been so widespread among American Indians. Beds are, for instance, found among the Hidatsa on the northwest coast of the USA and, above all, on the eastern slopes of the Andes (Montaña) in Peru and Ecuador. The bed used by the Indians in those regions is extremely basic. It consists of a wooden frame with a relatively short, elastic, palm-bark base. The feet rest on a support under which a small fire glows to keep the sleeper warm.

Aery dreams

Although tropical regions are found in different parts of the world, only the Indians of the South American rain forests had the inspired idea of having adults sleep in mid-air. It was they who invented the hammock – long before their path was so fatefully crossed by Europeans. In 1492, Columbus 'discovered' not only the 'New World' but also the hammock. As he recorded in his diary on 17 October of that year, 'a kind of woollen net is used as a bed and a blanket on which these people sleep'. At a somewhat later date, he noted that, in Cuba, these nets are called 'hamaca'.

The *hamaca* of the Aruak-speaking inhabitants of the Antilles gave rise to the English *hammock,* the French *hamac,* the Spanish *hamaca, amaca,* the Dutch *hangmak* and, a typical reinterpretation, the German *Hänge-Matte* or 'hanging mat'.

The hammock is an all-purpose piece of furniture. It is both bed and chair for the Indians. Suspended in mid-air, it offers protection against vermin and damp ground. At night, the sleepers are warmed by the glow of a fire, for the hours before dawn are notably cool in the tropics. Compared with beds, the hammock is very easy to transport and, folded away, takes up very little room, particularly since no other bedding is required. For the same reason, thanks to hammocks there is virtually no limit to the number of guests that can be put up in a house.

Every adult possesses his or her own hammock. Young, especially childless, couples share a large double hammock, while older couples sleep in separate ones. Infants and young children sleep with their mothers. Ham-

Gustave Courbet (1819–1877)
Le hamac, 1844
Oil on canvas, 70 × 94 cm
Oskar Reinhart Collection
Winterthur, Switzerland

In a memorable speech to an art congress held in Antwerp in 1861, Courbet claimed 'Realism is by its very nature a democratic art.' Courbet was a fighter, and Delacroix considered him a genius. At the Paris World Exposition in 1855 he created a sensation with his paintings (which he exhibited in a tent). Idealization in both subject and form – the prevailing taste of the classicism of the time – was rejected by the younger generation of painters. The revolutions of the age left their marks on painting no less than on society and politics. Everyday life was portrayed as it really was.

The young woman in Courbet's painting is shown just as she has fallen asleep in the hammock. We are drawn into her private sphere by her relaxed manner. She has unbuttoned her bodice, and her dress has slipped up to reveal her petticoat and stockings. Nothing – neither the girl's awkward position nor the bulges in the hammock made by her body – is glossed over. Courbet's observation is unfiltered and precise, and all the lines, hues and colours are accurate. This is exactly how the woman would look if she had been surprised in her sleep by a stranger.

AMERICA.

Americen Americus retexit, & Semel vocauit inde semper excitam.

Ioan. Stradanus inuent.
Theodor Galle sculp.

Jan van der Straet (called Stradanus)
America
Sheet 1 from *Nova Reperta*
Engraving, 20.2 × 26.9 cm,
engraved by Theodor Galle
Kupferstichkabinett, Basel

Amerigo Vespucci (1415–1512) explored South America first in the service of the Spaniards and later of the Portuguese. The newly discovered continent America was named after him. *Nova Reperta,* which reported these discoveries, contains illustrations by Jan van der Straet, called Stradanus, which were subsequently engraved by Theodor Galle. The first sheet shows Vespucci's arrival in a highly theatrical manner. He has rowed from his ship to the shore, where he lands in full armour, holding the navigator's sextant in his left hand and in his right the cross and flag. Discovery invariably meant that the ruler and the church took possession of the new land.

Exotic animals are shown frolicking. In the background, the sea and a rocky coastline are visible. In the middle ground, natives are roasting human limbs over a blazing fire. In the foreground, a statuesque woman is lying on a hammock suspended between two tree trunks. This type of bed was completely new for Europeans at the time. The woman is wearing a piece of jewellery on her lower leg and around her hips a feathered ribbon. From beneath her feathered crown, long, blond hair flows down her back. Vespucci stands in amazement. The naked woman, herself taken aback, rises to meet the stranger with an uncertain gesture.

Berthe Morisot (1841–1895)
Le berceau, 1872
Oil on canvas, 56 × 46 cm
Musée d'Orsay, Paris

Berthe-Marie-Pauline Morisot was a major artist. Born into an upper-class family, Berthe and her sister Edma persuaded their parents to allow them to take art lessons. Artists of the stature of Camille Corot and Edouard Manet were frequent visitors to the Morisot family home. From Corot, her first teacher, Berthe became interested in outdoor painting. Manet, with whom she had a close personal relationship, inspired her to attempt portraits and subjects from everyday life. He frequently used her beautiful face for his own work, for instance *Le balcon.* Berthe was later to marry Manet's brother, Eugène.

In the painting shown here, Berthe Morisot captures the atmosphere of a family scene, the young mother deep in thought as she keeps watch over her baby asleep in a cradle. The painting's poetic mystery emanates from the many shades of white. The white curtains behind the mother are suffused with a bluish light; the white covers on the cradle have a touch of delicate pink. Curtains and covers stand out against the warm, dark-brown background. This masterly painting, much admired by Monet and Renoir, seems almost to capture the sound of the child's breathing as it sleeps the sleep of the blessed. Berthe, disregarding Manet's advice, allowed the impressionists to include *Le berceau* in their first group exhibition, which was held in the studio of the photographer Nadar in 1874.

mocks are regarded as very personal property and are important objects of prestige. The number and quality of the hammocks in a family's possession is a yardstick of its standing and wealth. A family is considered rich if it owns at least ten splendid hammocks which enable it to do honour to its visitors.

The first Europeans in America did not take immediately to sleeping in a hammock. But as early as 1500, Vespucci enthused about the 'delights of sleeping in the hammocks' in a letter to Pierfrancesco de Medici. The Burgundian Calvinist, Jean de Léry (in Brazil from 1556 to 1558), after spending a year among the Tupinambas, wondered whether 'one did not sleep much better in these beds than in our normal beds, especially in summer?', and recommended introducing hammocks into the French army.

Being space-saving and versatile, hammocks became popular among sailors and soldiers and in this way gained a foothold on other continents, particularly Africa. By the 18th century, the hammock was a firm fixture of the colonizer's baggage. By the 19th century, it had become socially acceptable in Europe and North America. In the USA, indeed, efforts were made to 'extend the use of this Indian piece of furniture and to use it in new combinations' (Gideon[6], p. 515). The results of these endeavours were, however, sometimes grotesque, with hammocks being given wooden supports like those already 'invented' for the purpose in the 16th century [see the copperplate engraving by the Dutch artist Jan van der Straet (1534–1616)] and still encountered today, even though they are completely superfluous. Finally, just before the turn of the century, the hammock-based swing seat was developed.

The hammock gradually found its way into the visual arts. The mobiles of Alexander Calder are said to have been inspired by the 'suspended system that is always ready to change its position' (Gideon[6], p. 510), while Heckel, who together with Kirchner and Schmidt-Rottluff, founded the art movement known as the *Brücke,* very soon featured the hammock in lithographs and paintings. In Europe and North America, the hammock was relegated once more to the garden. In tropical regions, however, it is more or less ubiquitous, and not just among the Indians.

Rock-a-bye baby ...

In Indian tribes using the hammock, young children sleep in the same one as their mother. In other cultures, separate sleeping arrangements are made for children. Surprisingly, though enough 'hammocks' (in the sense of mats or bags suspended from beams or a trestle) for young children are found in, for instance, India, North Africa or Eastern Europe, it has never occurred to anyone that adults could use them too. Elsewhere, cradles take the place of hammocks, particularly in Europe and Asia. In Gujarat (India), artistically carved and gaily varnished cradles are produced.

Since sleep is considered even more 'dangerous' for children than for adults, their beds are protected against evil, in particular by amulets, which serve as an eye-catcher and a toy for the child.

Edouard Vuillard (1868–1940)
Au lit, 1891
Oil on convas, 73 × 92 cm
Musée d'Orsay, Paris

Vuillard, along with Sérusier, Denis, Bonnard and Roussel, was a member of the 'Nabis' group. They chose this name – it is Hebrew for 'prophet' – at a time of radical change when a new, expressive type of painting was emerging. At Pont-Aven in 1888, Gauguin had told Sérusier always to use the strongest colours on the palette. As evidence of the new style, Sérusier subsequently brought back to Paris a landscape painting which consisted of distinct zones of colour and which his admiring colleagues henceforth regarded as their talisman. The work by Vuillard reproduced here is a playful variant of *Art nouveau,* and entirely typical of the Nabis group. The family theme has been freely adapted. The surface of the painting is divided into large, contoured areas of beige which, without giving any effect of depth, organize the painting almost graphically. Each part is integrated into the whole but retains its autonomy. The line of the body and head – merely suggested – flows with the undulations of the bedclothes. The grey silence is all-enveloping, from the signature to the cross on the wall. For the observer, following this slow rhythm and its soundless cadences, it is as if the substance of the woman's sleep can actually be seen.

Young children need a lot of sleep. This probably explains why they are able to sleep almost anywhere: perched on their mother's hip in a strap or wrapped up in a shawl on her back, or even in a net bag or basket. In some societies, they are bound to woven frames so that they can be transported or laid down at any time. This approach is found particularly among the Pueblo Indians of North America, the Aztecs of Central America and the Mapuche in Chile (South America). Generally speaking, children can be left to sleep more or less anywhere — in washing baskets as in the time of Moses, or in drawers, chests or mangers (cribs). It is not for nothing that day-care centres are known as *crèches* or, in German, *Krippen*.

Rooms which are used *solely* for the purpose of sleeping are the hallmark of an urban, socially stratified society in which the classification of its members' social and economic functions goes hand in hand with a division of the functions of the home. The more the home is a site of economic *production* and not merely the place in which products are consumed, the more functions it assumes. We have observed a similar phenomenon with regard to the functions of furniture. Bedrooms already existed in the Mediterranean region in ancient times, particularly for married couples (e.g. the *cubiculum* of the Romans) and in India since the Moguls. At the same time, however, bedrooms often served as living-rooms for women, for instance in the Orient. In medieval Europe, the bedroom was used during the day for carrying out household tasks, for reading and for storing treasured possessions.

From the 14th century onwards, bedrooms were fitted out more luxuriously and there was a shift away from the intimate to public, representational functions. It was not until the 18th century that the bedroom and its fittings regained some of their earlier modesty. By the end of the 19th century, the bedroom was what it is today — mainly the room in which we spend our nights.

Bedrooms and beds have always been closely interrelated. By their very form, beds enable a room within a room to be created. All that has to be done is to raise the bedposts, cover the whole thing with a baldachin and hang curtains around it — a four-poster bed. Canopied beds of this kind were already known in ancient Egypt, where the curtain not only preserved the sleeper's modesty but also protected him against mosquitoes. The bed of Queen Hetepheres, the mother of Cheops (2690 BC), with its gold-encrusted baldachin and curtains, was famous. Four-poster beds were also popular in Asia.

Marco Polo was very impressed by the sleeping arrangements of the rich inhabitants of Maabar in 1281: 'The people have a kind of sleeping area or hut made of very light reeds. These are so ingeniously woven that the surrounding curtains they form can be tightly closed by pulling a string. In this way, they protect against tarantulas, flies and other vermin while at the same time allowing the air to pass through' (Marco Polo[8], p. 222).

The seclusion offered by the four-poster bed is certainly one of the reasons why it is so popular with married couples or lovers the world over. In Western and Central Africa, such 'bedchambers' are found among the

Of beds and bedrooms...

Peul and Shoa Arabs, whose spacious beds, which accommodate several people, are fitted out with several layers of matting and with elaborately patterned woollen blankets or rugs which can be rolled up or spread out as required. During the day, these bedchambers are used as storage or work space and for chatting and smoking in.

Four-posters were also extremely sought after in medieval Europe. The Gothic four-poster bed was completely closed in by curtains or, constructed with wooden walls and door, occupied the centre of the room, like a miniature house. The Baroque bed often stood in an alcove embellished with exquisite curtains. These rich and elaborate draperies were at their most elaborate in the first half of the 19th century and, by 1900, threatened to engulf not only the sleeper but also the entire interior.

Bedding, or the princess on the pea

Bed and bedding are as closely related as bed and bedroom. The bedding used for sleeping on the ground or on a stone platform is the counterpart of the 'mattress' used on beds. Strictly speaking, a mattress is a cover filled with grass, leaves (the *Lauberli*, from German *Laub*, that is still used in rural parts of Switzerland), brushwood, chaff, straw (hence the French *paillasse*), woodshavings, moss (or lichen, as in the *Lischensack* used in the Bernese Oberland), hair (horsehair mattresses) and feathers (feather-beds).

Like so many words connected with the home and its fittings (divan, sofa, pouf, tabouret, baldachin), the word 'mattress' is ultimately derived from the Arabic *matrah* and signifies 'a place where something is thrown'. The stuffing and design of the mattress also reflected the sleeper's social standing. In Europe, for instance, up to the First World War only the well-to-do could afford horsehair mattresses, and for a long time, feather-beds (duvets) were very greatly coveted in rural areas.

Head-rests also varied greatly with regard to material and form. Of course, sleepers can, if need be, use their arm, or do as Jacob did before he dreamed of the ladder reaching up to heaven: 'Taking one of the stones of the place, he put it under his head and lay down in that place to sleep' (Genesis 28, 11). Man seems, however, to have preferred other means, and there are no limits to the imagination that has been invested in developing head-rests.

These range from bundles of clothes or rags laid under the head and roughly hewn wooden cylinders to specially made head-rests and the finest of feather-pillows. The head-rests may be attached to the mattress or bedstead or may be quite separate and apart. In Sumba, the narrow side of a sleeping mat contains a woven pocket which is stuffed with leaves or kapok. Detached woven pillows with the same stuffing are found in Timor, Sumatra and Hawaii. In the Egypt of the 18th dynasty (1551–1306 BC), the sleeping area was sloped slightly, with a footboard to prevent the sleeper from sliding off.

Outside Europe, pillows with woven and embroidered covers tend to be found in 'highly developed' cultures rather than among 'aboriginal' tribes. Their existence depends very much on the sleeping, eating and seating habits of the peoples and on the way their dwellings are built. Hammocks and pillows, for instance, are mutually exclusive. Pillows are used wherever carpets are commonplace, for instance in China, India (since the first millenium BC), the Middle East and North Africa (upholstered divans). In the Americas, they have been found in pre-Columbian Peruvian graves. Among the inhabitants of Sumatra's coastal regions, embroidered pillows are put on display at marriage ceremonies. Their numbers and patterns reflect the wealth and social status of the owners.

In Europe, the medieval bed was piled up with bolsters. The addition of further pillows meant that the sleeper had to sit rather than lie, a habit that has persisted in Northern Europe into the present century. In Central Europe, too, the number and elaborateness of the pillows reflected the wealth of their owner, hence the rule of monastic orders that their members had to make do with a single pillow. Sleeping in less of an upright position only gradually became accepted in Europe in our century as progress was made in modern hygiene and medicine. Probably because the neck and head-rests of non-European peoples seem so alien to our culture, they have always been a source of fascination to Europeans, who forget that such aids were once also used in Alpine regions (Ticino, Tyrol and Bavaria) (Sarasin[9], p. 19f.). It is often forgotten that the things one finds comfortable, cosy and snug depend very much on the culture in which one has been brought up as a child.

Head-rests are relatively old. In their simplest form, gravel, they are found in neolithic (6000 years BC) graves. In Egypt, particularly elaborate head-rests were employed in the 3rd century BC. They were made from a variety of materials: wood, clay, alabaster or ivory. Head-rests are still widely found in Africa. They are considered to be highly personal belongings and may be used only by their owners. The Shona (Zimbabwe), for instance, smash the head-rests when their owners die. For the semi-nomadic peoples of Somalia and Kenya, head-rests are among the essential belongings from which they are never separated during their travels.

Head-rests have been known in India and China since the second millenium BC. In the 2nd century BC, the Chinese were making hollow, bronze head-rests which were filled with fragrant herbs, while 'cool' head-rests made of porcelain were being produced from the 7th century AD. From the 8th century AD, head-rests were being made in Japan from varnished wood and fitted out with small drawers for toiletry articles and hair ornaments (Falgayrettes[4]). The Chinese and Japanese head-rests were also lined with paper or cotton cushions. The Bedja of eastern Sudan combine head-rests with leather neckrolls lined with goat's wool and stuffed with basil leaves.

Head-rests are also widespread in Oceania. Among the Asmat, they include skulls, which are reserved for initiated males only. In New Guinea, head-rests carved in grotesque fashion from a single piece of wood (Graebner[7]) are also in many cases used only by men.

In America, even in regions where people sleep on the floor or on platform beds, head-rests are relatively rare and, as in Central Brazil, consist of a simple wooden cylinder. It should also be added that head-rests are used not only as a support for the head but also – shape and stability permitting – as a stool.

The fact that sleeping with the head slightly raised is so ancient and so widespread cannot be explained solely by physiological need. Even the need, as in Japan and certain parts of Africa, or in New Guinea on the eve of events associated with certain body decoration, to protect elaborate hairdos while sleeping does not provide a full answer. The use of head-rests can by no means be equated geographically with the custom of maintaining elaborate hairdos. Rather, the use of head-rests and, to some extent, of pillows seems to be connected with religious attitudes — many peoples believe that sleep is dangerous for human beings, and it is not only the Greeks who perceived it as being related to death. By lying with the head raised, it is felt — among other things — that the spirit is less likely to escape during sleep.

In the Egyptian New Kingdom, head-rests were embellished with representations of deities or with magic formulae in order to protect the sleeper against evil forces, including — it was hoped — the instigators of nightmares. Head-rests were also perceived as a guarantee of a gentle awakening. They were therefore given to the dead to facilitate their re-awakening in another world. For this reason, head-rests were an indispensable feature of Egyptian burial chambers.

Head-rests were also thought to bring pleasant dreams in Japan, while the Azera of New Guinea hoped that they would strengthen the sleeper spiritually. Through their close symbolic connection with dreams, head-rests were attributed a divinatory character and were used by priests and shamans to enter into contact with spiritual forces during dreams.

Similar ideas may well have existed in medieval Europe, given the belief in the nightly presence of demons. Even St Augustine regretted that 'sleep, which is supposed to bring repose', is visited by 'phantoms, terrors of all the bad things' that plagued the spirit and confused the senses. For this reason, the upper part of the sleeper's body was raised on wedge-shaped bolsters to ward off harmful elements. The custom of sewing fragrant herbs and blossoms into the pillows is again being encountered in Central Europe.

A further function of the head-rest is to prevent the head from coming into contact with the floor or ground. In Oceania, for instance, this is a feature of the initiation rites of young men.

'Being raised above the ground' is also a sign of social status and dignity (like the use of chairs, thrones and beds). This explains why the High Priest of the Dogon in Mali uses head-rests.

In Polynesia, both sleeping mats and head-rests are reflections of personal status, as was also the case in ancient Egypt (where status varied according to the materials used).

Blankets were attributed similar protective functions, i.e. both physical and spiritual. While we use different blankets and sheets for different functions (bedcovers, tablecloths, hand towels, bathtowels, dish towels, dusters, curtains or wall hangings), the functions are often interchangeable in non-European cultures and at the lower levels of a socially stratified society. The Aztecs of Mexico, for instance, used their mantles as blankets, while Andes farmers still wrap themselves up in their ponchos at night. The blankets or sheets of the upper classes are often made of expensive fabrics or involve elaborate production processes. Bedding of this kind is often given as wedding presents or form part of trousseaux. It includes, for instance, the woven cotton *qalamkar* of Persia and India, which are painted,

Albert Anker (1831–1910)
Auf dem Ofen (On the stove), 1895
Oil on canvas, 55.5 × 71.5 cm
Kunsthaus, Zurich

Albert Anker preferred scenes from the everyday life of the people in his native Bernese countryside or in his beloved Paris. His compositions, exhibiting great skill of draughtsmanship and colour, were very popular among his contemporaries. Anker's *Schlafendes Mädchen im Walde* (now in Lille) won him a gold medal in the 1866 Salon, at a time when his colleagues such as Monet, Gauguin or Cézanne, now so highly esteemed, had still failed to gain recognition. Anker did a number of paintings of sleeping children. These two girls are lying on the bench above the stove, whose warmth turns the living room into a blissful place to sleep. The red hair of the older girl rests on a blue pillow; the younger one has laid her blond head on her sister. A chair has been moved up to the stove to prevent the children from falling off the bench. The subdued colours of the chair, stove and wall bring out the sequence of blue, green and red hues, which are set off against the radiant colour of the children's hands and face. The girls are fast asleep, their limbs completely relaxed.

printed or patterned by means of the resist-dyeing process, and the quilts of America and India, which have also been known in Central Europe in the form of eiderdowns since the Middle Ages. In pre-Columbian Mexico and Peru, only the nobles were entitled to possess feather-beds and brightly patterned blankets of the finest cotton or vicuna wool. Similarly, only members of the highest caste in Gujarat (India) were allowed to possess *patola,* which were produced by the extremely laborious double *ikat* process and used, among other purposes, to cover marriage beds. Because of their patterns and the position of the caste that made them, they are considered particularly pure. Gujarat was already famous in the early Middle Ages for its soft, delicate, red and blue leather blankets embroidered with gold and silver threads. According to Marco Polo (1271–1295), there appeared to be a brisk trade in these blankets in Asia.

Marvellous *ikat* fabrics are also used as blankets by the Iban-Dayak people of Borneo, who consider that they help enter into contact with supernatural forces in dreams.

Linen sheets imprinted with lucky symbols are used as blankets in rural areas of China.

Thus bedding in the wider sense of the term served a variety of purposes both physical and spiritual. It also enabled its owners to demonstrate their ethnic roots and their social standing and wealth.

When I was looking for illustrations of sleepers, I was struck by their paucity not only among 'aboriginal' peoples but also in the hierarchically structured societies of pre-Columbian America, Oceania and Africa. We can look in vain for such illustrations of sleep in the art of the Maya, Incas or Aztecs, although representations of scenes of everyday life were by no means unknown in pre-Columbian America (e.g. in Western Mexico or among the Mochica in Peru), with sleep's brother, death, being very often depicted. The absence of portrayals of sleep in the art of these peoples is in marked contrast to Europe, the Orient and Eastern Asia, where sleep has repeatedly been depicted in art since antiquity. Outside these cultures, it was only with the arrival of the great discoverers that sleepers began to be depicted, either by the discoverers themselves or in drawings and paintings by members of their entourages. So the riddle remains unsolved: even though sleep plays such an important role in the mythology and legends of the native peoples of America and Africa, why are there so few depictions of sleep in their art?

Digression

References

1. Brunner-Littmann, B.: Textile Bettgeschichten; in: *Stoffe und Räume,* pp. 57–71. Langenthal: Création Baumann, 1986.
2. Dibie, P.: *Ethnologie de la chambre à coucher.* Paris: Bernard Grasset, 1987.
3. Dongerkery, K. S.: *Interior decoration in India.* Bombay: Taraporevala, 1973.
4. Falgayrettes, C.: *Supports de rêves.* Paris, 1989.
5. Fibicher, B.: Süsser Schlaf und Schattenseite dieses Lebens. Thesis, Biel, 1985.
6. Gideon, S.: *Die Herrschaft der Mechanisierung.* Frankfurt: Europäische Verlagsanstalt, 1982.
7. Graebner, F.: Kopfbänke. *Ethnologica 3,* 1–13, 1927.
8. Polo, M.: *Die Reisen des Venezianers Marco Polo.* Ed. M. E. Pabesamen. Munich: Heyne, 1963.
9. Sarasin, F.: Über die Schlafmethoden der Menschheit. *Verhandl Naturforsch Gesell 54,* I, 1–29, 1942–1943.
10. Seiler-Baldinger, A.: Le confort sauvage; in: *Stoffe und Räume,* pp. 9–25, 163. Langenthal: Création Baumann, 1986.
11. Visages du sommeil. *Rev Sci Hum 194,* 1984.

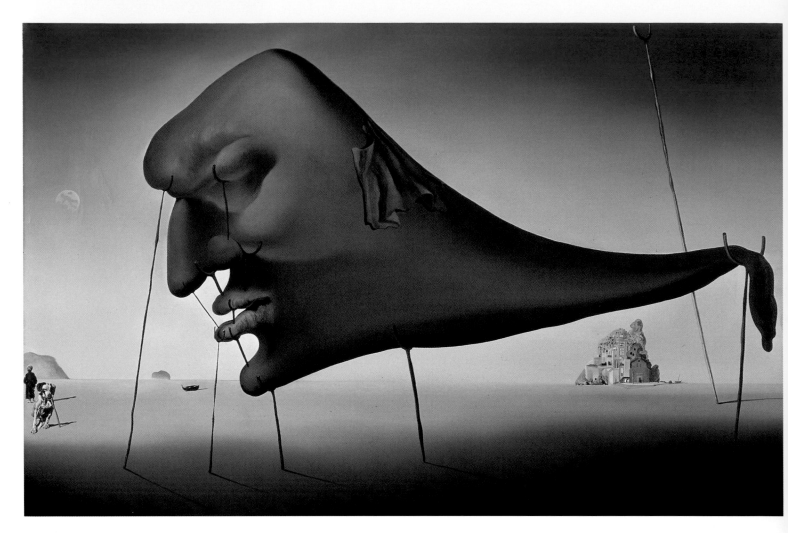

Salvador Dalí (1904–1989)
Sleep, 1937
Oil on canvas, 51×78 cm
Ophiuchus S.A., Geneva
© Demart Pro Arte B.V.

André Breton, the arbiter of Surrealism, made the anagram 'Avida Dollars' from Salvador Dalí's name. It is true that Dalí was very keen on money. This weird Spanish painter has been called a charlatan. That is also true. He was a snob who wanted to annoy people, and at the same time fascinate them. Dalí himself and many others have talked and written about his erratic life; many details are true, and many are apocryphal. What is true though, is that Dalí was a genius. He could paint as well as any Renaissance master. But he transformed, dissected and dismantled objects, landscapes, people, animals, organs, minerals and artifacts, discovering in the process relationships and combinations that, through his hypnotic composition, made fantastic

sense of what in reality should not have made sense at all. Dalí was certainly the greatest of the Surrealists, and Surrealism owes a great deal to his paranoid, critical approach, behind which Sigmund Freud lurks. Basically, all of Dalí's paintings are dream pictures of betrayal. One of the prime concerns of the orthodox Surrealist group led by Breton, Desnos and Crevel was the exploration of sleep. They held sleeping sessions to try to catch dreams in trance. This painting of Dalí's has become an emblem of Surrealism. A body in the form of a head lies exhausted, yet incredibly concentrated, on a fragile frame of crutches in an expanse that could be either ocean or desert. An insular city, an island and hills as well as a beached boat lie above the elusive horizon. In the clear sky above this, in turn, is an indistinct moon. At the far left of the picture are a person with his back to the viewer and a dog on crutches. There is no sound or movement. In a text com-

posed in 1930 Dalí wrote: 'The relationships between dreams and love and a sense of dissolution common to both have always been clear to me. Sleep is a type of dying or at least one way of taking leave of reality. In fact, it is the death of reality, but reality dies in love just as in dreams. The bloody osmosis of dreams and love occupies people for the whole of their lives. During the day we unconsciously search for the lost visions of our dreams.' Dalí painted them.

Every night, when Brahma sleeps, the world is destroyed. Every morning, when he awakes, it is recreated.

(Wisdom of the Vedas)

Sleep and Dreams in Myths
by Robert Th. Stoll

Scipio's dream

Cicero (106–43 BC) concluded the sixth and final book of the treatise *On the Commonwealth* with the famous dream of Scipio. As military tribune in North Africa, Scipio visited King Massinissa of Numidia, an ally of the Romans. The two friends talked late into the night about the kingdom and the Roman republic and about their famous close friend, Scipio Africanus. Afterwards, P. Cornelius Scipio fell into a deep sleep. His grandfather, Scipio Africanus, appeared to him in a dream, and advised him on matters of state, justice and the law. The dead man, with the wisdom born of experience, instructed the active statesman, who was destined for great things. Scipio's dream, and the entire work *De re publica,* ends with the terse sentence: *He departed; I awoke[1].* These three steps form the basic pattern of myths that deal with sleep: falling asleep – dreaming – waking up.

Transitions

Heraclitus (about 550–480 BC), the deep Ephesian, realized: *Alive or dead, young or old, awake or asleep: what is inherent in things does not change. For this changes to that, and that, in turn, changes to this[2].* Human life, like all creation, is full of rhythms and flux. Breathing, drinking and eating, being awake, making love or sleeping are basic human needs. The myths of all cultures and religions record them in word and image. These myths are particularly common in those transitional states that are absolutely essential to human life. To remain in one state is a threat to life itself, producing exhaustion, then coma and eventually rigor mortis. The richness of life becomes apparent in the transitional states, where the people are afforded great insights: falling asleep to dream, which makes of sleep another, wider and deeper life; and awakening to insights, which, as though a gift of the gods, are suddenly crystal clear. That *the Lord gives to his beloved sleep* (Psalm 127), puts into words a primordial human experience. There are many words of wisdom in this respect, for instance that one should always sleep on important decisions.

Novalis

The philosopher poet, Novalis (Friedrich von Hardenberg, 1772–1801) called sleep an *intermingled state of the body and the soul. In sleep, body and soul are chemically united . . . Waking is a divided, polarized state[3].* Removed from the external stimuli of his senses, in sleep man is suspended in another world that is yet his own. *We dream of travelling through the universe: is the universe not in us?* asks Novalis in his notebook[4]. For the way of mystery leads into ourselves. *We are close to waking when we dream we are dreaming[5].* Into our waking

181

state we bring images drawn from deeper, more universal layers of humanity, which are the stuff of myths.

Myths

Man cannot live without myths: all religions and cultures bear testimony to this. When old myths seem to lose their hold on man, new myths appear, as science fiction proves. Myths travel and merge, are transformed in the process, acquire new features, yet remain the same. Mircea Eliade wonders whether there is an adequate definition of myth. Myths narrate a story about events that took place in the fairy-tale world of our earliest history[6]. Mythos can be translated both as 'word' and 'speech'. Johann Jakob Bachofen (1815–1887), the great Basel scholar of symbols, whose research on matriliny is currently being reassessed, refers to myths as the sacred words of cosmic events, 'hieroi logoi', closely associated with poetry. Myths must be interpreted so that what they conceal may be given to others. The first step is to read and study the literal text of a myth. In other words, the context of a myth must be examined to learn what the message of its images and words means. Bachofen knows that *the myth is the exegesis of a symbol*[7]. By extension, myths can also be described as 'true legends'[8]. In the second song of the *Odyssey*, in which Telemachus secretly prepares to go and search for his father, J.H. Voss interprets the expression 'mythos' as: *Only one knows the secret* (II/413). Myth goes hand in hand with 'legein', mythology as the poetic interpretation of the archetype in word, the word *as direct evidence of that which was, is and will be, as the self-revelation of being in the time-honoured sense that does not distinguish between word and being*, in the words of Walter F. Otto[9].

Symbol

This concept derives from 'symballein', to join together, in this case the visible with the instinctive. A symbol is always more and something else than can be expressed in words. To start with, a tree is just a tree. Accordingly, the symbol, whether a tree or an animal, whether a stone or a mountain, whether a square or a circle, is always part of reality, but also transparently points to other realities. From the tree we get the family tree, the bridestake, the tree of life, Meru, the tree the Indian Vedas place at the centre of the world, the Norse ash tree Yggdrasil, that reaches from the deepest depths to the highest heavens. In the ancient Jewish mystical tradition of the cabbala the tree of the ten mysteries is the unspeakable highest being, the Sephirot, with its roots in heaven, and grows towards the earth and the people of God's kingdom. The symbol is mirrored in the pictorial

Hartmann Schedel's *World Chronicle*, 1493
The Birth of Eve
Woodcut
Edition Libri illustri, Ludwigsburg

This hand-coloured woodcut is one of the 1809 illustrations in Hartmann Schedel's *World Chronicle*. In the Middle Ages, such lavish productions were usually reserved for the *Bible* and liturgical books. But the times were changing: besides faith, people now wanted knowledge too. *Fides* had to share with *scientia*. This tome of 596 pages was the must important publication of an age that represented the threshold to modern times. The *World Chronicle* was put together from the large private library of the Nuremberg medical practitioner Hartmann Schedel. This fund of learning was distilled to a manageable encyclopedia in understandable German, so as to be accessible to people at large for their own instruction. A history of the world, it starts with Adam and Eve and ends with events occurring at the time of publication. The text was set in Schwabacher type at Anton Koberger's famous printing works in Nuremberg, where more than one hundred journeymen worked on 24 printing presses. The pictures of scenes and events, the portraits and panoramic views of well-known cities were done by accomplished illustrators, among them the young Albrecht Dürer. The all-pervasive spirituality of the text and illustrations is rooted in the humanistic conviction that it is possible to identify the good and apply it for the benefit of all mankind. Our woodcut depicts the creation of Eve, as described in Genesis v. 21–25, beginning with: 'So the Lord God caused a deep sleep to fall upon the man.' The event is set in an open landscape. God the Creator holds His right hand in a gesture of power, while with His left hand He draws the already perfectly formed Eve by her wrist from Adam's side, who is asleep, apparently oblivious to what is taking place. What is going to happen to the man and woman is already a cause of concern to the Creator: against the light of a cruciform nimbus, his face is furrowed in worry.

representation of concentric circles: our reality is at the periphery; the way we can see and touch the tree can be understood by reason. The symbol, however, quickens in the ever denser inner circles, which cannot be grasped by reason and will: they are accessible only through meditation and quiet contemplation of the mystery. The symbol is alive to the cosmos as the transcendent order. It can only be comprehended with the proper approach. Only those with feeling can grasp it.

In the Upanishad there is a tale from the Indian cosmogony that recounts the actions of the triad of the three chief gods, Brahma the Creator, Vishnu the Sustainer and Shiva the Destroyer. Indra, the most celebrated god, wants to build himself a palace on the cosmic mountain at the centre of the world. His ideas grew and grow. The master builder complains to Brahma. Brahma sits down on the sacred lotus, the symbol of divine power and beauty. However, the lotus grows out of the navel of Vishnu, whose dream is the universe. He knows and can do everything, and accordingly provides the solution to all problems[10]. Although transformed, the tree of Jesse in the Christian version of salvation is recognizably similar. The Prophet Isaiah prophesied that a branch would grow out of the tree of Jesse and bear fruit. Isaiah is depicted lying, even sleeping, with the tree of Jesse growing out of his navel. Sleep also plays a role in the story of creation in the *Old Testament*. In the second chapter (Genesis 2, 7), the creator forms man out of dust from the ground and breathes into his nostrils the breath of life. But Adam is lonely, and God decides he needs a partner. So, 'the Lord God caused a deep sleep to fall upon the man, and while he slept Yahweh Elohim took a part of his side (an acceptable translation for rib, because the sounds of the Ancient Hebrew are labial) and made (it) into a woman', and she was called Eve (Genesis 2, 21–22).

    Let us take another example from the Norse sagas of the gods. In the *Edda There was neither sand nor sea / nor saltwater waves, / Nor the skies above, / Nor the earth below: / Endless emptiness.* But the spirit of the Allfather was at work, and he separated south and north. Ymir, the giant hermaphrodite, emerged from the land of fire, Muspelheim. And he fell into a deep sleep, and while he slept, a male and a female being grew out of his armpits. But Odin and Wili and We slew Ymir; and his blood became the water, his flesh the earth, his hair the trees, his teeth the rocks, his skull the sky and his brain the clouds[11]. At this point, it is not out of place to mention Franz Kafka's story, 'Metamorphosis', whose horror is heightened by Kafka's crystalline, poetic language: *One morning, when Gregor Samsa awoke from restless dreams, he found he had been transformed into a monstrous insect, while lying in his bed[12].*

Sleep and creation

The Vision of Buddha's Father, 1793
Hand-coloured Chinese woodcut,
31.7 × 28.4 cm
Völkerkundemuseum, Heidelberg

One night King Suddhodana had seven dreams. The first showed Indra, the living image of ancient Indian kings, passing through the East Gate. In the second dream, Siddhartha rode through the South Gate on a white elephant. In the third, he left the city in a splendid carriage via the West Gate. In the fourth dream, a decorated wheel passed out through the North Gate. In the fifth dream, the crown prince was beating a drum. In the sixth, he cast jewels from a tower to the crowds below. In the seventh dream the king saw six people grieving. The dreams disturbed the king greatly and so he had a Brahman interpret them for him. The first dream showed that the crown prince would become a wandering ascetic. The second showed that the prince's efforts would be rewarded. In the third, he passed through the four stages of fearlessness. The fourth told that he would become a buddha, the next that he would spread his word. The sixth predicted that he would gain a wide following, and the seventh told of the despair of the teachers that had shown him the wrong way. 'O Great King,' said the Brahman, 'the Buddha's future will fill you with happiness and confidence!' This subtle Chinese woodcut gives graphic form to a legendary oneiric experience.

Hypnos and Thanatos,
5th century BC
White-ground lekythos
The British Museum, London

In the classical age of ancient Greece it was the custom to place lekythoi on the funerary stelae of the honourable departed as a mark of constant remembrance. The narrow-necked oil flask was made of red clay and usually covered with a white slip, on which scenes of death, tributes to the dead, and life in the other world were painted in fine, mat contours. These white-ground lekythoi are among the best of Attic pottery of the 5th century BC. Our picture shows a detail of the painting on an exceptionally beautiful example. A funerary stela in the shape of a smooth round column and decorated with ribbons stands on a rectangular pedestal in the centre. On the stela one can distinguish the painted outline of a solider's helmet. In front of the stela the winged brothers, Hypnos, the fair god of sleep, and Tha-

natos, the dark god of death, together are laying a dead warrior in cuirass in his grave. Is the departed the Lycian King Sarpedon, the bravest among Troy's allies? According to Homer, Sarpedon was the son of Zeus and Laodameia. He was killed in the Trojan War by Patroclus' spear. Zeus ordered Hypnos and Thanatos to bear his beloved son back to Lycia, so that he could be laid to eternal rest with the appropriate honours. The repetitive twenty spirals of the meander in the decorative band above the stela tell us that he will live on. In other words, the band is far more than an ornament: for the passerby it has the interpretative power of a symbol.

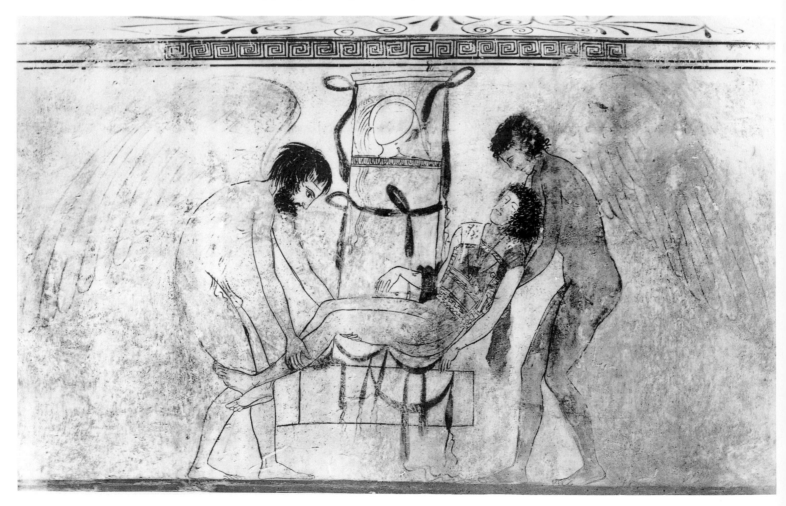

Ancient cosmology tells of primordial Chaos. His first-born was Gaea, goddess of the earth, followed by Tartarus, the underworld, and Erebos, the god of darkness, as well as Nyx, the goddess of the night. Some ancient sources include Eros, the god of creative love, among these primordial gods; others take him to be the son of Aphrodite. Without conceiving of man, Nyx, goddess of night, gave birth to Morus, the personification of fate; Ker, the personification of doom, the Three Fates, who control the destinies of the lives of man, and Nemesis, the goddess of retribution and vengeance. Nyx was also the mother of the twin brothers Thanatos, the god of death, and Hypnos, the god of sleep. They are usually depicted as winged youths, Hypnos fair and Thanatos dark.

Hypnos lived in a cave on the island of Lemnos, though some sources place it in the land of the Cimmerians, a region of perpetual darkness at the edge of the world. Lethe, the river of forgetfulness, flows through the cave, and Hypnos is surrounded by his sons, all the countless dreams. Hypnos often intervenes in the ancient history of the gods and man. Once, he took the form of a nightjar, and sitting in a pinetree on Mt. Ida, sang Zeus himself to sleep, so that Hera could punish Heracles. On another occasion, at the request of Zeus, Apollo, the god of the sun, sent the twins Hypnos and Thanatos to fetch the corpse of King Sarpedon of Lycia, son of Zeus and − according to Homer − Laodameia, Bellorophon's daughter, from the battlefield in front of Troy, where Patroclus had slain him with his spear. Ancient Greek figured vases show this scene: Hypnos and Thanatos are not only twins by birth; they belong together, because they represent, each in his own way, the deeper worlds − sleep and death − for which man leaves his everyday life, the worlds we learn about in myths.

In his epic on the five ages, the Theogony, Hesiod (ca. 700 BC) the farmer and poet from Boeotia, says that the people of the first, the golden age, lived *as easily as the gods, and died as though sleep descended on them*[13].

Plato's myth of Er

Plato's great dialogue about justice and the just 'state' concludes with a famous myth[14], which Socrates recounts to Glaucon. It is the myth of the Pamphylian called Er. Er fell in battle and his body was taken back home. On the twelfth day, lying on the funeral pyre about to be cremated, he awoke to life. He gave an account of his experiences in the other world. He told how his soul, after it had left his body, started on its journey. *At a wonderfully strange place* it had been able to watch how a judge fastened the badge of their judgement on the breast of each and every dead person in accordance with their deeds. (This may call to mind Kafka's story of the

'Penal Colony'[15].) Er's detachment is as in a dream experienced as reality. He reports that in the evening all the dead drank of the waters of the Ameles River, called the forgetful or carefree river, and thereupon fell into a deep sleep in which they forgot everything. At midnight, like shooting-stars, they were all suddenly swept up and away 'to be born'. However, Er had not drunk of the water of forgetfulness. 'He could not tell by what manner of means he returned to his body, but suddenly he opened his eyes and was lying on the pyre.' And Socrates, making a point about the immortality of the soul concluded the dialogue with the words: *And so, my dear Glaucon, the myth was preserved from perishing, and, if we remember it, may well preserve us in turn*[16]. In this myth, death is portrayed as sleep from which man can awake.

Leopold Robert (1794–1835)
Femme de brigand veillant sur le sommeil de son mari, 1827
Oil on canvas, 47 × 38 cm
Musée des Beaux-Arts,
La Chaux-de-Fonds
Dépôt de la Fondation
Gottfried Keller

One school of thought holds that every painting is, in some way, a self-portrait. This view of brigands may well substantiate this thesis. Although the elder Robert wanted his son to follow a good, solid business career, Leopold refused. He wanted to become an artist, and went to Paris to work in the studio of the court painter, J.L. David, who became his mentor. On a journey to Rome, he met a band of brigands, whom he became friends with and painted. Their unconventional way of living appealed to him, and it became his great subject: brigands in their traditional costumes, their customs and practices, their pride and their dignity. 'Vivere pericolosamente' became his motto, too. Eventually, though, he married the daughter of a Piacentina countess, and accepted fame, admiration and membership of the *Légion d'honneur*. Then he was off again, to Venice, where he died in 1835. This painting ('The Brigand's Wife Watches over Her Sleeping Husband') encapsulates the Robert legend: constantly on-the-run, yet seeking rest; courting danger, yet able to look after himself. It tells even more of his life: the beautiful woman, watchful, alert and, at the same time, calmly protective, while the fashionable bonnet on the ground, the watch, the dagger, the cartridges in the belt and the hand on the rifle are aspects of both brigand life and his own. To rest completely, one needs to sleep long and deeply, secure in the knowledge that one is safe, even under the stars in an open countryside that stretches from the mountains to the sea. Sure of this, Robert's brigand has abondoned himself to sleep in a symphony of red and black.

Max Kämpf (1912–1982)
Traumflug, 1944
Oil on canvas, 201 × 299 cm
Kunstmuseum, Basel

In this canvas, 'Dream flight', Kämpf has modified the entry he submitted in a competition to select a mural for the entrance façade of the Basel orphanage. Unfortunately, his prize design was never executed. This composition of interacting lines, cool colours and balanced *chiaroscuro* is impressive in its simplicity. The children fly off on a paper kite into the innocent reality of their dreams. As the trapezium swings up to the moon, its long tail decorated with shaggy tufts of paper traces the path of its melodic curves. In the clear night the silver lunar crescent responds in the same playful spirit. The world is left behind in darkness, though the golden weathercock still shimmers. The little girl turns towards it with a dreamy look on her face, stretching out her hands in a gesture that is both invitation and farewell in one. The little boy has snuggled up against her and is already far away in the Land of Nod. The children lie innocently united under a blanket of stars and signs of the zodiac. This masterpiece is deeply poetic, one of the most beautiful paintings of a dreamed vision, created from the gentle sounds of an inner music.

Die schlafenden Jünger, ca. 1160
Tempora on wood, ca. 92×92 cm
St Martin in Zillis, Grisons, Switzerland

The mountain village of Zillis lies south of the Via Mala gorge on what, in the Middle Ages, was the main north-south route over the Splügen Pass to Italy. The simple church was built about 1130. The wooden ceiling of the 20-metre-long nave is painted: 153 square panels in 17 by nine rows. They constitute a well-thought-out theological programme. What moved some unknown person to donate such an impressive work to a village church is a mystery, as is the name of the painter, who kept a workshop with a number of apprentices. Forty-eight panels around the edge show fantastic sea-monsters. Seven panels are dedicated to the life of St Martin, the patron of the church. The 98 tables in the centre present the genealogy, life, work and suffering of Jesus up to the crowning with thorns; the Crucifixion and Resurrection are not shown. Our picture – 'The sleeping disciples' – shows the disciples in the Garden of Gethsemane (Mark 14, 33). Exhausted, they have fallen asleep, while the Lord is praying in his hour of need. He returns to them twice to ask them to watch with him. Both times they doze off again. The composition is both simple and superb. The vegetation of the garden is shown at the lower edge. But there is no depth. The sleeping disciples are painted frontally in horizontal bands of colour. The black lines of the drawing are reminiscent of woodcuts. The paints are natural earth colours, finely ground and mixed with wax, resin and paste. All heads lean in the same direction; their eyes are closed. The disciples with their expressive hands lie in flowing robes; the round haloes heighten the aura of rest. This is not folk art, but the work of a great master, who probably stopped on his way over the Alps to create a masterpiece that ranks among the very best of romanesque painting.

In the *Old* and, particularly, the *New Testament* sleep and dream appear as steps to salvation and raising the dead. The third Psalm is one of King David's laments. He is lamenting because he is in need, but he knows that the Lord will hear and save him: *I lie down and sleep; I wake again, for the Lord sustains me* (Psalm 3, 5). For the Lord had long since promised his chosen people: *And I will give peace in the land, and you shall lie down, and none shall make you afraid; . . ., and the sword shall not go through your land* (Leviticus 26, 6). And in Proverbs the Lord promises: *If you sit down, you will not be afraid, when you lie down, your sleep will be sweet* (Proverbs 3, 24). For *He who keeps you will not slumber. Behold, He who keeps Israel will neither slumber nor sleep* (Psalms 121, 3).

Dreams associated with the child Jesus

Joseph was troubled that Mary was with child. Unwilling to put her to shame, he resolved to divorce her quietly. But *an angel of the Lord appeared to him in a dream, saying, 'Joseph, son of David, do not fear to take Mary your wife, for that which is conceived in her is of the Holy Spirit'*. And Joseph did as the angel commanded him (Matthew 1, 19–23).

In the same way, an angel appeared to the Three Wise Men from the East who had come to the crib of the new-born King, and warned them not to return to Herod (Matthew 2, 12). And yet another message used sleep: *Now when they had departed, behold, an angel of the Lord appeared to Joseph in a dream* and ordered him to take Mary and the Child and flee to Egypt to escape Herod's evil designs (Matthew 2, 13). But when Herod died, *the angel appeared in a dream to Joseph in Egypt* and told the family to return to the land of Israel (Matthew 2, 19).

In the *New Testament*, the three synoptic gospels contain the story of Jesus sleeping. He had got into a boat on the shore of Lake Gennesaret, and his disciples followed him. There arose a great storm *so that the boat was being swamped by the waves; but he was asleep* (Matthew 8, 24). The disciples were afraid and woke him and said: *Master, Master, we are perishing! And He awoke and rebuked the wind and the raging waves; and they ceased, and there was a calm* (Luke 8, 24).

Thus, in Jesus's miracles, bodily death is no more than sleep. When He went to the city of Nain, and drew near to the gate of the city, He saw that the only son of a widow was being carried out to his tomb. He had compassion on the weeping woman and said to the young man in the bier, *I say to you, arise. And the dead man sat up, and began to speak* (Luke 7, 11–15). Another time Jesus passed the house of Jairus, a ruler of the synagogue, whose daughter had just died. *All were weeping and bewailing her; but He said, 'Do not*

Petrarch (1304–1374)
The Triumph of Love, late 15th century
Bibliothèque nationale, Paris

Petrarch has fallen asleep in the well-kept garden of his studio in the Vaucluse near Avignon. What he is dreaming about is shown in the triumphal procession on the other side of the fence, in a landscape that stretches away to the blue mountains in the distance. A gathering of richly dressed men and women appear in front of the grove in the foreground. The naked, blindfolded god of love with his beautifully coloured wings stands on fiery embers, bow and arrow in his hands, as he heads purposefully towards the goddess of love, Venus. In expectation of his adoration, she waits on an altar in her temple. This elaborate illumination decorates a late-15th-century French edition of Petrarch's songs 'The Triumph of Love'. Two angels hold a scroll with the opening words in Old French. Petrarch's lyric poetry was very popular in the Age of Humanism that led into the Renaissance: after the Minnesang, it was the second wave of erotic poetry to enjoy international acclaim. Petrarch was born in Arezzo in 1304, grew up in Avignon and studied law and theology. He was the leading classical scholar of his time, imbued with the spirit and tradition of antiquity. In 1341 he was crowned as poet in Rome, and dreamed of his unattainable love, Madonna Laura, who had died young. This dream-world of love lost dominated his philosophical and poetic work almost up to his death in the Euganean Hills near Padua in 1374. His tercets in Early Italian are moral allegories celebrating the triumph of time and divinity, of fame and death, of chastity and love: 'Tired of tears, there under thatch / asleep, I saw before me dawn / a light....'

weep; for she is not dead but sleeping.' And they laughed at Him (Luke 8, 52–53). Mark describes the scene more dramatically: Jesus put the weeping and wailing women outside and went in to where the child was lying. *Taking her by the hand He said to her, 'Talitha cumi',* which means, *'Little girl, I say to you, arise'. And immediately the girl got up and walked* (Mark 5, 41–42).

John gives an even more dramatic account of the raising of a man from the dead. Lazarus, the brother of Mary and Martha, Jesus's friends in Bethany, Judea, fell seriously ill, and his sisters sent Jesus an urgent message for help. He, however, took His time. He said: *Our friend Lazarus has fallen asleep, but I go to awake him out of sleep.* But His disciples thought that he meant taking rest in sleep. Then Jesus told them plainly, 'Lazarus is dead.' Now when Jesus and His disciples came to Bethany, they found that Lazarus had already been in the tomb four days, and the sisters chastised Jesus. But He said, *I am the resurrection and the life; he who believes in Me, though he die, yet shall he live,* and deeply moved in spirit and troubled He asked where the tomb was, and told them to take away the stone from the cave, even though there be an odour, and *cried out with a loud voice, 'Lazarus, come out.' The dead man came out, his hands and feet bound with bandages, and his face wrapped with a cloth. Jesus said to them, 'Unbind him, and let him go'* (John 11, 1–44).

After the *Bible's* account of the raising of Lazarus from the dead, we turn to the Eastern Church for the wonderful story of how Mary ended her life on earth: the koimesis, which is celebrated for the faithful in the ikons carried on great feast days. Mary did not die; the Mother of God passed away surrounded by the disciples, and her divine Son raised her up directly to the eternal glory of God[17]. For, as St Paul tells us: Christ was *raised from the dead, the first fruits of those who have fallen asleep* (1 Corinthians 15, 20).

Lacteur

Combien que la co̅mune et vniuersellement approuuee sentence des bons et
anciens expositeurs soit que au commencement dung liure plusieurs choses
sont diligentement a considerer Ce neantmains pour ce que si nous vuillios
raporter et mettre par escript toutes les choses qui se pourroient bien escrire
en leuure presente Il nous semble que plus tost encourrions en supfluite
et obscurite que en elucidation et clarte du liure pour quoy nous
suffira p̅r le p̅nt declarer a̅nre propos quatre choses seulement

St Mark's Relics are brought to Venice
Early 12th century
Mosaic
St Mark's, Venice

One of the most beautiful mosaics in the cycle depicting the legend of St Mark is on the vault of the organ gallery. St Mark was one of St Paul's companions. Later he preached Christianity to the Venetians. In his old age he became Bishop of Alexandria, where he was cruelly martyred. According to the legend, in the 9th century his mortal remains were stolen by Rustico and Tribuno, two Venetian merchants, who wanted to transport them to Venice. They packed the corpse in a basket and smuggled their precious prize past the Muslim customs officers. Accompanied by the Bishop Stauracio, they sailed across the Mediterranean, where they had to contend with pirates and storms. Exhausted by his efforts, Stauracio fell asleep on the wicker coffin. St Mark appeared to him in a dream and admonished him that the ship had already passed the islands and was entering the lagoon. The waves have

been calmed and, its sails struck, the ship glides towards the church. This mosaic, in the Venetian Byzantine style, is one of the earliest in the basilica of St Mark's. Small cubes of natural stone in their natural colours have been laid directly into the wetplaster. Typical of the Venetian style is the generous use of gold tessere, small glass cubes containing real gold-leaf. On account of the material, the presentation of the subject has been kept very simple. The wooden boat with two rudders, three masts and furled sail progresses against a background of golden waves. The gestures of the men are expressive. Stauracio wears the hat and robes of a monk-bishop. Not only is St Mark's name mentioned, he is also set apart by his vestments and nimbus.

People about to undergo a serious operation that requires a general anesthetic may be afraid of not waking up again. This fear of not regaining one's senses is also a reason why many refuse to let themselves be hypnotized. On the other hand, psychiatrists may be informed by patients, in their desperation, that they wish never to have to wake up again. They want to evade everything. Mythology in its various forms of fairy-tale, saga and legend tells of sleep as transport. This removal from actual time may take the form of quick motion, slow motion or eternity.

The myth of Endymion, King of Elis, son of Aethlios and grandson of Zeus, is just such a sleep of transport. Selene, the goddess of the moon, fell in love with the handsome youth Endymion; in keeping with the phases of the moon, their relationship produced fifty daughters. The moon goddess was deeply in love with the youth, and although she repeatedly vanished, she always returned. Because she could not accept that Endymion, as a human, would die, she transported him into an everlasting sleep. Ever since, he has lain in a cave in Mt. Latmos, eternally young and beautiful.

The Kyffhäuser legend is a Teutonic version of this myth. Removed to the eponymous mountain, and asleep until he wakes when his time comes, the great Emperor Frederick Barbarossa lives, ageing and hidden. He sits at a round table of stone, with his head in his hands, lost in his own world. His beard, growing through the table, according to some, growing around it, according to others *must reach such a length* before he awakes that it will encircle the table *thrice*[18]. There is also a tale of a shepherd who whistled so beautifully that a dwarf led him into the mountain to Barbarossa. The old emperor asked him: *Do ravens still fly around the mountain?* When the shepherd affirmed this, he cried out: *Now I have to sleep yet another hundred years*[19]! What is it that he must wait for?

Another German legend concerns another emperor: Charlemagne. He lives hidden in the magic mountain Unterberg. Whereas Barbarossa sleeps alone, a sleep with very rare, brief interruptions, the Emperor Charles I, he too with a long, grey beard, golden crown and sceptre, is in a hall in the company of other noble lords. He is awake, and friendly towards all his subjects. The legend ends with the sentence: *Why he stays there, and what he does, God alone knows*[20]. However, some sources think that he is awaiting the coming of the Antichrist for the decisive battle before the Last Judgement. Then he will come out to fight.

Epimenides

Epimenides, the author of a theogony, was probably a real person who lived about 600 BC, although very little is known about him. In his day, the plague broke out in Athens, because the right of asylum had been violated by murder. To expiate the crime, the government summoned Epimenides, a miracle-worker, from Crete. And, with all due ceremonial, he did indeed succeed in ridding the city of the plague. However, the mythology of antiquity tells not so much of this deed as of Epimenides' sleep. It is said that when he was still young, he fell asleep and was transported from his fellow men, and spent the next 57 years in an age full of menace, danger and need. When he awoke, he was a fund of prophecy and wisdom. For Epimenides, as for the Emperor Frederick Barbarossa, this sleep has become a symbol of destiny.

The Seven Sleeping Youths of Ephesus,
Greek, 18th century
Icon on wood, 26 × 19 cm
S. Amberg Collection,
Kölliken, Switzerland

According to Orthodox belief, an icon is a holy image, in other words, a liturgical object. Because icons spread the word of God and the salvation of man, they have an inner radiance which imparts to them a beauty that, to the modern eye, makes them works of art. This Greek icon shows seven men asleep in a dark cave in a bleak, mountainous landscape. A basket of bread is hanging from the ceiling. Luminous red and gold predominate. An account of the Seven Sleeping Youths is found in the *Legenda aurea,* a collection compiled in the 13th century, which is our chief medieval source of Christian legends. In different ages the seven men have been known by different names. As early Christians in Roman Ephesus, they were persecuted during the reign of Emperor Decius (about 200–251). To escape, they concealed themselves in a cave on Mt. Celion, taking nothing with them but a little bread. Their pursuers walled up the cave. Almost two centuries later, a shepherd broke open the cave in the hope of finding hidden treasure. Instead, he found the sleeping men. They awoke and went out into the light of day, and into another time and world. The faithful saw in the seven young men proof of the resurrection and venerated them. Out of this expression of faith arose the tradition of this icon.

Goethe reworked this myth about Epimenides in a play he was commanded to write for the festive occasion of the return of the Tsar and the King of Prussia from the Napoleonic wars. The writer withdrew to the quiet of Bad Berka, where he composed a play in two acts titled 'Epimenides Awakes'. Goethe commented that *the gods let the miracle sleeper pass away a second time so that he will not experience an age of great misfortune, but also so that he will gain the gift of prophecy, which had been refused him up to now* – by whom Goethe meant the King of Prussia. Although a feeble allegory for a particular occasion, this piece requires an imposing stage upon which warring armies, courtiers, and demons of intrigue and oppression appear and destroy all existing structures. Through faith, hope and charity, personified by joyful characters, green again starts to cover the ruins. Epimenides awakes from his sleep and is able welcome the new world: *Now I see my pious hope / Realized through wondrous deeds: / How great to trust in the Highest. / He taught me know our age. / Now shall my glance be kindled, / And greet the coming of new times*[21].

The Seven Sleeping Youths

This myth of sleep as a means of preserving people from danger and for the benefit of later times has remained alive, as the early Christian legend of the Seven Sleeping Youths of Ephesus illustrates. At the time of the persecution of Christians by the Roman Emperor Decius they refused to renounce their Christian faith. The fled to a mountain cave, where they were walled in and fell into a deep sleep. When they awoke and emerged from the cave almost two centuries later, their home town Ephesus, like Rome and Byzantium, had become Christian. Ikons depict this miracle.

Rip van Winkle

The American writer Washington Irving (1783–1859) used the myth of sleep as transport in his story 'Rip van Winkle', published in 1819. Rip had gone hunting in the Catskill Mountains with his dog and rifle. Descending into a ravine, he chanced upon a gathering of strange people, joined them in a number of glasses of spirits and fell into a deep sleep. When he awoke, he thought he had simply spent a night under the stars. Then he noticed that his rifle was rusted and the butt eaten away. And his joints were stiff. In short – the night had lasted twenty years, and Rip had slept through the War of Independence. The people in the village no longer knew him, but remembered that one of their number had disappeared a long time ago. The inspiration for Washington Irving's story came from a book he owned, viz. J.J. Büsching's anthology, *Sagas, Fairy-tales and Legends,* published in

Leipzig in 1812, and in particular the legend of the shepherd Peter Klaus, one of the Kyffhäuser tales. The myth of sleep keeps within the dimension of time, which, objectively, is the same for everybody, an unchanging succession of day and night. But the experience of time is subjective, and it may even be forgotten in times of great joy, passion or sadness. And in all ages, people were and are tempted to use whatever means they have at their disposal to gain control of time, that is, to dilate, contract or suspend it. In our own century, José Luis Borges[22] deals with this subject in his incomparable writings, and Stanley Kubrick visualized it in his fascinating science-fiction film '2001: A Space Odyssey'.

A dream of the prophet Mohammed is one of the most beautiful visions of such transformation of time. Lying on his bed, the holy man is transported to different paradises, hells and heavens. There he exchanges 90,000 words with God. Back on earth, he finds his bed still warm, and water is still running out of a jug that has been knocked over[23].

Sleep for evil

The final great panel of the folding winged altar-piece Master Matthias, called Grünewald, painted for the convent hospital run by the nuns of St Anthony in Isenheim before 1515 depicts a nightmare of the patron of the order, St Anthony the Hermit. The bearded old man is lying on the floor, surrounded by demons — and yet not lying. A syphilitic has torn away his pocket prayer-book, a chimera is biting the monk's right hand, in which he is still able to hold his rosary. St Anthony has opened his mouth to scream in terror, but in his horror he cannot utter a sound. He is caught in a nightmare of destruction. But salvation is nigh, in the shape of angels of light descending from heaven, who will drive off the spirits of shades of darkness[24].

Menacing nightmares of this nature can befall people in their sleep. Sheet 43 of the 'Caprichos', a series of etchings by Francisco Goya (1746–1828)[25] shows the artist asleep. He lies bent over his work-table surrounded by his instruments and tools. On the base of the table are written the words: *El sueño de la razón produce monstruos*. The enlightened painter is warning that, when reason falls asleep, demons take power. If man's reason, which keeps him under control, is turned off, his instincts take over, and he becomes evil, destructive, superstitious and Hobbesian: *homo homini lupus*. In sleep such dreams may occur and pictures emerge, full of horror, a danger for both the dreamer and others.

Ferdinand Hodler's great painting *Night* is an artistic expression of the development of such fear, culminating in paralysing horror.

El sueño de la razon produce monstruos

Francisco Goya (1746–1828)
El sueño de la razón, 1798
Sheet 43 of the 'Caprichos'
Etching, aquatint, 18.1 × 11.9 cm
Print Collection, Basel

The young Goya was an extraordinarily gifted portraitist of the *ancien régime* Spanish court in the latter half of the 18th century. It is another Goya we admire today, the product of troubled times and his own loss of hearing. These tribulations produced a keen observer of his own person and his contemporaries. Henceforth he depicted his society and the people around him utterly realistically, with new techniques that influenced future painters right up to Picasso. Over the years he produced 80 sheets of 'Caprichos', in which he etched his criticism of society, the state, the royal court and the Church. His portrayal of human behaviour is often shocking in its honesty and directness. Sheet 43 ('The sleep of reason') is a key picture. In this self-portrait the artist has fallen asleep at his work table, in the midst of his tools. Sinister demons crowd in from the surrounding night. Goya has scratched his dreadful experience on the base of the table: 'El sueño de la razón produce monstruos.' When human reason falls asleep, monsters awake in dreams at night, to do their deeds by day: when people discard reason, their superstition and intolerance lead to the Inquisition; they become base, mendacious and power-hungry, and torture and kill those weaker than themselves. Goya himself gave the title *Idioma Universal* to a preliminary sketch for this etching, now in the Prado. The 'Caprichos' are an enlightened appeal for humane behaviour.

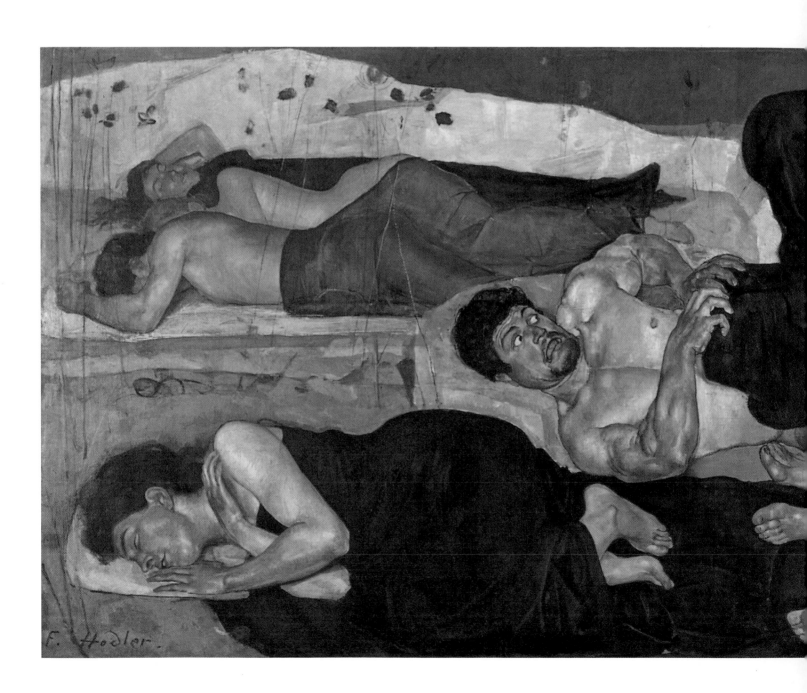

Ferdinand Hodler (1853–1919)
Die Nacht, 1889/90
Oil on canvas, 116.5 × 299 cm
Kunstmuseum, Berne

This major work ('Night') by Hodler is a carefully considered artistic construction. Whereas in contemporary France the dominant Impressionist style concentrated on catching the play of light and colour in paint, the determining elements in this picture are line and the balanced disposition of the figures, here united in sleep, dream and horror. This picture was first shown at the 1881 Salon. At the time, symbolism was just gaining acceptance, and Hodler's use of it, together with his predilection for parallelism in composition, attracted a great deal of attention, winning the Swiss painter the fame denied him in his own country. In the four corners of this exceptionally broad canvas people are asleep: two single individuals and two groups in the diagonally opposite corners respectively. The man in the centre is Hodler himself, torn awake by the dark, draped nightmare. He wrote: 'I call "Night" my first work. I view it as a symbol of death.' Hodler grew up in poverty and disease, and knew death at first hand through those of his father and siblings. He started out as a house-painter and then worked as a painter of vedutas. But that did not satisfy him, and he moved to Geneva, to Calame's works and to the painter Barthelemy Menn (1815–1893), who recognized Hodler's talent. Here, Hodler, a man with a mind of his own, developed his inimitable artistic signature. Once the Parisian Symbolists had acclaimed him, his fellow Bernese were prepared to acknowledge him too. Hodler was the leading Swiss painter of his time. His paintings of the Alps and Lake Geneva are incomparable. He died on the shore of Lake Geneva in the spring of 1919, a wealthy and much honoured man.

Vittore Carpaccio (ca. 1455–1526)
Il sogno di Sant'Orsola, 1495
Oil on canvas, 274×267 cm
Accademia delle Belle Arti, Venice

The medieval collection of the lives of the saints, the *Legenda aurea,* gives a full account of the life and martyrdom of the Breton princess Ursula and her bridal journey to Rome with 11,000 virgins, during which they all prayed for the conversion of Ursula's heathen bridegroom. In a dream, an angel appeared to Ursula and announced that she would by martyred by the Huns on her return to Cologne. Many artists have treated this subject, among them the Fleming Hans Memling. But the greatest work is the cycle of nine scenes by the Venetian painter Carpaccio. Carpaccio trained in the solid Venetian tradition of Gentile and Giovanni Bellini, and, despite great success and originality, even in his maturity remained essentially an artist of the Quattrocento. Characteristic features of his work are a love of ornament and fantasy. He tells his stories in richly appointed rooms and lavish surroundings. The bedroom in 'The Dream of Saint Ursula' is no exception. It is painted in strict perspective and natural colours. Unlike his modern contemporaries, who had the viewer standing on the floor, as it were, of the space depicted, here the viewer is looking from above. It is obvious that Carpaccio has had much pleasure organizing the depth of the room. At the back, an open door leads into a second room, in which a cupboard is standing open. Through an open double-window one can see outside, but the vanishing point is abscured by a latticework garden wall. Myrtle and a bunch of carnations stand on the window-sill, symbols of pure love and of marriage. Ursula is sleeping alone in the large double-bed, at the foot of which is the crown of victory and a little dog that symbolizes faithfulness. All the objects in the room are lovingly painted in great naturalist detail, such as the holy picture with holy-water font and sconce, the chairs and small table with bookcase, the classical figures of the sopraportas and even Ursula's shoes on the bedside rug. In the clear light of morning, as if borne by the light of God, the angel of the dream enters the room through the door on the right, carrying the palm-leaf of martyrdom.

Prophecies from the *Old Testament*

In his prophecies about the fall of Jerusalem, the greatest of the messianic prophets, Isaiah (mid-7th century BC) sees the approaching afflictions in the images of a dream and a vision of the night (Isaiah 29, 7–8). *And the multitude of all the nations that fight against Ariel, all that fight against her and her stronghold and distress her, shall be like a dream, a vision of the night. As when a hungry man dreams he is eating and awakes with his hunger not satisfied, or as when a thirsty man dreams he is drinking and awakes faint, with his thirst not quenched, so shall the multitude of all the nations be that fight against Mount Zion. . . . For the Lord has poured out upon you a spirit of deep sleep, and has closed your eyes, the prophets, and covered your heads, the seers* (Isaiah 29, 7–10).

In both the *Old* and the *New Testament* the event of sleep is often the cause of decisive turns in the fate of peoples and people. The sleep of Noah after he drank of the wine and became drunk and lay uncovered was the prelude to his cursing Ham, his youngest son, the father of Canaan, and blessing his two elder sons, Shem, from whom Abraham is descended, and Japheth. For the words of curse and blessing are very strong words (Genesis 9, 18–27).

The strength of a powerful person can be broken by a deed carried out while he is asleep. Samson lost his strength when his mistress Delilah had the locks shaved off his head (Judges 16, 4–21). In eight oracles the prophet Zechariah (about 520 BC) announced the ordeals facing God's people as well as the approaching messianic age: *I saw in the night, and behold, a man . . .* (Zechariah 1, 8–6, 8).

Joseph's interpretation of the dreams of Pharaoh's chief baker and chief butler had severe consequences (Genesis 40, 5–41, 36): the chief baker was hanged and the chief butler restored to his office. Of far greater enormity were the consequences of Pharaoh's dreams of the seven sleek and fat cows and the seven gaunt and thin cows that come up out of the Nile. Joseph interprets them as seven years of plenty followed by seven years of famine. And when famine forced Joseph's brothers to come to Egypt to buy wheat, *Joseph remembered the dreams he had dreamed of them* (Genesis 42, 9).

Raphael (1483–1520)
Vision of a Knight, 1504/05
Oil on canvas, 17 × 17 cm
The National Gallery, London

Norse sagas

In the world of sagas and fairy-tales, sleep and dreams play an important role in developing and resolving the stories. Odin, the supreme god in Norse mythology, is the greatest master of the art of poetry. But there is a tale to this. The most malicious of the black elves had put Kwasir, the omniscient dwarf, to sleep with a magic potion. While he was in this deep sleep, they opened his arteries and collected his blood in three pails and sweetened it with honey. Whoever drank of it would become a wise bard. They hid this magic potion. But Odin's raven reported everything to the god, who soon set off, eager to drink of this mead. After overcoming extraordinary dangers he reached the mountain, the cave and the vat. In the form of an eagle, he bore this magic potion to the gods in Asgard. Since that day, Odin's poetry is known as the drink of find, catch and give, or the drink of the Aesir [26].

The *Edda* recounts yet other happenings of Odin associated with sleep and dreams. When all the beings in the great ash tree Yggdrasil were put to sleep by the singing of the birds, the goddess Idun drew of the mead Odin kept for the gods from the well where Odin stored it and poured it over the ash, that it might never wither. Yet the time of decay arrived. Then Odin despatched his raven Hugin to learn the meaning of these grave signs. But the dwarves Dain and Thrain – which mean dead and rigid – who knew the future, lay caught in heavy dreams of the coming horrors. The morning after the dark night Frigg appeared in Odin's camp and reported that Balder, the son they loved above all, had had bad dreams and that Hel, the pale goddess of the dead, had appeared to him and given him a sign to follow her. Now the Aesir, gods and goddesses, cast the lot-sticks to ascertain Balder's fate, and the rune for death fell uppermost. Loki the giant, who had always been jealous of his much-loved brother Balder, had him killed with a bough of mistletoe, and Balder vanished into grey Hel.

The composition of this square canvas is symmetrical: a tree in the centre, two women to the left and right and a young knight in armour asleep in front of it. He is dreaming of his future, a crucial dream whose content the women and the landscape represent. All is symbolic. The severely dressed woman to the left is holding out a sword and book to the dreamer, representative of the traditions of just laws and proper order. A path leads from her helmet up to the castle on the hill, the seat of knightly duty and good government, towards which riders are climbing. The woman on the right is richly dressed, her veil and gown moving in the breeze. She is offering the young man a stem with five white star-shaped flowers against a wide landscape of lakes that stretches to the blue mountains on the horizon, a life in freedom and beauty. Which path will the young man choose on waking from his sleep? Behind him, his tree of life rises from the ground high into the clear skies. The artist of this small panel is Raphael, one of the greatest masters of the Renaissance. The same epoch that brought forth some of the world's finest art was also an age of bloody power struggles between princes and rulers. As an apprentice in the workshop of Perugino in Perugia, the twelve-year-old from Urbino observed an incidence of the latter at close quarters, as the Baglioni family tore itself apart in internecine strife. This horrific experience is reflected in Raphael's art insofar as, in the words of Jacob Burckhardt, Raphael's most prominent personal trait is 'not of an esthetic, but of a moral nature'. This small masterpiece painted in Florence in 1505 supports this thesis in its clarity of line and radiance of colour as well as in the balance disposition of the symbols. Seen in this light, the square format itself acquires symbolic significance. The square is the geometric expression of the four elements, seasons and positions of the sun, and, as such, a symbol of the world in its perfect state, of cosmic order. The square is one of two shapes favoured by the Renaissance – the other is the divine circle – an attitude Leonardo captured in his 1492 drawing of man in relation to the square and circle.

Pieter Bruegel the Elder
(1525/30–1569)
Land of Milk and Honey, 1567
Oil on wood, 52×78 cm
Alte Pinakothek, Munich

The early myths of various cultures tell of a land of milk and honey. It is common in fairy-tales. In antiquity, the country was called 'Cucania' (Cockaigne). Even the *Bible,* in its unique manner, alludes to it in Psalm 127, 2. The story of Cockaigne is man's age-old dream of regaining the lost paradise. In Bruegel's painting the table is fully laid under a tree. In front of it, people lie stretched out on the ground, like spokes in the wheel of fortune: the soldier with his lance, the farmer with his flail and the scholar with his book. A knight is standing beneath a hut whose roof is stacked with loveas of bread, just waiting for roast pigeons to fly into his mouth. To get into this promised land of unending laziness one has to eat one's way through a mound of dough, like the man falling into Cockaigne with a spoon in his hand and his trousers down in the upper right-hand corner. Bruegel worked in Antwerp and Brussels, and painted this picture at a time when Flanders was suffering under the Spanish yoke. The picture is a dream in paint, in which cooked geese lay themselves on the platter, roast suckling pigs bring along a carving-knife with them and boiled eggs roll themselves towards their devourers.

The brave and eager Valkyrie Brunhild appears in the mythologies of the *Edda* and the Middle High German *Nibelungenlied*. Because she disobeyed Odin's will and helped the warrior Agnar to victory, she was imprisoned in a castle surrounded by a ring of flickering flames and put into an enchanted sleep with a prick of the thorn of sleep. To save her, Siegfried rode through the ring of fire, found the sleeping maid in the hall and loosened her shirt of mail, upon which she awoke. *I have slept long and without dreaming. Who has broken my sleep?* With that the spell over the castle and the servants was broken. Despite Brunhild's pleas that he remain, Siegfried rode out into the world in search of new adventures.

For his 'Ring der Nibelungen', Richard Wagner used the Younger *Edda*, in which Brunhild and Siegfried appear as lovers, though fate was to keep them apart.

There are also other dreams in the *Nibelungen-Saga*. A particularly nice one is that of Kriemhild, the jewel of the Burgundian court at Worms on the Rhine. She dreamed that she held a beautiful falcon, which was torn to pieces before her eyes by two eagles. Her mother Ute interpreted the dream for her weeping daughter: *The falcon symbolizes a knight whom you wish to win. May God protect him, otherwise he is lost.* After many deeds, Siegfried married Kriemhild in Xanten, and for ten years they lived in peace. But Brunhild's jealous feud with Kriemhild ended in Siegfried being treacherously stabbed in the back.

Fairy-tales

Sleeping Beauty is an exemplary fairy-tale for this subject. In his joy over the birth of a daughter, the king had invited twelve wise women to the feast, that they might each wish the child something good. But a thirteenth, who had not been invited, cursed the child, saying she would die of a spindle-prick in her fifteenth year. The twelve wise women were able to intervene in time, so that instead of dying, the princess would *fall into a deep sleep for one hundred years*. The curse was fulfilled on the princess's fifteenth birthday. And a heavy sleep covered the whole castle and everyone in it; even the well in the courtyard ran dry. A hedge of thorns grew around and over the castle. Many brave young men lost their lives trying to enter the castle. But when one hundred years had passed, a prince appeared. The thorns turned to flowers and let him pass. He climbed through the castle as it lay in its deep slumber, until he reached the Sleeping Beauty's bedchamber. And when he kissed her, she awoke to new life, and with her the entire castle and all its inhabitants.

In the fairy-tale 'The White Serpent' the young man despaired of ever carrying out the task the proud princess had set him, and wanted to lie under a tree and fall asleep, because he was very tired after his long walk. At this point the magic raven brought the golden apples from the tree of life he had been seeking and dropped them into his hand. And he and his princess could live happily ever after.

Sleep and dreams for good

Ancient Egyptian dream stelae

The dream of Thutmosis IV before the Sphinx of Gîza is famous. The Sphinx, with its body of a lion and royal head, was carved out of the stone next to a quarry used for the great pyramids during the Old Kingdom. It is a symbol of divine power which fills the pharaoh with new life when the sun awakes on the eastern horizon in the shape of Re Harachme. With her gaze fixed on eternity, she guards the divine mountains of royal pyramids behind her in the west. It is recorded that Amenophis II, a mighty pharaoh of the XVIII Dynasty, had dreamed about the promise of the Sphinx that he would achieve great fame in the New Kingdom. His successor, Thutmosis IV (about 1400 BC) had a similar dream. As a young man he was hunting near the Sphinx, which by then was almost buried, when he grew tired and lay down in the shade. He dreamed that the sun god Ra promised him that he would become pharaoh and famous, if he freed the Sphinx from the sand and restored it to its former glory. He became pharaoh, and before the first year of his reign was over, Thutmosis IV had a chapel erected in front of the Sphinx as well as the stela on which is inscribed the account of the dream.

In the Cairo Museum there is a stela that records the dream of the Nubian King Tanut-Amon. In the first year of his reign he had a dream that encouraged him to embark on a campaign against Lower Egypt to rescue the country for the Assyrians. The hieroglyphics carved into the stone read: *In the first year of his kingship, his Majesty had a dream at night, in which he saw two serpents, one to the right, the other to the left of him. This caused him to wake up, but he could not find the serpents. He asked: Why has this appeared to me? The dream was interpreted thus: you already have the land of Upper Egypt — take the land of Lower Egypt as well. Then the serpent and the vulture, the symbols of the rulers of the two countries, will shine on your head. The king set out to realize his dream, like God to the people who follow him. And his Majesty realized: The dream is true*[27].

A third dream stela is of a later date, and is now in the Museum in Naples. It comes from the temple of Hari-Shat in Herakleopolis. It tells of the dream in which the god of the world, whose eyes are the sun and the moon, advised the district administrator Smatawi-Tefnacht to return home to Egypt from the wars of Alexander the Great against the Persians[28].

Texts in the pyramids

In the pyramid texts, related to the mysteries of Osiris, the myth of his resurrection is made known as an awakening from the sleep of death and rigidity to new life. Horus commands: *Do what I command! You, who hate sleep, and who are tired, get up . . . , prepare your good bread and receive your power*[29].

Osiris's sleep to new life is symbolically shown in the ritual of burying corn in the earth: as the final step, a wooden tub in the shape of the mummified, standing Osiris in profile is laid in the tomb. In the shallow hollow lies muddy soil from the Nile, in which three seeds of cereal are sown. The seed, lying in the sleeping body of Osiris, the god of earth, quickens to new life. The bodies will start to germinate in the tomb, the grains will sprout like seed in the field. In the eyes of the believers, the myth of the god returned to new life closes the circle.

Edda

The *Edda* relates a similar account of life restored through sleep and dream, though with different imagery. In the primordial world, when there was no life and no breath, only rigidity and silence, the ship of dwarves sailed over the motionless see. In it, Bragi lay asleep. As Odin's son he had the power of divinely invigorating song. As the ship glided past the threshold of Naim, the dwarf of death, Bragi awoke, and started to play on his golden harp, singing the first song of life. Upon this, nature awoke out of its rigidity, and Iduna, the goddess of spring and beauty, sprouted from the depth of the earth. Bragi married her, and achieved everlasting life. The fairy-tale of 'Jorinde and Joringel' tells the story of a enchantress, who turns the beautiful girl Jorinde into a nightingale and carries off her bridegroom Joringel. He was very sad. *Finally, one night he dreamed that he had found a blood-red flower, at the centre of which lay a big and beautiful pearl. He picked this flower and took it to the castle of the enchantress. And everything he touched with this flower was freed from the enchantress's spell. He also dreamed that he had regained his Jorinde.* When he awoke from his dream, he started looking, and on the morning of the ninth day he found the blood-red flower, at the centre of which lay a large dew-drop, as big as the most beautiful pearl. And with the flower of his dream now reality, Joringel was able to break the power of the enchantress and free Jorinde[30].

Dreams of the future

The large body of sagas contains several dreams that reveal the future to sleeping rulers. Thus, when King Charles the Fat wanted to take a rest after Christmas Mass, a person appeared to him in a dream and said: *Now your spirit will leave your body, to appear before the Lord your Judge and your Saviour!* A bright red thread was tied around the thumb of his right hand, and he started the tour through the valleys of the sulphur springs and over the montains of the dragons. There he met ancestors that had to suffer, because as rulers they had brought dissension, not peace. In an open valley he saw his son Louis coming towards him. King Charles tied the bright band around his hand and gave him the kingdom. The account concludes with the words: *Thereupon Charles's spirit returned to his body, tired and worn out*[31].

Parinibbana Buddha, 12th century
Granite
Height: 12 m
Gal Vihara, Polonnaruwa
Sri Lanka

Polonnaruwa succeeded Anuradha-pura, the traditional seat of government, as the capital of Ceylon from the 11th to the 13th century. The twelve kings who ruled here endowed the city with as much spendour as was in their power. They built public halls and palaces, irrigation systems and lotus-shaped bathing pools. Above all, they erected temples and dagobas. But the most beautiful objects are the stone figures of Buddha.

Buddha was born in northern India about 560 BC, the son of the local rulers. As a young man he renounced a life of luxury and spent seven years as an ascetic seeking the meaning of life in inner enlightenment. He found it while sitting under a bodhi tree in a deer-park near Benares. For over twenty years he spread his teachings throughout India, accompanied by Ananda, his most devoted attendant. Gautama preached that man must free himself from the centrifugal emotions of lust and sorrow, so as to find the centre of complete harmony in the turning wheel of life. When he does he will be free and, as a buddha, enter Nirvana, the nothing of everything that is the fullness of everything. Gautama Buddha himself passed into eternal salvation at the age of eighty. A long time was to pass before people started to create images of him.

King Ashoka, a pious Indian ruler who sent his son Mahendra to Sri Lanka in the 3rd century BC to spread the teachings of Buddha, began the tradition of paintings of Buddha. Since that time, Sri Lanka has been a centre of Buddhism. Even though the old royal city of Polonnaruwa, the 'serene city', lies in ruins, it is still a centre of pilgrimage. The most beautiful Buddhist images there are these from Gal Vihara, the 'rock shrine'. These master-pieces of Singhalese art were chiselled out of solid granite in the 12th century. There is a sitting, meditating Buddha, a cave Buddha with Brahma and Vishnu as well as a seven-metre-high standing figure not of Buddha, but, as the arms folded in veneration indicate, of his favourite disciple Ananda. His master lies on cushions next to him, his eyes closed, as in the sleep of healing. Ananda is silent witness to Buddha's passing on, to the 'parinibbana', the Buddha's soundless transition into Nirvana.

On his journey along the Main, the Rhine and the Neckar, J.W. Goethe composed the poem of four lines:

Ich gedachte in der Nacht
Dass ich den Mond sähe im Schlaf;
Als ich erwachte,
Ging unvermutet die Sonne auf.
During the night I thought
That I saw the moon in my sleep;
When I awoke,
The sun rose unexpectedly.

Genesis 28 tells of Jacob's flight to Haran. He came to a certain place and, as it was after sunset, he wanted to stop for the night. Taking a stone, he put it under his head and lay down to sleep. *And he dreamed that there was a ladder set up on the earth, and the top of it reached to heaven; and behold, the angels of God were ascending and descending on it! And behold, the Lord stood above it and said, 'I am the Lord, the God of Abraham your father and the God of Isaac; the land on which you lie I will give to you and to your descendants.'* Then Jacob awoke from his sleep and said: *Surely the Lord is in this place; and I did not know it.* In the morning he set the stone up as a pillar, and called the name of that place Bethel, the house of God. The Lord appeared to Jacob in this dream, and now Jacob knows where his salvation lies and will order his life accordingly.

In the rites of the ancient Egyptian ceremony of Hebsed, the feast of a pharaoh's rebirth, the ruler, as an initiated mystic, had to descend into the depths of the chamber of serpents in the temple of Dendera in Upper Egypt. There he took fright and was purified. Then he was shown the way out of the darkness to the height of rebirth. He climbed the narrow way in the temple walls up to the roof, where on the divine bed under the stars he consummated the priestly marriage with Nut, the goddess of the heavens, and lapsed into the sleep of re-creation. Strengthened with new divine powers, he then descended to the people, appearing in the centre of the temple, in the naos of the cella, where he presented himself to his priests, before showing himself in a solemn procession to the faithful as the reborn pharaoh.

Every healing is a rebirth. For it is the power of nature gaining the upper hand over the spirit and the body again. Man can only help; nature takes care of the crucial aspects itself. Aesculapius's wise saying is as true today as it ever was: *Medicus curat, natura sanat.*

Sleep and dream as healing

Mysteries

The successors to the acient cults of Egypt, Greece and Rome were never fully informed about them. The secret of the mysteries was largely kept, precisely because the initiates were bound to silence. Even the loquacious Herodotos[32], who may have learnt quite a bit on his travels, makes a point of his silence here and there.

The eleven books of the *Metamorphoses* of Apuleius (124–180) include the story of 'The Golden Ass'. In it, an initiate tells about the mysteries of the Isis cult in words that conceal as much as they reveal. The hero is Lucius. Because he reveals too much, he is turned into an ass; the spell can be broken only by roses. He flees to the sea, where he falls asleep exhausted. When the full moon rises, he awakes and asks Isis to either save him or help him die. She appears out of the sea in a jet black coat covered with stars (like the star-covered Queen of the Night in Mozart's 'Magic Flute'). In her hands, she is holding a sistrum and a container with the serpent in it. Isis promises to save him. To this purpose, she appears to the high priest of the Isis mysteries in a dream, so as to give him instructions. Lucius is freed from the spell on the occasion of a procession. His background, education and scholarship did not help him at all; it was the goddess alone[33].

Incubation in Epidaurus

Epidaurus is a very old sanctuary. From its hills, it has a view through the fertile valley to the broad expanse of the sea, where initially the god of Malea, the god that brought nature back to life, was honoured. Later the Greeks identified him with Apollo. Asclepius, the divine doctor[34], was regarded as Apollo's son. Anyone who came to Epidaurus to be treated had to make his first sacrifice at the temple of the Maleata; this ensured succession. Asclepius acquired his knowledge of the healing powers of nature from the Chiron, the centaur. As the god of healing, Asclepius appears at the source in the shape of a serpent; in human form he supports himself on the Aesculapian staff, the rod and snake. He is accompanied by his daughter Hygieia. Often he receives visits at night from dwarflike figures in Capucian robes, 'Telephoros', Accomplisher – which can be death too – and 'Akesis', Healing.

Epidaurus is the largest and most important of Asclepius's sanctuaries. It is a full sanatorium, specializing in psychic ailments. Every healing process went through different phases. Drinks made with healing herbs, infusions, compresses, washings and baths served to relax and rest people. The crucial step, though, was the healing sleep. This is the root of our modern psychotherapy. But we do not have complete knowledge of all the processes used in Epidaurus.

The holy serpents in the base of the labyrinth of the tholos, the important circular temple at the centre of the holy area, were also important for the healing process. So that people who want to be healed would fall into a deep sleep, they were placed in the long hall at the back of the temple of Asclepius. The god of healing worked through sleep and dream.

Sleeping Woman, about 3500 BC
Terracotta
National Museum
Valletta, Malta

The Hypogeum of Saflieni is one of the most astonishing testimonies to the Neolithic period on Malta. Three storeys below the surface of the rock, a series of staircases, corridors, chambers and halls at different levels and in various arrangements form impressive underground sacred architecture. Only towards the end of the Bronze Age did it become a burial ground for thousands upon thousands. We can only guess at the earlier ceremonies. In the centre of the Hypogeum is a large room with gallery and frieze, possibly the central point of a sanctuary. Next to it is a room with spiral frescoes and red bands, perhaps an oracle room, adjoining which is a cave chamber. The whole construction is similar to the megalithic temples on Gozo and Malta, such as Ggantija, Hagar Qim, Mnajdra and Tarxien with their arched chambers, phallic menhirs and vaginal, V-shaped depressions for the libations of a fertility cult. The numerous large

and small female figures found on Malta indicate that the rites were part of a cult of the life-giving *magna mater.* Our sculpture of a sleeping woman, the size of a stretched hand, is a particularly splendid example. Characteristic of all Maltese Neolithic figures of the *magna mater* are the powerful torso, the severely tapered legs and arms and the small head. The woman is lying on an upholstered bedstead, fast asleep. One interpretation is that her sleep is incubative. Might the Hypogeum of Saflieni be a very early example of an incubation chamber where people were healed by sleep, the equivalent in a matriarchal society of the practices in the Aeskulapium in Epidaurus, the god of healing's centre in classical antiquity?

Epilogue

In the *Edda* it is reported that after the twilight of the gods and their fall a new day will begin for the world. New life will sprout on earth: grass will shoot, trees flower, birds sing and animals frolic around. And two young humans, a youth and a virgin, who, at the will of the father of the universe, have survived the burning of the world in deathlike sleep, will awake in amazement.

Constantin Brancusi (1876–1957)
La muse endormie IV, 1920
Polished bronze
Length 28.5 cm
Le Musée national d'art moderne, Paris

The Rumanian-born sculptor Brancusi was never part of any school. He studied at the Bucharest School of Fine Arts until 1902, after which he headed west, crossing much of Central Europe on foot and finally reaching Paris in 1904. Rodin immediately recognized Brancusi's creative power and invited him to enter his workshop. Brancusi refused, on the grounds that nothing flourishes in the shade of great trees. Brancusi was not interested in sculpting in the classical tradition, and experimented with symbolic forms he felt were rooted in the strength of myths. His work is unmistakeable and incomparable. Four times he treated the sleeping muse, reducing the form to its essence, slowly peeling away externalities to reveal the inner being as perfect, tangible form. The first version was in marble, the second in patinated bronze and the third in alabaster. Our photograph shows a cast in bronze as polished as a mirror, whose form is the essence of economy and simplicity. The face is calm and collected, both beginning and end of the world in harmony. It has the pure form of the egg, as is found in numerous ancient cultures, like that of the Indian Vedas, at the beginning of each new cosmic life.

Notes

1. Scipio «Über den Staat» 1990, p. 148.
2. In: «Antike Geisteswelt» 1964, p. 93.
3. Novalis «Werke und Briefe» 1942, p. 347.
4. Ibid. p. 419.
5. Ibid. p. 423.
6. Mircea Eliade «Mythos und Wirklichkeit» 1988, p. 15.
7. Johann Jacob Bachofen «Urreligion und antike Symbole», Ed. C.A. Bernoulli, Vol. I, 1926, p. 281.
8. Karl Kerényi «Auf den Spuren des Mythos» 1967, p. 291; idem, «Antike Religion» 1971, p. 13ff.
9. Walter F. Otto «Die Gestalt und das Sein» 1955, idem, «Gesetz, Mythos und Urbild» 1951, q.v. also: Leopold Ziegler «Überlieferung, Ritus, Mythos Doxa» 1948.
10. Joseph Campbell «The Power of Myth» 1988, p. 63.
11. Eckart Peterich «Götter und Helden» 1971, p. 198f.
12. Franz Kafka «Gesammelte Schriften» Vol. I, 1935, p. 69.
13. In: «Antike Geisteswelt» 1964, p. 457.
14. Plato «Sämtliche Werke» Vol. IV, 1974, p. 510ff.
15. Franz Kafka op. cit. p. 181ff.
16. Plato op. cit. p. 520.
17. Robert Th. Stoll «Ikonen», Exhibition Kunsthalle Basel, Catalogue No. 19.
18. Brothers Grimm «Deutsche Sagen» Vol. I, p. 50.
19. Ibid. p. 51.
20. Ibid. p. 53.
21. J.W. Goethe «Werke, vollständige Ausgabe letzter Hand» Vol. XIII, 1928, pp. 260, 313.
22. José Luis Borges «Gesammelte Werke» Vols I–IX, 1982ff.
23. Cf. G.F. Hartlaub «Das Unerklärliche, Studien zum magischen Weltbild» 1951, p. 284; q.v. also: Sahih al-Buhari «Nachrichten von Taten und Aussprüchen des Propheten Mohammed» 1991.
24. Robert Th. Stoll «Matthias Grünewald» 1956.
25. Idem, Robert Th. Stoll «Goya», Exhibition Kunsthalle Basel, 1953, Catalogue No. 230.
26. Eckart Peterich op. cit. p. 213.
27. Günther Roeder (ed.), von «Zauberei und Jenseitsglauben im Alten Ägypten» 1961, p. 369ff.
28. Ibid. «Die ägyptische Götterwelt» 1959, p. 214ff.
29. Ibid. «Mythen und Legenden um ägyptische Gottheiten und Pharaonen» 1960, p. 159ff., in particular p. 179.
30. Brothers Grimm «Kinder- und Hausmärchen» Vol. I, n.d., p. 489.
31. Ibid. «Deutsche Sagen» Vol. II, op. cit., pp. 122–124.
32. Herodotos «Historien» Deutsche Gesamtausgabe, Ed. H.W. Haussig, 1955.
33. Marion Giebel «Das Geheimnis der Mysterien» 1990, p. 172.
34. Karl Kerényi «Der göttliche Arzt, Studien über Asklepios und seine Kultstätte» 1948.

Contributors

Katharina Eder Matt, Swiss Museum of Ethnology, Basel, Switzerland

Dr Silvia Evangelisti, Academy of Fine Arts, Bologna, Italy

Lorenza Melli, Department of Psychology, University of Florence, Italy

Professor David Parkes, MD, Department of Neurology,
Institute of Psychiatry, University of London, UK

Professor Pier Luigi Parmeggiani, MD, Institute of Human Physiology,
University of Bologna, Italy

Professor Piero Salzarulo, MD, Department of Psychology,
University of Florence, Italy

Dr Hartmut Schulz, Psychiatric Clinic and Outpatient Department,
Free University of Berlin, Federal Republic of Germany

Dr Annemarie Seiler-Baldinger, Director of the Americas Department,
Swiss Museum of Ethnology, Basel, Switzerland

Dr Robert Th. Stoll, art historian, Basel, Switzerland

Dr Irene Tobler, Institute of Pharmacology, University of Zurich,
Switzerland

Photographs

Joachim Blauel, Artothek Peissenberg (Germany), 35, 42, 67, 206

Luca Carra, Milan, 114

Degonda & Siegenthaler, Zurich, 109

David Heald, Peggy Guggenheim Collection, Venice, 104

Peter Heman, Basel, 26, 190

Silvia Hertig, Archeological Collection, University of Zurich, 37

Hans Hinz, Allschwil (Switzerland), 13, 189

Bruno Jarret, ADAGP, Paris, 127

Yves Siza, Geneva, 161